MW00573389

CONCRETE JUNGLES

Recent Titles in

Global and Comparative Ethnography
Edited by Javier Auyero

Violence at the Urban Margins
Edited by Javier Auyero, Philippe Bourgois, and Nancy Scheper-Hughes

CONCRETE JUNGLES

Urban Pollution and the Politics of
Difference in the Caribbean

Rivke Jaffe

OXFORD
UNIVERSITY PRESS

OXFORD
UNIVERSITY PRESS

Oxford University Press is a department of the University of Oxford. It furthers
the University's objective of excellence in research, scholarship, and education
by publishing worldwide. Oxford is a registered trade mark of Oxford University
Press in the UK and certain other countries.

Published in the United States of America by Oxford University Press
198 Madison Avenue, New York, NY 10016, United States of America.

© Oxford University Press 2016

First Edition published in 2016

All rights reserved. No part of this publication may be reproduced, stored in
a retrieval system, or transmitted, in any form or by any means, without the
prior permission in writing of Oxford University Press, or as expressly permitted
by law, by license, or under terms agreed with the appropriate reproduction
rights organization. Inquiries concerning reproduction outside the scope of the
above should be sent to the Rights Department, Oxford University Press, at the
address above.

You must not circulate this work in any other form
and you must impose this same condition on any acquirer.

Library of Congress Cataloging-in-Publication Data
Jaffe, Rivke, author.
Concrete jungles : urban pollution and the politics of difference in the Caribbean / Rivke Jaffe.
pages cm.—(Global and comparative ethnography)
Includes bibliographical references and index.
ISBN 978–0–19–027358–3 (hardcover: alk. paper)—ISBN 978–0–19–027359–0 (pbk.: alk. paper)
1. Urban pollution—Caribbean Area.   2. Environmental sociology—Caribbean Area.
3. Social classes—Caribbean Area.   4. Equality—Caribbean Area.
5. Urban ecology (Sociology)—Caribbean Area.   6. Human ecology—Caribbean Area.   I. Title.
GE160.C27J34 2016
363.7309729—dc23
2015027018

9 8 7 6 5 4 3 2 1
Printed by Webcom, Canada

CONTENTS

CONTENTS

LIST OF FIGURES

ACKNOWLEDGMENTS

Completing this book has been a long journey; the final manuscript materialized only gradually through a range of writing projects and extended conversations that developed as I traveled through various institutional settings. I am indebted, first of all, to the many people in Curaçao and Jamaica who shared their ideas on cities and environmental issues with me, both the residents of the four research neighborhoods and the environmental professionals in these countries. In Willemstad, I am very grateful to Lloyd Narain and Yvette Raveneau for their long-term friendship and support. Their desire to work toward more inclusive, locally rooted forms of environmentalism has been a source of inspiration. Rose Mary Allen's anthropological work and her friendship over the years have also meant a lot to me. Thanks also to Ivan Cordero for being a great *amigu*. In Wishi/Marchena, I am especially grateful to Kenneth Valpoort, a great *lider di bario*, and to Jamel Gregorius, Norvin Louisa, Eddy Zimmerman, and Shon Benchi. In Seru Fortuna, many thanks to Migarda Wijngaarden, Ivy Cicilia, Veronica and Zieck at the *Sentro di Bario*, Kenneth Girigori, Aretha, and Jacqueline Hortensia-Louisa and her children. Elsewhere on the island, thanks go out to the staff of the Central Bureau of Statistics, the National Archives, Mongui Maduro Library, and Selikor. In Jamaica, nothing would have been the same without Miss Gwen Whittaker, her extended family, and the larger Red Light community. In Riverton, my thanks go out to Miss Likkle, Kevron McKay, Raymond, Sonny Dread, and Dean, Neville, Tony, and Brian Duncan. In Rae Town, I am grateful to Vincent "Bones" Gordon, Fana, Elvis, Jamar, Dwight and Stevie, Monique, Auntie Joy, Jackie, and Tamara. Thanks also to the staff of the National Solid Waste Management Authority, the United Nations Development Programme Local Initiative Facility for the (Urban) Environment, the Jamaica Information Service, and the National Library of Jamaica, and to Esther Figueroa for her critical engagement with my work.

In writing this book, I have benefited immensely from the insights and feedback offered by colleagues and friends along the way. The initial research began at Leiden University and the Research School of Asian, African and Amerindian Studies (CNWS), with my supervisor Peter Nas, whose support and enthusiasm for urban environmental research were invaluable, and with the friendship of Alex Geurds, Liza de Laat, and many others. A post-doc position at the Royal Netherlands Institute of Southeast Asian and Caribbean Studies (KITLV) with Rosemarijn Höfte was the start of my engagement with historical research and broadened my understanding of the Dutch Caribbean. At the University of the West Indies, Mona, I learned much from colleagues such as David Dodman, Mark Figueroa, Kevon Rhiney, Robert Kinlocke, and the late Barry Chevannes. Returning to Leiden as a lecturer in the anthropology department, my thoughts on how to develop this book project were helped significantly by working and co-teaching with inspiring colleagues such as Sabine Luning, Ratna Saptari, Marianne Maeckelbergh, Bart Barendregt, Erik Bähre, Maarten Onneweer, Roos Gerritsen, and Annemarie Samuels. At the University of Amsterdam, I am grateful to geographers such as Fenne Pinkster and Wouter van Gent for sharpening my understanding of the politics of place-making, and to Marcel Heemskerk for creating maps of Willemstad and Kingston. Working with Ph.D. students at the University of Amsterdam, especially Alana Osbourne and Tracian Meikle, has shown me new ways of understanding Kingston. Other colleagues whose comments and feedback helped improve the manuscript include Deborah Thomas, Mimi Sheller, Tim Barringer, and Rose Mary Allen. I am especially happy to have been able to work together with Eveline Dürr for over a decade in developing an anthropology of urban pollution.

Financially, the initial research was made possible by the support of the Jacob Gelt Dekker Institute in Curaçao, the CNWS and the Leids Universiteitsfonds at Leiden University, and the sponsoring of tickets by KLM Royal Dutch Airlines. A Visiting Scholar Award from the Yale Center for British Art allowed me to explore the historical and aesthetic dimensions of the project more fully.

I am grateful to James Cook at Oxford University Press for his editorial support for this project, and to the two anonymous reviewers whose constructive comments helped me to refine and strengthen the arguments I make in this book. Thanks as well to Javier Auyero for welcoming this contribution to the Comparative and Global Ethnography series at OUP, and to Dennis Rodgers for suggesting the possible fit between my manuscript and the series.

Parts of this book developed in the context of other publication projects. Some of the text in Chapter Six, on Uptown environmentalism, has been published as the book chapter "Unnatural Causes: Green Environmentalism, Urban Pollution and Social Justice in the Caribbean," in *Environmental Management in the Caribbean: Policy and Practice*, edited by Elizabeth Thomas-Hope (Kingston: University of the West Indies Press, 2013). A section of Chapter Three, on the Jamaican cholera epidemic, will appear as part of the chapter "Dirt, Disease and Difference in Victorian Jamaica: The Politics of Sanitary Reform in the 1852 Milroy Report" in *Victorian Jamaica*, edited by Wayne Modest and Tim Barringer (Durham: Duke University Press, forthcoming). Thanks are due the editors of these collections for their encouragement in developing these texts.

I might never have completed this book without a group of dear friends, with whom I shared countless hours typing away in libraries and cafés in Amsterdam, The Hague, and Kingston, and on writing retreats in Groningen and Limburg: Anouk de Koning, Hebe Verrest, Guiselle Martha, Petrina Dacres, and Claudia Hucke. I am especially indebted to Anouk, whose anthropological knowledge, sharp editorial eye, and patient encouragement improved the manuscript immensely.

Finally, all my love to Wayne Modest—husband, best friend, and astute critic—whose empathy, patience, and erudition have sustained me throughout much of this project. Our continuing conversations about difference, inequality, colonialism, and the Caribbean have inspired me intellectually and personally, and there is no one with whom I would rather continue this journey.

CONCRETE JUNGLES

INTRODUCTION

On my first trip to the Caribbean island of Curaçao, I joined a nature hike to help clean up the *mondi*, as the island's wild nature is called in the local vernacular of Papiamentu. We left Willemstad, the capital city where the vast majority of the population lives, early in the morning and drove out to a meeting point. A volunteer who was employed by the national Department of Environment and Nature led our group of assembled hikers as we started off into the *mondi*. As we walked through a landscape of small trees, dry brush, and *dadu* and *kadushi* cacti, the volunteer regaled us with stories about the different plants and their uses. One type of cactus, for instance, is used to make Curaçao's traditional *sòpi di kadushi*, a soup that will congeal enough to make your spoon stand up straight if you don't eat it immediately. We continued until we reached a big pile of garbage, mostly construction materials, in the middle of the wilderness. Here, each of us was given a special pair of thick gloves and a special white garbage bag with the name of one of the island's environmental nongovernmental organizations (NGOs) printed in green (Figure 1.1). After only a few minutes of hefting concrete blocks into these bags, we stopped our efforts because the next group of hikers had almost reached the garbage site, and we needed to move on. We continued our trek and ended up at the main meeting point, where we stretched our legs and had drinks and snacks.

Over the decade that followed, researching urban environmental problems in Curaçao and Jamaica, I came to see the significance of this first nature hike. First of all, despite the ubiquity of garbage and litter in Willemstad, we had traveled outside the city to do our clean-up. As I argue in this book, it is no coincidence that to practice environmentalism we had to leave the city, polluted as much of it was, to protect and purify nature and the non-urban

FIGURE 1.1 Cleaning up the *mondi* in Curaçao.
Photograph by Irene Rolfes.

environment. The various environmental organizations that are active on both islands largely saw urban pollution as a regrettable but also normal situation, whereas pollution in or of nature was perceived as an offensive phenomenon that prompted collective environmentalist action. In addition, it struck me that most of those participating in the hike to the *mondi* were either White or light-skinned (*koló kla*), and included many Dutch expatriates as well as Curaçaoans. The language used was also Dutch, rather than Papiamentu. The composition of this group, so different from the majority of the island's population, over time also proved indicative of the social distance separating environmentalists from "ordinary people." Finally, our few minutes of stuffing construction waste into garbage bags seemed a rather symbolic act unlikely to affect any of the issues underlying problems in solid waste management. I came to wonder to what extent environmentalism not only was a problem-oriented ideology and social movement, but served as a practice that marked social, and specifically class, distinction.

As I continued my research, I began to realize that even on these small islands, there were distinct versions of environmentalism that articulated with class, ethnicity, and urban space. Comparing the perceptions, behaviors, and organization of environmental professionals and "lay" citizens in Willemstad, Curaçao, and Kingston, Jamaica, I began to distinguish

"Uptown environmentalism" from "Downtown environmentalism."[1] These two forms of environmentalism acted as analytical and normative frameworks, outlining different definitions, causes, and consequences of urban and environmental problems, as well as possible solutions to them. These two socio-ecological spheres were not completely opposite or entirely separate, nor do I mean to suggest that these are the only two spheres or positions possible. However, they were connected to urban divisions that resonated broadly with the lived experience of residents of Kingston and Willemstad.

In this book, I explore the ways in which urban inequalities and the socio-spatial fragmentation of Caribbean cities both reflect and reinforce diverging discourses and practices pertaining to the environment. I contend that political economy approaches to environmental injustice are insufficient, and that we must expand our focus to include the cultural politics that naturalize the unequal distribution of pollution. To do so, I examine the ways in which pollution—understood here as a phenomenon of entangled material and symbolic components—intersects with urban space in the construction of social hierarchies and the unequal distribution of environmental burdens and hazards. Connecting environmental anthropology and urban studies, I attempt to understand how the politics of difference are played out through environmentalism and urban space.

Throughout the book, I link analyses of discourses on the environment and on the city to their material effects and contexts, most specifically by focusing on urban space. What effects do specific environmental narratives have—that is, what forms of social power do they legitimate, where and for whom do they create jobs, and whose activities do they constrain and stigmatize? Who gets to define what constitutes an environmental problem and what is the best way to solve it, and who benefits from those definitions? How are the residential and professional spaces within which policymakers circulate reflected in the focus of environmental policies, and what effects do those policies have on urban spaces not considered to be environmental priorities? Nature, the environment, and the city are produced socially and discursively, and these discourses result in physical and economic changes to urban and natural environments and the people who live in them. At the same time, these discourses are not unchanging, nor do they emerge in limbo. They are developed in specific material spaces of power and powerlessness: the government ministry, the university, and the boardroom, as well as the ghettoized neighborhood, the street, and "the gully." Even as these discourses—and the stories, visual images, policies, and songs that constitute them—are produced in particular spaces, they help reproduce those same spaces as different and sustain the social distance between the groups of people who dwell in them.

This book is based on extensive ethnographic fieldwork among residents of low-income, polluted urban neighborhoods and professional environmental practitioners. This twin focus on "grassroots" and "professional" actors reflects what is known as a "vertical slice approach" (Nader 1980). Such an approach expands anthropology's traditional "on-the-ground" focus by "studying up": studying communities and issues in connection to other strata of society and as situated within broader spheres of power. I also draw on auto-ethnographic approaches, incorporating and reflecting on my own urban experiences and encounters as a White-identified middle-class woman to analyze the emplaced and embodied construction of raced, classed, and gendered difference and behavioral norms in Willemstad and Curaçao.

Much of my fieldwork was concentrated in four low-income neighborhoods, locations selected on the basis of their proximity to environmental problems and their socio-economic status. Additional factors in the selection of these research sites were physical accessibility and perceived safety, as well as social accessibility through gatekeepers, such as community leaders and key informants. Because their environmental characteristics make them easily identifiable, I have chosen to use the real names of these communities. However, the names of all residents have been anonymized throughout, unless otherwise indicated, as in the case of prominent neighborhood leaders. At this "grassroots" level, I combined qualitative and quantitative approaches, incorporating a range of methods, including in-depth semi-structured interviews, unstructured interviews, and numerous informal conversations. In Kingston, the two research neighborhoods were Riverton, a community at the edge of the city that bordered on Jamaica's largest landfill, and Rae Town, a downtown fishing community on Kingston's polluted harbor that suffered major sewerage issues. In Willemstad, my fieldwork took place in Wishi/Marchena, a central neighborhood located downwind from the Isla oil refinery, and in Seru Fortuna, an area on the urban periphery that was experiencing a degrading social and physical infrastructure, including issues related to sewage and garbage.

In both Willemstad and Kingston, I worked with members of governmental and nongovernmental environmental organizations, studying the development of these groups over time and their real or potential influence on policy and on urban and environmental discourse. This research included interviews with strategic individuals and an extensive analysis of online and printed sources, including numerous policy documents, news reports, and social media. In addition to interviews and policy and media analysis, I attended NGO activities such as meetings, lectures, nature hikes, and so on. I worked with an urban environmental NGO in Kingston to organize a stakeholder meeting, coordinating activities and raising funds for the construction of a solid waste barrier in a gully in my research community Rae Town. Because these organizations and their leaders are often prominent, with well-known public campaigns and opinions, I sometimes refer to them by name.

Jamaica and Curaçao present useful case studies for a comparative urban environmental analysis, offering different vantage points from which to study the interconnections among the social, natural, and built environment, and to explore the ways in which the trope of "pollution" organizes relations between classed and raced bodies and urban space. The two islands were selected as research sites in part because of their distinct characteristics in terms of size, colonial history, current political situation, economy, and ecology. Jamaica, the largest island within the British West Indies, with a current population of around 2.7 million, gained independence from the United Kingdom in 1962. Some 700 miles to the south lies Curaçao, a much smaller territory. The majority of its 150,000 inhabitants are Dutch citizens, as the island remains a nonindependent part of the Kingdom of the Netherlands. While Jamaica's economy was historically dominated by plantation agriculture and now relies heavily on tourism, Curaçao's semi-arid climate resulted in a nonagricultural economy reliant on trade, the petroleum industry, and only recently tourism.

Beyond these differences, the two islands also share various commonalities: they were positioned similarly within European empires and share histories characterized by slavery, institutionalized racism, and associated models of colonial urban development. In the twenty-first century, both are integrated in comparable ways into global environmentalism's dominant organizational, financial, and ideological structures. The specific but recognizably Caribbean historical trajectories of both cases have shaped patterns of urban development in which discourses of pollution link imaginaries of tropical nature to racialized space in distinct but analogous ways. In the next chapter, I elaborate on the possibilities and pitfalls of analyzing the socio-ecological politics of Willemstad and Kingston within such a Caribbean and comparative urban framework.

Caribbean cities

Willemstad and Kingston are both cities whose origins lie in the colonial past. The islands of which they are the capitals, Curaçao and Jamaica, were both Spanish possessions until they were conquered in the seventeenth century by the Dutch and the English, respectively, and populated with enslaved Africans. Like most of the urban Caribbean, these two cities were hubs of colonial trade and control. In processes of what can be seen as "proto-globalization," these urban centers facilitated the movements of free and unfree people, goods, capital, and ideas between the Americas, Europe, and Africa. Caribbean cities linked their hinterlands to European metropoles. As important nodes in global networks, they foreshadowed what would come to be known, centuries later, as global cities. In the context of slavery, such cities were characterized by high levels of social stratification. In Willemstad and Kingston, as throughout the region, skin color, class, and urban space were intimately connected in constructing and maintaining inequalities, as enslaved Africans and their descendants were separated socially and spatially from European colonial populations. These historical divisions are still evident in contemporary Caribbean cities, where socio-economic and spatial differences continue to correlate with ethnicity and skin color. Despite major shifts in the political context, the built environment that was created by and for colonial powers continues to mediate present-day social, ethno-racial, and environmental inequities.

In many ways, the representation of the Caribbean in foreign imaginations has also remained remarkably constant. The region has been imagined primarily as a space of nature, although the meanings and values attached to its nature have often been multiple, contradictory, and unstable, ranging from source of spiritual salvation to moral and health hazard, from bounteous economic resource to imperiled ecological repository. Caribbean islands have long been seen as tropical Edens: lush, tropical, green spaces that stand in contrast to the urban, civilized, temperate spaces of Europe and later North America. From colonialism into the postcolonial era, the tropics have featured as "the site for European fantasies of self-realisation, projects of cultural imperialism and the politics of human or environmental salvage" (Driver 2004, 3). The exotic imaginary of the Caribbean attracted colonial adventurers from botanists and buccaneers to planters, and it continues to draw millions of tourists to the region annually (Sheller 2003; Thompson 2006). In the twenty-first century, the islands' designation as relatively pristine "biodiversity hotspots," characterized by exceptionally diverse ecosystems and endemic species, underlines their significance for transnational environmental organizations.

Cities, however, sit awkwardly in this vision of an unspoiled, natural Caribbean. Historically, cities have been framed as simultaneously utopian and dystopian spaces. In one conception, they have been imagined as beacons of civilization, representing progress and modernity. This positive image does not mesh well with portrayals of a primeval, pristine Edenic nature that has remained unaffected by the march of time, or with depictions of easygoing and rather backwards "natives." Modern, civilized cities do not fit the idea of a tropical Caribbean paradise, whether that tropicality emphasizes unruly jungles, fertile plantations, or sandy beaches. Such utopian images of urban order and modernity tend to be accompanied by dystopian notions of cities as spaces of blight, where dirt, disease, and moral decay prevail. These notions of socially and physically polluting cities do not match dominant representations of the Caribbean either, antithetical as such urban areas are to unspoiled landscapes of natural purity. Imaginaries of Caribbean natural purity are so strongly entrenched that the concept of a Caribbean city would almost seem to be an oxymoron. Indeed, while the Caribbean is one of the most highly urbanized regions in the world, anthropological and historical research on the Caribbean has tended to disregard urban areas. In a region that has long been represented through a focus on nature, cities are an ambiguous and disruptive element as loci of both progress and pollution.

Both historically and in the contemporary Caribbean, the production and imagination of nature and the environment connect to the production of social difference, as is evident at both the national and the urban scale. At the level of the island territory, and in the cases of Jamaica and Curaçao, the social production of tropical nature has historically been tied to racist colonial representations of Afro-Caribbean people as backwards, childlike creatures, incapable of managing their natural surroundings sensibly. These representations have then been contrasted with European colonizers who were adept at rendering the fertile soil economically productive (through enslaved labor) and who built cities both to control the rural hinterland and to provide the island with military protection against other European forces. These racialized divisions supposed that non-Europeans were somehow closer to nature: less capable of mastering nature and, in relation to this, less human, or at least less civilized. Both non-European bodies and natural landscapes were seen as ripe for cultivation and productive management by Europeans (see Moore et al. 2003).

Within cities, analogous narratives of difference played out. Dystopian and utopian urban imaginaries became entangled with social divisions. Enslaved Africans and later the Afro-Caribbean lower class came to be associated with dirt, disease, and disorder. These connotations, while related in part to the actual living and working conditions under which the darker-skinned urban poor suffered, drew heavily on racist and classist narratives circulating more broadly within European empires. In contrast, the European rulers, and later the light-skinned elites, assumed a social position they sought to legitimize by claiming an association with metropolitan modernity, cleanliness, and order. Pollution, both as a physical threat to health and as a symbolic threat to civilization and the social order, became a discursive frame that served to justify repressive measures against the non-European urban poor. While urban space and the built environment act as traces of empire that can be reactivated in the present day, this trope of pollution also continues to be invoked in ways that normalize historically rooted inequalities.

Nature, environmentalism, and the city

For quite similar reasons to those that have almost elided the urban from popular imaginaries and academic studies of the Caribbean, cities have rarely been the focus of environmental anthropology, or of mainstream environmental activism. "Nature" and the "environment" tend to be conceptualized as outside of, and autonomous from, the urban. This ontological separation stems from the broader "culture–nature" divide that Bruno Latour (1993) has theorized as being integral to the project of modernity. By severing society from nature, the latter could be studied, understood, and finally controlled by the former, furthering human emancipation and progress. Within this culture–nature dichotomy, which structures so much of science and society, cities often represent the cultural antithesis of nature. In her discussion of the relationship between nature and urban life, Maria Kaika (2005) brings Latour's argument to bear on the urban, arguing that the opposition of "the city" and "nature" is the spatial expression of this modern dualism. If one views cities not so much as things but as continuous processes of the urbanization of nature, these ontological categories of "city" and "nature" can be understood as intertwined hybrids that are neither purely natural nor purely human. Yet even as they constitute each other, discursive processes of purification have rendered them distinct and mutually exclusive.

The construction of nature–culture dualisms has become an important focus within environmental anthropology. This makes it all the more ironic that within the subdiscipline itself the urban is almost completely absent as either a topic or a physical setting of research. Most research within the field has emphasized rural areas and wilderness, studying human–environment interactions mainly in the context of agriculture, natural resource management, and conservation, and privileging issues of depletion over those of pollution. Over the last two decades, much work has emphasized the complexity of power relations in environmental knowledge and practice and the global interconnections and collaborations that structure them (e.g., Tsing 2005; West 2006; Li 2007; Dove et al. 2011). Despite its attentiveness to scale making and the politics of place, this work has tended to privilege non-urban, "green" environmental concerns (e.g., rainforest conservation) as the focus of environmental anthropology. "Nature" and the "environment" in the bulk of these studies still tend to be researched as—implicitly or explicitly—conceptually outside of, and antithetical to, the urban. "Brown," urban environmental problems such as solid waste, sanitation, and air pollution rarely feature in such work.[2]

Early anthropology had as its preferred subject "natural" (i.e., "primitive") Man, who tended to dwell far outside the modern city.[3] Cities, as modern and modernizing sites, have long featured as spaces that erode "traditional culture," anthropology's original focus. It is only since the 1960s that the urban has begun to feature as a valid field of inquiry within the discipline rather than as a non-object or a "problem space." Anthropology itself has, of course, been complicit in the project of modernity, as it separated culture/the urban from nature/the non-urban, relegating the non-West to the latter sphere. Cities, representing both impurity and civilization, stood in opposition to both the broader project of early anthropology and, more recently, that of environmental anthropology. Urban anthropology, which emerged relatively recently within this context, absorbed the "modern" dualism and, with a few notable exceptions (e.g., Aoyagi et al. 1998; Checker 2005; Rotenburg 2014), has not taken nature or environmental issues on board.

These conceptions of nature and the city as mutually exclusive, the legacy of modernity's nature–culture divide, are not only evident in academic paradigms. They also structure mainstream environmental policies and environmental activism, as will become evident throughout this book. Mainstream environmentalism as a social movement has overwhelmingly prioritized green issues such as biodiversity, wildlife conservation, deforestation, and global warming. Traditional conservationist discourses within environmentalism are also strongly invested in the "purification" of nature (see, e.g., Head and Muir 2006). Such discourses construct a "pure" or authentic nature that is marked by wilderness and endemic, indigenous, or endangered species. Conservationist strategies have traditionally framed "nature out of place," such as pests, exotic and genetically modified species, and "non-nature," including humans, and particularly urban humans, as pollutants that should preferably be removed from nature. These discourses tend to frame civilization and human activity as the problem, and the city as the main source of pollution and depletion of natural environments (which are conceived of as pure and ontologically distinct from the urban). Cities appear as the sources of problems, and occasionally as the source of solutions.

As my research in Curaçao and Jamaica progressed, I became increasingly intrigued by the extent to which environmental organizations both in and outside the Caribbean focused on turtles, whales, and pandas, rather than on garbage dumps, oil refineries, and leaky sewage pipes. These specific identifications of what constitutes an environmental problem are not coincidental; they reflect the priorities and concerns of those who have the power to define such agendas at national and international scales. Such definitions—that elide cities and urban environmental problems—also have concrete, material consequences, as they influence the social and geographical destinations of government and NGO funding.

These green prioritizations have been challenged to some extent by the emergence, from the 1980s on, of the environmental justice movement (Bullard 2000; Checker 2005; Sandler and Pezzullo 2007). This form of environmentalism, concentrated mostly in the United States, links poverty and inequality to urban environmental degradation and the spatial distribution of environmental hazards such as polluting industry and toxic waste sites. The type of environmentalism that I encountered in the low-income neighborhoods of Curaçao and Jamaica reflected some of these associations but rarely coalesced into long-lasting forms of collective action. Environmental justice activists in the United States have argued that the conservation focus of mainstream environmentalism reflects the interests of its predominantly White, middle-class membership, ignoring and excluding the environmental concerns of racial minorities. Rather than seeing the city as the problem, an environmental justice perspective posits the unequal distribution of pollution within the city as its main issue.

In a parallel move, but drawing more explicitly on Marxist analyses, the academic field of urban political ecology has advocated the conjoined study of cities and nature, emphasizing the relations of power that permeate urban environments. Studies within this field focus first on the unequal socio-ecological relations that shape and are shaped by urban environments, and second on conceptualizing those environments as nature–culture hybrids. David Harvey (1996, 435) calls for the recognition "that the distinction between the [natural] environment as commonly understood and the built, social and political-economic environment is artificial and that the urban and everything that goes into it is as much a part of the solution as it is a contributing factor to ecological difficulties." The intimate connection and mutual constitution of nature and the city are theorized as systems of urban metabolism, with natural, social, economic, and political inputs and outputs.

Several urban political ecology studies have focused on water (e.g. Gandy 2004; Swyngedouw 2004; Kaika 2005; Ioris 2012), while others have examined urban forests, lawns, and green space (Heynen 2003; Robbins and Sharp 2003; Kitchen 2013). Work in urban political ecology explicitly brings nature back into the discussion, arguing for an understanding of urbanization as an ongoing process of socio-ecological and political-economic transformation of nature (Swyngedouw 1997). While largely dominated by geographers, urban political ecology crosses disciplinary boundaries, drawing on urban studies, critical theory, and science and technology studies. However—in contrast to broader, non-urban political ecology—anthropological theory and methodology do not feature very prominently. Specifically, very few studies in urban political ecology have a strong ethnographic basis.[4] In addition, like the environmental justice movement, most work is rooted geographically in North American and, to a lesser extent, European cities.

Grounding urban political ecology theory more solidly in ethnographic research can enhance our understanding of how environmental injustices are normalized through everyday practices and popular knowledges. Incorporating anthropological methods and connecting Marxist approaches to poststructural theory can help uncover the multiple meanings that nature, pollution, and depletion take on in the lived realities of diverse urban residents. In addition, ethnographies of environmental injustice can shed light on the more micro-level conditions that may facilitate urban social movements (Checker 2005) or, conversely, inhibit collective action (Auyero and Swistun 2009; Auyero 2012). In addition to the methodological benefits that such a dialogue with anthropology could entail, it might also broaden the geographical scope of our understanding. Recent work in urban political ecology has emphasized the need to broaden the focus of the field beyond North American cities. As Mary Lawhon, Henrik Ernstson, and Jonathan Silver argue in their call to "provincialize" urban political ecology, much of this research "tends to overlook the situated understandings of the environment, knowledge and power that form the core of other political ecological understandings as well as recent work in Southern urbanism." Extending the analysis to more explicitly include theories and case studies from cities of the global South, they suggest, would result in "a more situated UPE [urban political ecology] which creates the possibility for a broader range of urban experiences to inform theory on how urban environments are shaped, politicized and contested" (Lawhon, Ernstson, and Silver 2014, 498). Such a geographical refocusing would also enable a better understanding of how multiple histories of European imperialism have informed the racialization of urban ecologies in ways that may diverge from North American experiences.

Building on urban political ecology approaches, this book explores the broader significance of thinking through the "natural" aspects of urban space in connection to the cultural politics of difference in colonial and postcolonial settings. If we understand politics as embedded in both the natural and the built environment, this points our attention to how forms of urban difference and inequality are *naturalized*. Garbage, sewage, and air pollution are central elements in the nature–culture hybrids of cities no less than urban water, greenery, and wildlife. They play a critical role in the cultural construction and legitimation of urban inequalities. In this book, I draw on anthropological analyses of how alterity and inequality are produced and reproduced through (post)colonial socio-ecological governmentality and everyday practices and discourse. In so doing, I am interested not only in understanding how the discursive-material "production" of nature affects different urban groups—whether racial, ethnic, or socio-economic—unequally, but also in emphasizing the extent to which the production of nature is complicit in the construction and reproduction of categories of social difference in urban space.

Nature, space, and the politics of difference

"Nature" is produced through human physical and intellectual labor, not only materially, but socially and discursively as well. Nature is made and remade, produced and transformed, within a system of capitalism. The mechanisms of capitalism are complicit in the production of uneven geographical development through the production of socially unjust natures and, more broadly, the skewed distribution of resources (Smith 1990; Harvey 1996). In the non-urban Caribbean this has meant, historically and through the present, that the profits of plantation agriculture and nature-based tourism have gone to local and foreign elites, leaving only marginal land for farming and residence by the Afro-Caribbean lower classes. Uneven development is equally evident in the urban areas, where the price of land and housing in cooler, greener neighborhoods places them out of reach of the urban poor, who are consigned to hotter, more crowded, and more polluted sections.

This uneven geographical development, the material-spatial expression of historical inequalities, needs to be understood within the discursive frames that have served to produce and justify it. Understanding these connections requires being attentive to "imaginative geographies" (Said 1978; Gregory 1995): the discursive production of social difference in and through space. David Harvey (1996, 6) states that "spatial and ecological differences are not only constituted by but constitutive of . . . socio-ecological and political-economic processes." However, there is a cultural, more symbolic side to these processes as well that approaches strictly oriented toward political economy often overlook. The production of nature and the production of social difference occur through similar processes and are often intertwined, particularly when representations of nature serve to naturalize social relations and power structures. The logics of colonial domination in particular produced ideologies and imaginaries that acted to control both ecologies and people. Tropical natural landscapes and the colonized "natives" who inhabited them both served as untamed "Others" to the European colonizers, who sought to prove their civilization and superiority by dominating and exploiting both. The equation of non-White people with nature and natural landscapes worked as a dehumanizing strategy that attempted to naturalize their enslavement and exploitation. Moreover, nineteenth-century race theories mobilized nature to produce the "fact" of racial difference and "innate" social hierarchies. Theories of environmental determinism, contrasting the effects of tropical and temperate climes on their inhabitants, bolstered the race theories that justified imperialism and its "civilizing mission" (Robbins 2004, 64; Sheller 2003; Argyrou 2005).

These imaginative geographies that legitimated colonialism and slavery continue to legitimate oppression and exploitation in the present. The construction of difference through spatial categories and relations has received increasing attention in anthropological work. An important concern has been with large spatial categories such as "East" and "West," or "tropical" and "temperate" zones. However, these spatial techniques of differentiation work more generally through what Akhil Gupta and James Ferguson (1992, 7) call the "assumed isomorphism of space, place and culture." Associations between space and culture have been naturalized through ethnological and national naturalisms (Gupta and Ferguson 1992; Malkki 1992): the equation of "cultures" and nations, respectively, with specific territories. Cultural differences and identities are territorialized through the naturalization of connections between people and places.

Ethnological naturalisms located—or incarcerated (Appadurai 1988)— the original anthropological "native" statically in the non-urban non-West, as discussed previously. In a related move, national naturalisms have attached the imagined communities of the nation to specific territories. These national territories form the "natural habitats" of the citizens of a nation. They are often constructed in relation to specific landscapes (mountains, deserts, lowlands) and through natural metaphors (roots, blood, kinship) and metonyms (national trees, flowers, birds, and other "totemic" species). Through such naturalisms, national belonging becomes a static concept that is inscribed in a specific territory and defined by a natural or ecological law (Olsen 1999; Comaroff and Comaroff 2001). Similar processes of spatially mapping and naturalizing difference can be identified at a variety of scalar levels, such as between the city and the countryside or between gendered spaces within the household. Across scales, though, the cultural construction of spatial meaning is a political process, with economic interests and material effects (Lefebvre 1991).

In this book, I combine this idea of politicized place-making with the production of nature in urban space. I develop the concept of "urban naturalisms": the equation of specific urban populations with specific traits and specific types of spaces. How are the associations of certain types of bodies with certain urban places naturalized? How do these naturalizations in turn legitimate urban inequalities, and specifically urban environmental inequalities? And how does the socio-spatially unequal distribution of environmental pollutants and hazards reproduce the original urban naturalisms? I argue that, for the Caribbean cities studied here, this production of difference through nature, the environment, and urban space entails a number of distinct but intertwined and simultaneous processes that rely heavily on constructs of pollution.

Urban naturalisms

This book attempts to problematize and de-naturalize the way difference is produced and reproduced in the context of urban space. Pollution is an important trope in these urban naturalisms. As Greg Garrard (2004, 9) notes, any environmental trope can be appropriated and deployed to serve a range of potentially opposed interests. Pollution as a trope can function to maintain an oppressive social order, but it equally has the potential, such as through the inversion of its application, to interrogate or undermine the dominant order. I focus on this trope here to understand the entanglement of material and symbolic forms of pollution: the ways in which physically measurable, quantifiable forms such as garbage, sewage, and air pollution interact with cultural concepts of contamination. The materiality and sociality of urban pollution are relational entities that produce each other, making pollution a nature–culture hybrid similar to the city itself. Pollution, in this sense, can be used as a lens through which to dissect the social and cultural intricacies of the urban environment, space, and power.

In this book, I explore the different ways in which these hybrid forms of pollution are implicated in the production and naturalization of urban difference in the Caribbean and beyond. I discuss the ways in which certain bodies—classed, raced, gendered—are culturally classified as pollutants that threaten the urban and social order. These bodies are associated with specific "dirty" marginal places in which material and symbolic pollution converge: marginalized people are seen to pollute the places where they live and work, and conversely, dirty places come to be understood as the proper site for such bodies. These associations of people and places can be used to legitimate the unequal distribution of environmental hazards or physical pollution in blame-the-victim policies. This institutionalizes the spatial concentration of material-symbolic pollution in specific places. To contain it there and to preclude contagion of cleaner, healthier parts of the city, segregation and other spatial techniques of domination are employed. If these are somewhat successful, the conflation of people, places, and pollution can become sufficiently strong to generate environmental determinism, reproducing the urban naturalism.

I argue that mainstream, professional environmentalism—what I call "Uptown environmentalism"—both developed within the force field of this urban naturalism and feeds back into it. This dominant form of environmentalism operates within colonially shaped geographies of purity and pollution that depoliticize environmental problems and frame the urban poor as socio-ecological threats rather than as victims. Its inattention to urban environmental problems reproduces the "natural" association of poor Afro-Caribbean populations with polluted ghettoized neighborhoods. The "Downtown environmentalism" that developed within the main spaces of social and material pollution cannot be understood outside of this same urban naturalism. By recognizing the underlying relations of power that distribute both social groups and environmental problems in urban space, this "lay" form of environmentalism offers the possibility of de-naturalizing the conflation of material pollution with marginalized people and places. It prioritizes brown environmental problems over green ones and connects them to social, economic, and political issues, noting, for instance, that the economic benefits of polluting industries accrue to groups who remain at a social and spatial distance from those industries' environmental effects. While displaying a historically shaped ambiguity toward wilderness and untamed nature, Downtown environmentalism depicts humans and nature as interconnected and expresses religiously informed ideas of balance.

Divergent environmentalisms, emplacement, and embodiment

In recent decades, most Caribbean governments and NGOs have tended to prioritize green environmental problems such as biodiversity, the marine environment, and nature conservation within a framework of sustainable tourism. This professional environmentalist focus, however, is not shared by residents of low-income neighborhoods, who are confronted on a day-to-day basis with brown environmental problems such as waste management, sewage, air pollution, and flooding. I argue that this green prioritization can be explained through specific classed interests and orientations that reflect the socio-spatial divisions of Caribbean cities such as Willemstad and Kingston. On the one hand, a commitment to an image of the Caribbean as tropical paradise, linked to the economic significance of tourism and the funding priorities of global actors, accounts for the concern with conservation. On the other, popular blame-the-poor rhetoric that naturalizes the association of poverty and pollution underlies the lack of attention to the problems that are concentrated in inner-city areas. A historical contextualization of these two tendencies can help us understand the general neglect of urban pollution.

Within cities such as Willemstad and Kingston, the urban poor and other marginalized social groups bear the brunt of pollution. Social movements that are themselves classed and racialized seek to address environmental problems but sometimes end up crafting their own exclusive regimes of environmental knowledge. Despite widespread global institutional support for participatory approaches, and the incorporation of "local knowledge" in environmental and natural resource management, strong hierarchical divisions in practice still exist between different types of environmental knowing. Formal environmental knowledges and the politics, policies, campaigns, and flows of funding that accompany them have economic and material effects on urban space and the people who live there. Definitions of environmental problems and their causes, consequences, and solutions can enable or constrain livelihoods, reward or penalize urban activities, and maintain or transform the urban built environment. If smoke and air pollution are associated with economic growth and progress, they may be tolerated as inevitable side effects of a positive development, rather than classified and managed as an environmental problem. If the causes of urban pollution—such as garbage, for instance—are located in social pathologies of the poor, the outcome for polluted spaces and the urban poor will be markedly different than if socio-ecological inequality is taken to be the root cause. The elision of cities and urban environmental problems from environmental policy and practice, then, undermines the rights of the urban poor.

The way nature and the environment are imagined and defined must be understood within spatially embedded and embodied contexts (Goldman and Schurman 2000). Different environmentalisms are developed in different spaces of residence, work, and leisure by people whose classed, raced, and gendered bodies experience their social and physical urban environments in different ways. The constitution of environmental knowledge and practice cannot be understood as separate from urban, national, and global regimes of power and their politics of difference. In this book, I argue for an emplaced and embodied approach to urban ecologies in order to understand the complex ways in which environmentalism is implicated in the reproduction and spatialization of power, difference, and inequality.

Structure of the book

The chapters that follow analyze the mutually constitutive dynamics of Caribbean environmentalism, urban space, and the politics of difference. Chapters Two, Three, and Four provide a detailed historical and ethnographic analysis of Caribbean urban space, from the colonial past into the contemporary postcolonial period. These chapters dissect the colonial character of Willemstad and Kingston and demonstrate how the built environment in particular constitutes those traces of empire that continue to be reactivated in the twenty-first century. The politics of difference continue to play out through shifting configurations of color, class, and urban space. These politics and their imprints on the social, natural, and built environments are situated within changing global political economies.

In Chapter Two, I provide a historical background to the two case studies, detailing the historical development of Willemstad and Kingston within a comparative Caribbean urban framework. Considering the potential of comparative urbanism more broadly, the chapter reflects on the salience of "Caribbean cities" as a framework of analysis, given the diversity of urban development trajectories within the region. This is followed by sections that outline the socio-spatial and political development of the two islands and their capital cities, highlighting both similarities and divergences in their historical trajectories. The chapter ends with an introduction to the four research neighborhoods, focusing on their social and ecological characteristics and their positioning within the larger urban landscape.

Chapter Three builds on this discussion of urban development in historical perspective through an exploration of colonial socio-ecological relations, proposing that these relations can serve to contextualize contemporary forms of environmental injustice in the urban Caribbean. The chapter connects colonial interventions into Caribbean natural and built environments to discourses and narratives of difference and inequality. It focuses first on early colonial discourses and practices that worked on and through natural landscapes, exploring how the imaginative geography of "tropical paradise" shaped proto-environmentalist action and occluded the centrality of cities to colonial commerce and control. Moving to the nineteenth and twentieth centuries, the chapter presents a discussion of colonial urbanism, investigating how the imaginative geography of the pathogenic urban slum functioned within post-emancipation strategies of control.

Chapter Four examines how historically shaped geographies of exclusion are experienced and narrated in twenty-first-century Caribbean cities, offering an ethnographic exploration of the discursive construction and social use of urban spaces. It discusses how residents of Kingston and Willemstad differentiate between sections of the urban landscape and between forms of urban mobility, and how these differentiations are central to the reproduction of urban inequalities. In order to understand how the fragmentation and segregation of these cities has come to seem natural, the chapter considers the complex ways in which raced, classed, and gendered bodies are emplaced within the broader urban landscape and within micro-places such as a car, an office, or a street. Urban privilege is emplaced and embodied; it involves both physical distance from, and insulation against, the dirty and violent spaces of the urban poor. The chapter considers how, in their everyday spatial practices and narratives, residents of Caribbean low-income neighborhoods both reproduce and subvert these dominant spatial and bodily regimes.

In Chapter Five, I delve more deeply into the role of pollution in constructing and naturalizing urban inequalities, connecting concepts of cultural pollution to the distribution of material pollution and examining their co-production in urban space. In Kingston and Willemstad, physical contaminants such as uncollected garbage, raw sewage, and toxic smoke are conflated with certain places and populations, and are justified through references to social pathologies. While these justifications of environmental injustice are not always explicitly racist or classist, they draw directly on colonial patterns of urban development and historically developed portrayals of darker-skinned Afro-Caribbean persons and their surroundings as unhealthy, unsafe, and unmodern. The chapter dissects the workings of the urban naturalisms that make instances of environmental injustice appear normal. I consider the various spatial and discursive tactics that residents of polluted neighborhoods such as Riverton and Wishi/Marchena use to negotiate socio-ecological discrimination, showing how these tactics involve the simultaneous rejection, deflection, and reproduction of urban naturalisms.

The next two chapters examine two broad types of environmentalism that I encountered, understanding their development against this background of socio-spatial fragmentation and exclusion. I suggest that not only do different social spaces—in this case, Uptown and Downtown areas—produce different kinds of urban and environmental practice and knowledge, but in addition, these different practices and knowledges produce different kinds of urban and environmental subjects (cf. Lora-Wainwright et al. 2012; Singh 2013). Because Uptown environmentalism is the formal, institutionalized type of knowledge and ties into global epistemic and funding structures, this social distance between urban environmental subjects has political-economic repercussions. The urban landscapes of Kingston and Willemstad, then, contain the traces of empire, and the geographies of exclusion shaped by colonial power structures are reactivated through contemporary environmental discourse and practice.

Chapter Six focuses on the Uptown environmentalism of environmental professionals in governmental and nongovernmental organizations. This form of environmentalism is concerned with green environmental issues such as biodiversity, wildlife, coral reefs, and the marine environment. Urban environmental problems such as air pollution, sewage, and garbage tend to feature peripherally, if at all. This focus is analyzed in relation to the class and ethno-racial composition of these organizations, many of which are headed by either foreigners or largely light-skinned members of the middle class. This green focus reflects the importance of tourism to Caribbean governments and business elites and the green environmental agenda pushed by global stakeholders and funding. In addition, environmental concern is increasingly a symbolic marker of class distinction. Discursively, NGO and governmental environmental campaigns draw on national naturalisms that frame the islands as pure, unspoiled tropical landscapes. These discourses indirectly frame the environment as something that needs to be protected from poor people and their problems.

Chapter Seven contrasts this type of discourse with Downtown environmentalism, a loosely organized framework of causality and blame that positions poor people as a group who need to be protected from environmental problems. This form of environmentalism stresses brown environmental problems such as garbage, air pollution, and sewage, and links them to an inequitable social context. Residents of environmentally degraded and hazardous urban areas connect environmental problems to their status as low-income, politically marginalized communities. Downtown environmentalism emphasizes the combined and interrelated effects of environmental and infrastructure degradation, poverty, violence and crime, and social disintegration. Environmental issues are seen in the light of socio-economic inequities at the urban and national levels, which are evident in a lack of political concern for the living conditions of the urban poor and an inability on their part to mobilize effectively against or influence policy that affects them.

The politics of difference that are at work in creating divided environmentalisms and divided cities are strengthened by these same environmental and spatial discourses. Situating different environmental discourses in urban space, within larger national and global political economies, can help us understand how citizens' understandings of the environment both reflect and reinforce a socially and spatially divided urban landscape. Forms of environmentalism that implicitly or explicitly understand cities as opposed to nature, and poor people as a threat to environmental purity, contribute to urban naturalisms that further normalize social hierarchies and the unequal distribution of environmental problems.

CARIBBEAN CITIES IN COMPARATIVE PERSPECTIVE

A superficial comparison between Willemstad and Kingston would appear to present two very different cities. Willemstad, with a population of about 140,000, curves gently around Curaçao's Schottegat Harbor. It has a clearly defined city center, which has been designated a UNESCO World Heritage Site for its distinctive Dutch Caribbean colonial architecture. Many of these colorful monuments have been carefully restored, and the streets swarm with Dutch and American tourists who sip cold drinks in sidewalk cafés, visit the city's various museums, and sample the duty-free shopping before they return to their beachfront hotels or their cruise ship. Kingston, on the other hand, is a sprawling city with about 600,000 inhabitants that is considered a no-go area by most visitors to Jamaica, who tend to stay in the all-inclusive tourist zones of the north coast. Attempts to "revitalize" the historic city center, which was devastated by an earthquake in 1907 but sports a variety of art deco buildings, have proved largely futile. Political and gang violence, accompanied by a lack of state investment and corporate speculation, have resulted in a devastated inner-city full of burnt-out hulls of buildings, its streets strewn with garbage and its walls marked with political graffiti.

As the apparent contrast suggests, Willemstad and Kingston differ in many respects—they are each marked by specific colonial histories, political systems, economic emphases, and ecological conditions. Yet the two cities also have much in common, with each other and with a broad variety of other Caribbean cities. The region's diverse territories share similar historical trajectories, characterized by European colonialism, slavery, and institutionalized racism. Following Sidney Mintz, the Caribbean can be understood as an *oikoumêne*, a framework within which historical processes combined to produce specific results. Mintz (1996, 297) underlines that "the societies of the Caribbean are differentiated not only internally in terms of class, ethnicity and other criteria, but also cross-culturally. [T]he similarities between [Caribbean societies] are not, properly speaking, cultural in nature. ... The Caribbean, in other words, is not a culture area." Rather, a more loosely defined Caribbean *oikoumêne* that took shape had its basis in "the imperial intentions of its rulers, even though those rulers, taken together, represented different cultures with different ideologies," and was shaped more broadly by "the social frameworks created for culturally diverse migrant peoples who were subjected to centuries-long processes of mostly forced cultural change by European rulers; and [by] the long-term effects of those processes upon Caribbean life."

In the context of this book, I take as my starting point the historical trajectories and associated models of colonial urbanism that have shaped patterns of Caribbean urban development in Curaçao and Jamaica, as elsewhere throughout the region. As Michel-Rolph Trouillot (1992, 22) argues, "Caribbean societies are inherently colonial. . . . . [T]heir social and cultural characteristics . . . cannot be accounted for, or even described, without reference to colonialism." The centuries during which colonial power was manifested through urban planning and architecture have created classed and racialized geographies of exclusion that continue to reverberate in the twenty-first century. Within this framework of shared histories, I seek to also highlight the intra-regional differentiations and divergent patterns that characterize the *oikoumêne*.

This chapter reflects on the diversity and commonalities of Caribbean cities and, more broadly, on the possibilities of comparative urbanism. It presents a broader comparative framework for understanding Willemstad and Kingston, emphasizing the historical trajectories that have shaped them in the present. In addition to marking the parallels and "Caribbean" characteristics that these two cities display, I elaborate on the contrasts between the two cases and flesh out the implications they have for analyzing urban pollution in relation to differentiations of race, class, and space. The chapter starts with an overview of the region's historical urban development, exploring what the parameters of a Caribbean urbanism might be. This is followed by two sections that present a more detailed and explicitly comparative treatment of the historical development of Willemstad and Kingston, providing context for the comparisons and ethnographic discussions that follow later on in the book. These sections also present the four urban research neighborhoods in more detail, including background information on their socio-economic characteristics and an overview of the environmental problems that affect them.

Comparative urbanism in the Caribbean
Comparative urbanism and area studies

Both anthropological and historical work on Caribbean cities have tended to focus on single case studies. Even in urban studies more broadly, ideographic single-city studies have been the norm, a tendency reflecting the late-twentieth-century aversion to overly schematic city models or typologies. More recently, however, urban geographers in particular have begun to call for a "comparative urbanism." While recognizing that every city has a unique and idiosyncratic character, and eschewing the universalizing, nomothetic positivism of early comparative studies, these scholars point to the benefits of developing explicit comparative methodologies and conceptual frameworks. Such frameworks could involve, as Michael Dear (2005) suggests, concentrating on urban processes rather than cities per se in order to tease out common dynamics and tendencies. However, other authors argue that a new comparative urbanism needs to move beyond commonalities to study both convergence *and* divergence. Jan Nijman (2007a, 1), for instance, holds that comparative urbanism should involve "the systematic study of similarity and difference among cities or urban processes . . . [and address] descriptive and explanatory questions about the extent and manner of similarity and difference."

Such an approach, which may involve studying one city in the light of another comparable case, can take into account both place-particularity and "deep analogies," teasing out more general mechanisms while recognizing the limits of urban generalizations (Nijman 2007b). The comparison between Kingston and Willemstad pursued in this book builds on such approaches, practicing a form of comparison that attends to analogous historical and contemporary socio-ecological processes while explicitly acknowledging the specificities of different localities and points in time. Within these two cities, my focus on four research neighborhoods offers the possibility to also highlight differences and similarities at a smaller level of scale. In addition to exploring this type of comparative ethnography, I also draw inspiration from studies in global ethnography that direct our attention to broader transnational relations and connections—such as those associated with imperialism or environmentalism and their epistemic cultures—in order to contextualize the comparison between these two cities (e.g., Burawoy et al. 2000; Holmes and Marcus 2005).

Comparative urbanists have in part been interested in contrasting cities across different geopolitical regions. In particular, much debate has concentrated on comparing cities in the global North with those in the global South, drawing on urban anthropology and postcolonial approaches to critique the Euro-American bias in urban theory and to "provincialize" those universalisms rooted in empirical work in the Northern cities (Robinson 2004, 2011; McFarlane 2010). However, scholars have also drawn on these new comparative approaches to develop and study intra-regional parallels and variations in ways that avoid schematic typologies of "the Asian city" or "the African city" (Ernstson et al. 2014; Ren and Luger 2015; Waley 2012). In reflecting on the possibilities connected with the development of a comparative urbanism within Asia, for instance, Julie Ren and Jason Luger (2015, 145) ask, "How do we approach this 'regional' topic in a way that both resists categorizing the 'Asian City' as an exotic 'other,' elevating it onto a mythical pedestal, yet appreciates its differences, localisms and unique 'cosmopolitan vernacular'?" This type of comparative urbanism seeks to retain the advantages offered by an area studies approach—such as an attentiveness to the specificities of history, territory, and place and the importance of proximity—without suggesting regional exceptionalism or developing new forms of parochialism.

Such explorations of regional forms of urbanism connect to larger debates on urban theory and area studies. Urban studies scholars such as Ananya Roy (2009) have called for a critical epistemological examination of the "geographies of theory." Emphasizing the locatedness of urban theory, she argues for more attention to the particular "conceptual vectors" that emerge from specific historical contexts and intellectual traditions, and have shaped the area-based production of knowledge. This scholarship recognizes and interrogates genealogies of regional theorization in a process that both locates and dislocates urban theory. Such a process involves developing an area studies approach to cities that uses the framework of the region as a heuristic device, in a strategically essentialist fashion, but explores the connections between multiple area-based knowledges. Building on these insights in the context of Africanist urbanism, for example, Henrik Ernstson, Mary Lawhon, and James Duminy (2014, 1564) seek to "develop new theoretical insights rooted in, and relevant to, African cities with broader significance for urban studies."

Similarly, this book explores the possibilities of bringing a rich tradition of regional, Caribbeanist scholarship into dialogue with broader theoretical discussions on cities, ecologies, and the politics of difference. Caribbean studies has emphasized the lasting legacies of colonialism, connecting the region's positioning within global hierarchies of value to more localized social hierarchies structured around intersections of race, class, and gender. Caribbean urbanists have noted how these global–local power structures worked in and through urban space, while ecocritical work on the region's tropical island landscapes has emphasized how the natural environment has been harnessed to projects of both domination and resistance.[1] Combining these different strands of Caribbeanist research, I draw on a closer examination of two cities within the region to propose new approaches to urban environmental injustice that may shed light on the material semiotics of pollution in cities.

Caribbean urbanism

Within the Caribbean, there has been a limited exploration of a regional tradition of urban theory. However, recent genealogies of Caribbeanist theory, and Caribbeanist anthropology in particular (Slocum and Thomas 2003; Thomas and Slocum 2008), point to the importance of distinct themes, concepts, and categories and locate them within specific academic traditions. There has been a strong school of Caribbean political economy, studying plantation economies, global capitalism, and labor relations. Other important theoretical emphases within Caribbean studies have included social integration and disintegration (expressed in the plural society and creolization debates); the connections among colonialism, nationalism, and identity politics connected to intersectional hierarchies of class, gender, and race/ethnicity; and globalization, migration, and transnationalism.

These themes have also been evident in studies of Caribbean cities, which have largely concentrated on colonial urbanism (see Jaffe et al. 2008). A significant body of historical geographical work has focused on patterns of urbanization in the context of colonialism, mercantile capitalism, and plantation economies (e.g., Cross 1979; Potter 1989). This work has emphasized the extent to which the form and functions of many contemporary Caribbean cities, expressed in their spatial, social, and economic features, reflect a shared past of colonialism and economic dependency. The mercantile capitalism that shaped the region in the first centuries of colonization has been associated with a classic pattern of dependent urbanization without industrialization oriented toward the economies of western Europe. Within a global system of urban places, the region's port cities served as nodes connecting their hinterland to the colonial metropole in Europe.

The role of colonial cities was to extract surplus, expand the market for European commodities, and maintain political stability within the larger colony (King 1990). As the role of Caribbean plantation economies within the infamous triangular trade network expanded, coastal settlements founded as fortresses developed into commercial gateways for the transportation and trade of enslaved Africans, agricultural products, and manufactured goods. In contrast to mainland Latin America, there was little indigenous urbanization in the insular Caribbean, and the rapid death or deportation of most of the native inhabitants made it easier for the European colonizers to treat the islands as *terra nullius*, empty land. Unlike most other regions where urban development took place within a rural context, historical circumstances meant that Caribbean cities developed prior to the rural hinterland. Rather, the population of the rural areas, proceeding outward from the urban centers of military defense and administrative control, only took place as plantation agriculture grew in importance.

The more anthropological Caribbeanist themes of societal (dis)integration, colonialism, and identity politics can be recognized in both historical and contemporary urbanist work that focuses on urban fragmentation along ethno-racial, class, and gender lines, often in relation to strategies of colonial control (e.g., Mohammed 2008; De Barros 2002; Ulysse 2007; Dinzey-Flores 2013). In circumstances marked by extreme ethno-racial inequality and exploitation, colonial "integration" was often achieved through spatial techniques of domination and, in particular, through colonial urban planning and policing strategies. These reflected a concern with preventing urban uprisings among enslaved people and the post-emancipation non-White underclass by controlling their movements and expanding the possibilities of surveillance. Planners and administrators ensured that the principles of colonialism were expressed in the urban built environment, from the layout of the city and its quarters to the shapes of its streets and buildings. Residential segregation featured as a central fact of colonial rule, creating and reiterating intersectional categories of social difference and identity along lines of race, ethnicity, occupation, income, and gender.

The aesthetics of the built environment also reflect such identity politics and negotiations of authority. Colonial authorities and elites sought to express or consolidate their power through the built environment by erecting impressive architecture, from stately government offices and churches to splendid storefronts, or mandating strict regulations on specific dimensions, building materials, styles, or colors to be used in the construction of buildings and streets in formal city districts (Mohammed 2008). While certain measures were implemented from a public health perspective, as described in the next chapter, such policies also served to deliberately demonstrate colonial authority through the imposition of respectable, "civilized," or "European" norms in architecture and urban layout. In less formal lower-income areas, often located on the urban periphery, laissez-faire approaches on the part of the colonial authorities enabled the development of vernacular, hybrid forms of using and adorning the built environment. These shantytowns, communal yards, and building and decorating styles offered opportunities for the elaboration of aesthetic and political positions outside the control or interest of elites (e.g., Römer 2003; Raymond 2013).

The Caribbeanist interest in globalization, migration, and transnationalism is also evident in analyses of the region's urban development and city life, from discussions of the "proto-globalization" associated with imperialism and mercantile capitalism (e.g., Rupert 2012; Cañizares-Esguerra et al. 2013) to an engagement with the acceleration and intensification of global flows of people, capital, goods, and ideas in the late twentieth and early twenty-first centuries. The latter body of work has studied how urban form and social relations have been influenced by global economic flows associated with mass tourism or export-processing zones; by migration; and by policies propagated by global financial institutions, particularly those related to structural adjustment (e.g., Portes et al. 1997; Potter 2000; Gregory 2007).

This broad sketch of themes in discussions of Caribbean urbanism, with its emphasis on the historical trajectories, political strategies, and global interconnections associated with colonialism and its legacies, serves to frame the more specific historical development of Kingston and Willemstad, presented in the sections that follow. Both contexts are also marked by colonial patterns of dependency and domination, by racialized negotiations of authority and identity, and by contemporary global connections. However, these contexts also differ significantly in terms of political, demographic, ecological, and economic developments.

One obvious difference is Curaçao's nonsovereign status as a country within the Kingdom of the Netherlands, which has shaped urban conditions in more than one way. The standard of living is significantly higher in Willemstad than in Kingston, although socio-economic inequality and environmental injustice within Willemstad (and indeed within the Kingdom) are stark. In addition, Curaçao's lack of independence is associated with its large population of wealthy White Dutch expats, who often live in segregated urban enclaves and are often driven by a semi-colonial "will to improve" (Li 2007) the island. More broadly, Kingston has had a less varied migration history in recent decades than Willemstad. Not only does the latter city have a larger White population because of its continued relationship with the Netherlands, but in addition, the presence of large numbers of light-skinned but relatively low-status Latino migrants, who tend to be concentrated in low-income *barios*, has also somewhat disrupted historically established color–class correlations. Finally, the different island ecologies—Curaçao's semi-arid climate and location near oil reserves, and Jamaica's tropical climate and fertile soils—are connected to different economic histories, with Willemstad developing as a commercial and later an industrial town while Kingston grew more directly in relation to its agricultural hinterland of plantations. Together, these various factors inform different understandings of which urban places and populations are considered "dirty," who is seen as responsible for solving environmental problems, and what solutions are considered feasible.

Kingston, Jamaica
From port town to troubled capital

Jamaica, with an area of some 11,000 km^2, is the third-largest Caribbean island after Cuba and Hispaniola and the largest of the Anglophone islands. [2] Following its occupation by the Spanish in 1509, nearly all the indigenous Taino people died. The English forces who gained power over the island in 1655 proceeded to develop lucrative sugarcane plantations, making extensive use of enslaved labor until full emancipation was achieved in 1838. A plantation society developed, characterized by economic dependency and "an abiding Eurocentrism which puts everything European in a place of eminence and things of . . . African origin in a lesser place" (Nettleford 1978, 3). The population was divided into roughly four different social groups: Whites; "Free Coloreds"; enslaved Blacks; and Maroons, who had escaped slavery to live in the island's mountainous interior. The White elite was always both diverse and very small; Europeans never represented more than a few percent of the population.

Soon after capturing Jamaica from the Spanish, the English erected several forts to guard the large natural harbor formed by the Palisadoes, a long thin peninsula that runs parallel to the shoreline. Kingston itself was not founded until 1692, after a large earthquake destroyed the naval and commercial town of Port Royal, which was located on the opposite side of the harbor on the Palisadoes. The colonial capital at the time was Spanish Town (named after its previous role as the main Spanish settlement, when it was called Villa de la Vega), and Kingston's principal role in the eighteenth century was the collection, storage, and export of sugar to Britain, and the import, storage, and dispatching of enslaved Africans and British manufactured goods to the plantation estates. Kingston's advantageous location on an accessible natural harbor facilitated its development as an important regional center within the transatlantic system of mercantile capitalism. The city's population grew as a result of (involuntary) immigration from Africa and Europe and in-migration from the plantations, increasing from under 5,000 in 1700 to 25,000 in 1790 to 30,000 in 1807 and 35,000 in 1828, before decreasing to 27,400 in 1861 following the cholera epidemic described in the next chapter (Clarke 2006a, 5). Kingston's social order was liberal compared to the estates, but still very much related to color, with a strong color–status correlation. Initially, spatial segregation was not very rigid, but as the city expanded, richer people chose to live in the cooler, less dusty hills to the northeast of the city, so that a more definite relationship between income and spatial distribution developed. Colin Clarke describes Kingston in its early stages as "a transplanted European town, designed by the white elite to fulfil its own requirements," noting how building regulations that stipulated that huts and housing compounds could have only one entrance functioned to enable searches by the authorities (2006a, 9, 11).

In the late nineteenth century, following the abolition of slavery and with the onset of the free trade era, Jamaica and Kingston's economies slumped. Kingston's role as a trade center diminished, and so too did the harbor's commercial activities. With the exception of a small economic comeback when Kingston replaced Spanish Town as the island's capital in 1872 and a short banana export boom in the 1890s, this economic recession lasted until early in the twentieth century. Despite this, Crown colony rule—introduced by the British following the Morant Bay Rebellion in 1865—brought about a certain level of modernization and improvements in infrastructure and healthcare. The divisions between the three main social strata of "Blacks," "Coloreds," and "Whites" became more established in this period, even as small but relatively influential groups of Syrians, Chinese, East Indians, and Jews settled in Kingston.

The 1920s and 1930s were decades of civil and labor unrest as well as the growth of Black nationalist movements such as Marcus Garvey's Universal Negro Improvement Association (UNIA). These movements played a significant role in revalorizing Blackness and in fomenting the political consciousness that resulted in the attainment of universal suffrage in 1944 and independence in 1962. In the 1940s and 1950s, Kingston's population once again grew explosively as a result of urbanization, but the majority of rural migrants found themselves impoverished and living in the city's tenement yards. Social conditions were and remained miserable, with high rates of unemployment, violent crime, and overcrowding. Post-independence "political tribalism" and gang warfare between supporters of the two major political parties starting in the 1960s and 1970s exacerbated the decline of the main commercial area in Downtown Kingston, and the corporate sector shifted Uptown with the development of New Kingston as a modern business district.

As the city began to expand, commerce and retail shifted to New Kingston and to U.S.-style shopping malls, while wealthier residents moved to suburban homes in the cooler hills surrounding the city. The original city center, which enclosed the old colonial residential and administrative district, became largely rundown. Urbanization in the late twentieth and early twenty-first centuries has taken its toll on the natural environment and urban resources. Housing conditions are often miserable, with increasing numbers of people squatting in hazardous sites such as steep slopes and gully banks. Water supplies, sewerage, and waste disposal systems often lack the capacity to provide adequate services to the growing neighborhoods. There is a marked socio-spatial schism between the "ghettos" and "garrisons" of Downtown and the spacious, well-guarded gated communities and "residential" areas of Uptown, a disparity that is described in more detail in Chapter Four. While this classed divide is also racialized, the association of a dark skin color with poverty weakened in these years as educational opportunities, migration, and transnational networks enabled the emergence of a Black middle class (Robotham 2000; Thomas 2004). Meanwhile, the squatter settlements that popped up near Kingston's elite neighborhoods complicated the bipolar Uptown–Downtown divide.

Despite the poverty, crime, and physical degradation that have given Kingston a bad reputation at home and abroad, the city, known simply as "Town" throughout the island, is still seen as Jamaica's cultural, intellectual, and political heart. As Elizabeth Wheeler (1996, 174) elucidates: "What makes Kingston beautiful? Not its buildings nor its infrastructure— Kingston couldn't compete on that basis—but its lines of communication and movement." Kingston is a cosmopolitan site where things happen: socio-political movements, cultural transformations, innovations in the music industry, the newest fashion statements and dance moves: all come from Town.

Riverton and Rae Town

The two main Kingston research areas that I focus on in this book are both low-income neighborhoods located in Downtown Kingston (see Figure 2.1).

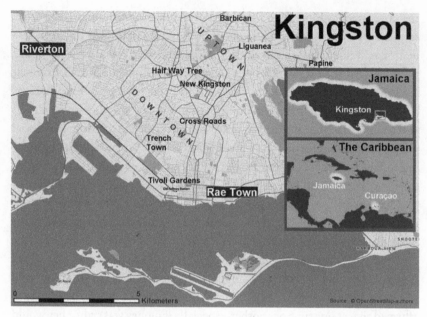

FIGURE 2.1 Map of Kingston, including location of Riverton and Rae Town

This half of the city is characterized by a variety of "inner-city" neighborhoods with different locations, histories, reputations, and levels of infrastructural development. Riverton lies on the urban periphery and developed as a squatter settlement in the 1960s, when political violence and the bulldozing of informal housing in West Kingston forced residents there to relocate. The neighborhood has a reputation as an area suffering from violence and extreme deprivation, related in part to its proximity to Jamaica's largest dumpsite. In contrast, Rae Town is located in Kingston's historical center, and its establishment dates back to the early nineteenth century. This neighborhood, which was built as a more formal district, has a middle-class past but was abandoned by its wealthier residents in the mid-twentieth century. Despite a history of political conflict with adjacent neighborhoods, many Kingstonians consider Rae Town to be a relatively safe inner-city area, a reputation due in part to its "Ole Hits" street dance, which attracts tourists and adventurous Uptown residents.

Riverton, with an estimated population of 2,340, or 812 households (Statistical Institute of Jamaica [STATIN] 2003, 31) at the time of my main fieldwork, lies off Spanish Town Road, a highway lined by industry, including a major brewery, a rum distillery, and a paint factory. A few rows of relatively sturdy and clean houses, built from cement and with fresh paint, stand near the entrance to the area. These dwellings were constructed as part of the government's Operation PRIDE, a program meant to upgrade squatter settlements that produced government-built houses that most Riverton residents could not afford to buy or rent. A bit farther in toward the dumpsite, the asphalted road disappears, the dust increases, and the stench from the landfill becomes more pungent. This is where the majority of residents live, as squatters in small one-room dwellings built out of wood, with zinc roofs and fencing, and illegal access to water and electricity. According to a Social Development Commission survey of living conditions, the majority of housing in Riverton is substandard in terms of building materials and access to toilet facilities (Social Development Commission [SDC] 1999a).[3]

Over the course of my research, I found that while on the outside these residences were a rather depressing sight, especially in combination with the dusty dirt road littered with rubble and garbage (see Figure 2.2), on the inside they were kept painstakingly clean and neat, with carefully maintained pieces of furniture crowding the small space. The garbage seemingly scattered about was not always waste in the literal sense; nearly all the people I spoke to affirmed that at one time or another, especially if money was tight, they would go search for sellable items on the landfill. At times these items would be set in front of houses, waiting for a buyer or a further destination. Around the time of my research over a third of the working population was unemployed, and many of those who did have work were employed at the dump or involved

FIGURE 2.2 Hog rummaging for food next to a zinc-fenced yard in Riverton

in (informal) recycling or small-scale farming (SDC 1999a). Data taken from the 2001 Population Census indicates that residents of Riverton were generally very young: over half of the residents were younger than 15, while almost 90 percent of the total population was under 35 (STATIN 2003).

More than other poor inner-city communities, Riverton is regarded by Kingston's Uptown public as a hellish no-go zone. Geographer Alan Eyre, who did research there in the early 1990s and in previous decades, termed it "the poorest and most desperate shantytown in the Caribbean" (Eyre 1997, 75). When I worked there, it was in fact very dusty, dirty, and smelly. The smell from the landfill bothered many residents, especially when garbage trucks dumped their loads nearer to the edge of the neighborhood or carried unusual substances such as chemicals. Another common complaint was the dust, which was a result not of the dump itself but of the garbage trucks that drove back and forth over the dusty, unpaved road all day. This dust, which could get "very wicked," made everything dirty and caused respiratory ailments. The dump was plagued by regular fires that sometimes raged for weeks, caused by spontaneous combustion or sometimes lit by residents, and the smoke from the burning garbage also presented serious health hazards. Residents were, obviously, aware of these hazards; as Mosiah, a young Rasta farmer, summed it up: "Chemicals come out, toxic waste and germs, it's not good for your health. It's really no good, you breathe it in, it internally pollutes." For many residents, however, the neighborhood represented economic opportunities through informal recycling. In fact, for the rural migrants who comprised one sector of the neighborhood's residents, the area provided improved access to urban facilities such as healthcare or education in comparison to the Jamaican countryside from which they had come.

In comparison to Riverton, Rae Town is a more established and centrally located neighborhood (see Figure 2.1) that a few years before I conducted my fieldwork there consisted of an estimated 790 households, or about 3,300 residents. Compared to Riverton, the community had fewer young people, but nevertheless nearly 75 percent of the population was younger than 35. While over a third of the working population was unemployed, the livelihoods of many residents depended on fishing and entertainment (SDC 1999b). Based on its location and socio-economic makeup, Rae Town is categorized as an inner-city or "ghetto" area, but because of its close proximity to the harbor, the neighborhood is cooler and breezier than most parts of Downtown Kingston. In addition, it is "cool" in a social sense, as it does not have the violent reputation of Riverton or, for instance, the adjacent neighborhoods of Southside and Dunkirk.

To the north, the community is bordered by the busy Windward Road; to the south, by the harbor and the fishing beach. The latter is a strip of sand on which a few dozen fishing boats wait to go out to sea, though not all are sufficiently seaworthy to be in use. A long line of gear sheds, tiny concrete roofed buildings, stand alongside the beach. Built under the Michael Manley government in the 1970s, these sheds were meant as a place to store fishing gear such as nets, engines, and so on. However, individuals, and sometimes even families who found themselves without a home after, for instance, a fire or a hurricane, have taken up permanent residence in a number of these dwellings. Since the construction of Michael Manley Boulevard, a highway that roars straight through the middle of Rae Town, the beach has effectively been cut off from the rest of the community. However, residents living in the upper parts of the neighborhood would wander down to "cool out" in the shade on the beach with the fishermen. Paradise Street, the neighborhood's eastern boundary, reflects Rae Town's past as home to a more moneyed class of occupants. Like most of the community's streets, it is lined by sturdy concrete houses from around the 1920s, surrounded by relatively spacious yards. After the prosperous former inhabitants moved Uptown, long ago, most of the old houses were converted into tenements, interspersed with zinc-fenced communal yards that accommodate several wooden one-room shacks.

Many of Rae Town's streets are dilapidated, with rundown houses and a few filthy empty lots. Facilities tended to be better than in Riverton[4]; following government development projects, most of the roads were paved, the basic school was upgraded, and garbage collection became fairly regular. In addition, community members had initiated beautification projects, such as the establishment of miniature plots of grass and a few plants or the placement of whitewashed tires with plants or flowers in them. However, a considerable and recurring problem was sewage, which ran down the sides of the streets in rivulets. An important sewage pump near the beach and the newly rehabilitated community center would regularly back up and overflow, effectively impeding use of the center. The local sewer system was never designed to carry the load it was handling, and as a result it often clogged, especially when it rained, resulting in raw sewage running down the streets—a health hazard compounded by the fact that children would play in the filthy water.

Despite regular garbage collection, garbage was still a problem in that it clogged the main gullies running through Rae Town on Paradise Street and Margaret Street. Garbage thrown or blown into the gullies locally or in other parts of the city clogged these drains, attracting vermin and increasing the risk of flooding during heavy rain. Solid waste and wastewater management

FIGURE 2.3 Rae Town's polluted Paradise Street gully where it enters Kingston Harbor

were interrelated, as households throughout the city that were not connected to the sewage system sometimes disposed of their feces in plastic bags, which were thrown into the gullies. The rubbish in the gully would then flush into the harbor and wash up on Rae Town's beach, causing further pollution and affecting fishing and recreational activities negatively (see Figure 2.3). Residents throughout the area complained of mosquitoes, ants, cockroaches, and "rats big as puss" roaming brazenly through their yards. The pollution from the gully also contributed to the polluted state of the harbor, one of the major complaints among those involved in fishing.[5]

Willemstad, Curaçao
From fortress to refinery town

A small island some 50 kilometers north of the Venezuelan shore, Curaçao was first sighted by the Spanish in 1499, during an expedition led by Alonso de Ojeda.[6] The Spanish did not invest much effort in the territory, and in 1634, they ceded Curaçao to the Dutch West India Company (WIC). The establishment of Willemstad began with Fort Amsterdam, erected on St. Anna Bay at the mouth of the larger Schottegat Harbor. The semi-arid island was initially used only as a garrison, but by the 1650s the fort was expanding into a walled trade settlement. The Dutch deported to the mainland the majority of the few hundred indigenous inhabitants who had survived the Spanish conquest, and until emancipation in 1863 much of the economy relied on the labor of enslaved Africans. While a system of plantations developed on Curaçao, the semi-arid climate meant that export-based agriculture was never the economic mainstay. Instead, the colony developed in the seventeenth and eighteenth centuries as an important transshipment hub for legal and illegal inter-imperial trade, including the slave trade with South America; enslaved Africans passed through the island in transit to Spanish colonies or were made to work for the WIC.

In addition to Dutch Protestant settlers and enslaved Africans, Curaçao's population in this period also included Sephardic Jews who had fled the Catholic Inquisition in previously Dutch parts of Brazil. The limited importance of agriculture on Curaçao resulted in a more urbanized population than developed on many other Caribbean islands, and one with relatively high numbers of Whites and "Free People of Color."[7] While the city was organized as an open port town to facilitate the trade interests and activities of the White and Sephardic merchant elites, this openness was balanced by the restrictive regulation of the mobility of the enslaved population (Rupert 2012, 135–136). In 1789, the city housed 11,543 inhabitants, more than half of the total island population. Until the mid-nineteenth century, the expansion of Willemstad remained within the walled urban area of Punda and three other neighborhoods also clustered around St. Anna Bay: Otrobanda, Scharloo, and Pietermaai.

The city's main expansion took place in the first half of the twentieth century following the economic boom associated with the Isla oil refinery. Established by Royal Dutch Shell in the 1910s, the refinery has arguably been the principal formative factor in the development of Curaçao's social and physical landscape. Its construction resulted in rapid population growth— from 34,000 in 1915 to over 90,000 in 1947—and spurred Willemstad's development until the urban area eventually encircled the entire Schottegat Harbor. The refinery largely shaped the island's socio-economic structure and the urban landscape; both the polluting refinery itself and its production of a segregated cityscape are forms of what Ann Stoler (2013) calls "imperial debris." As the island's largest employer and a major political force, Shell was actively involved in the development of Willemstad. Afro-Curaçaoan manual laborers who had moved to the city from the countryside were generally not provided with housing and lived concentrated in slum-like conditions in *barios* such as Wishi/Marchena (Weeber 2004) or in the same "dark neighborhoods" that the colonial officials discussed in the next chapter tended to characterize as dens of vice and disease.

However, Shell also attracted refinery laborers from all over the world and spurred urban development through the construction of company housing in previously undeveloped areas on the north side of the harbor. The company purposely promoted segregation by providing separate neighborhoods and housing for different groups of employees, ordering them by class and ethno-national origin (Gill 2008). White Dutch managerial and engineering staff lived in airy villas in Julianadorp and Emmastad, spaciously constructed gated enclaves built well out of range of the refinery's emissions; the only non-Whites granted entry were domestic servants. Manual laborers from Portugal, Suriname, Venezuela, and the British West Indies were housed in more crowded barracks in ethnically segregated camps in neighborhoods called Suffisantdorp and Surinamedorp (Figure 2.4). These groups of laborers and their families were followed by a flow of Lebanese, Indians, Chinese, and Ashkenazi Jews attracted by trading opportunities.

FIGURE 2.4 Barracks for refinery workers in Willemstad, 1951

Through occupational and residential differentiation, Shell's state-sponsored policies created and consolidated ethnic and class boundaries. As Shell's influence waned and immigration continued and diversified toward the end of the twentieth century, ethno-residential patterns became more complex. With the widespread availability of cars and expansion of the road infrastructure in the mid-twentieth century, the sprawling urban area came to incorporate previously semi-rural areas and former plantations. The various *barios* circling the harbor, connected by a ring road and a large bridge spanning the port, formed a heterogeneous agglomeration. Middle-class Curaçaoans relocated to new suburban areas, leaving the city center to immigrants and the poor. Public housing projects on the urban periphery, such as those in Seru Fortuna, were intended to improve the living conditions of the urban poor, but often ended up concentrating, rather than alleviating, poverty. Starting in the 1990s, a revitalization of the inner city began to take place, and nascent processes of gentrification have helped conserve Willemstad's monuments while displacing residents, including many undocumented Latino migrants. Meanwhile, rapidly proliferating "villa parks" (as gated communities are known locally) on the urban fringes have become a preferred residential environment for the large population of White Dutch expats.

These socio-spatial developments, associated in diverse ways with Curaçaoan and immigrant groups who were positioned differently within the ethno-racial hierarchies established during three centuries of Dutch colonialism, have resulted in an urban landscape patterned less clearly than that of Kingston in terms of class and race. The social mobility of many Afro-Curaçaoans, and the influx of light-skinned Latino immigrants, most of whom settled in Willemstad's low-income neighborhoods, also began to alter the association between a *koló skur* (dark skin color) and a disadvantaged socio-spatial positioning. While less explicit than in Jamaica, Black nationalism became a more prominent tendency in Curaçao through the processes of "Antilleanization" that followed the "revolt" of May 30, 1969. Constitutional reforms in the first decade of the twenty-first century—as the non-independent confederation of the Netherlands Antilles was disbanded and Curaçao became a non-independent country within the Dutch Kingdom—spurred another wave of public reassessments of Afro-Curaçaoan identity (Allen 2010). Nonetheless, the history of colonial and corporate policies remains evident in the overrepresentation of *koló skur* Curaçaoans and immigrants in Willemstad's *marginal barios*. While Curaçao has a considerably higher gross domestic product (GDP) than Jamaica,[8] the high levels of poverty, unemployment, crime, and environmental degradation in Willemstad's low-income neighborhoods contrast sharply with the neighborhoods of the largely *koló kla* (light skin color) rich, where tall electronic gates, security systems, and guard dogs shield large mansions with swimming pools in the backyard. Lower-class Curaçaoans scarcely enter these neighborhoods except as maids and gardeners—positions increasingly occupied by immigrants—while the wealthy rarely see the poorer *barios* other than while passing by on the ring road.

Wishi/Marchena and Seru Fortuna

Two of Willemstad's most well-known low-income neighborhoods are Wishi/Marchena and Seru Fortuna (see Figure 2.5). Unlike in Kingston, in Willemstad such *"marginal"* areas are not concentrated in one part of the city, but are interspersed with much wealthier areas. The categorization of *marginal* covers a broad range of *barios*, from derelict areas in the historical city center and former squatter settlements that developed during the refinery's boom years to more peripheral semi-rural areas that became incorporated into Willemstad's urban sprawl and public housing estates constructed

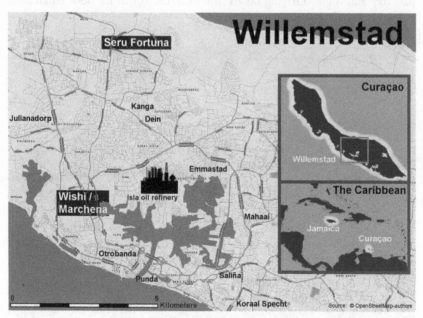

FIGURE 2.5 Map of Willemstad, including location of Wishi/Marchena and Seru Fortuna

in recent decades (Weeber 2004). Wishi/Marchena developed as a self-built *bario* in the 1930s, housing Shell laborers who had migrated from Curaçao's countryside. Later in the twentieth century, the neighborhood diversified as migrants from elsewhere in the Caribbean moved there as well. It had a *mal nomber* ("bad name") in these years, although this improved somewhat in the early twenty-first century. Seru Fortuna is located much more peripherally than Wishi/Marchena, and is a combination of a former rural estate dating back centuries and a public housing complex built in the mid-1970s. The latter section in particular became associated with the drug trade and violent crime around the 1990s, a reputation that has lasted into the twenty-first century. In contrast to other neighborhoods, it has relatively low numbers of foreign-born residents (Ministry of Social Development, Labor and Welfare [SOAW] 2012a, 2012b).

Wishi/Marchena lies on the southwest side of the harbor, downwind of the Isla. Because of the prevalent northeasterly trade wind, which makes the island's dry heat bearable, the refinery's emissions are always blown in one direction. This neighborhood receives most of the air pollution produced by the refinery's various petrochemical units and their dozens of chimneys, which spew smoke and flares day in, day out (Figure 2.6). The main ring road that circles Willemstad's harbor bisects the community, with cars zooming past day and night. Driving down this road, the sulfurous odor emanating

FIGURE 2.6 View of Wishi/Marchena, with Isla refinery in the background

from the refinery can be smelled from far off and becomes stronger as one nears the neighborhood. Marchena, the half of the neighborhood east of the ring road, is slightly more organized than Wishi to the west, with official street names and a layout that is more planned. Both small and large houses, often with a little *kurá* (yard), line the narrow allies. Wishi has a more scattered layout and no official streets. Unpaved and damaged roads curve up the hillier terrain, and empty patches of land, often used as informal garbage dumps, alternate with rows or clusters of houses.

Around the time of my study, Wishi/Marchena's population was estimated at 1,402, or some 600 households. A quarter of residents were under age 15, and 22 percent of the working population was unemployed (compared to 16 percent island-wide), of whom half had been unemployed for over a year. The youth unemployment rate was 43 percent. Almost half of the adult population were high school dropouts, and for 80 percent the first stage of secondary school was the highest level of education attained. The teenage pregnancy rate was considered problematically high. Government surveys classified some 13 percent of all housing as poor or very poor; most households had soak-away pits or septic tanks as toilet facilities. The community hosted a community center, a baseball field, a church, and a medical center, which, however, served a much larger area. At US$1,216 monthly, average household income was significantly lower than the island average of US$2,117. Over 20 percent of residents were not born on the island, and the *bario* housed many (documented and undocumented) immigrants from the region. Those from Suriname and the British West Indies had settled in the area several decades prior; recent immigrants included mainly female immigrants from the Dominican Republic (Central Bureau of Statistics [CBS] 2002, 2004; George et al. 2003; Arthur Andersen 1996).

The refinery, which most people referred to as "the Shell," featured prominently in discussions of the community's problems. Wishi/Marchena residents saw its smoke and soot as a big problem, mitigated slightly by the fact that the height of the refinery's smokestacks had been increased. Where pollution used to be an all-day constant, the intensity of the emissions now fluctuated. Nights were the worst, when the refinery emitted so much dust that the sky was misty. Residents were familiar with the technical details of the refining process and pointed out that conditions worsened when the catalytic cracker was started up. The dust that blew into the cracks of their houses settled on everything and necessitated constant cleaning, while the acid in the emissions caused cars and metal roofs to corrode. Many residents objected to the sulfurous smell, although others who had grown up in the area had become so accustomed to the fumes that the smell did not bother them, or would even evoke positive associations with home. However, they too immediately noted irregularities, such as changes in the makeup of emissions, based on the smell. The refinery's effects on health were a cause of concern, and a number of residents mentioned headaches and becoming out of breath quickly.[9] In addition to the refinery's emissions, another problem was the garbage throughout the neighborhood; while the public waste management company Selikor maintained regular garbage collection, the rubbish that piled up in the many abandoned houses and vacant lots was a nuisance to many. As it remained on private property and was not presented properly in garbage cans, this garbage did not fall under Selikor's responsibility. Residents complained about their neighbors dumping bulky waste in empty lots because arranging a special Selikor pick-up would be too expensive.

Seru Fortuna, which encompasses "Old" Seru Fortuna and the more recent public housing development Seru Papaya, is located on the northwest fringe of greater Willemstad and is built on elevated terrain—hence the name *seru* (hill). Seru Fortuna's total population around the time of my research was 2,404, with the majority living in the public housing section of Seru Papaya. Presumably because of the public housing system, the number of foreign-born residents was much lower than in areas such as Wishi/Marchena. The unemployment rate was a staggering 46 percent in Seru Papaya and 15.2 percent in Old Seru Fortuna, and the majority of residents had not reached further than the first stage of secondary education (CBS 1993, 2002, 2004; George et al. 2003; Arthur Andersen 1996).

The neighborhood is bordered on the north by the rocky northern coastline and is ringed by fairly busy through-roads that separate it from other areas, while a defunct football field and a polluted patch of *mondi* (bush) lie as a divider between the two sections of the *bario*. The public housing development was built in the mid-1970s in an attempt to solve the dire shortage of affordable housing in Curaçao at a low cost to the government. Cheap-looking rowhouses line loop-shaped streets off the main road, across which cars, motorcycles, and scooters zoom back and forth loudly. Somewhat larger houses with spacious yards can be found in the older part of Seru Fortuna. Before urban sprawl led to its incorporation into greater Willemstad, this area used to be a rural area (*kunuku*) where residents would plant small crops such as peanuts and pumpkins. People would go into the surrounding *mondi* to collect firewood or food, mainly the *kadushi* cactus, the basis for a traditional Curaçaoan soup.

FIGURE 2.7 Goats foraging in the polluted *mondi* near Seru Fortuna

Because of its location near the seaside and on top of the *seru*, Seru Fortuna is cooler than other parts of Willemstad, and many residents saw the view of the sea as a neighborhood asset. While not located "in" an environmental problem in the manner of the other neighborhoods where I did fieldwork, solid waste management posed serious problems (SOAW 2012b). Seru Fortuna was surrounded by polluted *mondi*, which functioned as an informal garbage dump where all kinds of trash had been discarded (Figure 2.7). The effects of occasional clean-up actions were soon undone, and one leaseholder was found using a plot of land to operate an illegal dump that accepted construction waste at cheaper rates than the public landfill.[10] In addition, wastewater was disposed of by way of a communal cesspit that did not always function properly. During my fieldwork this cesspit had overflowed; as a result, sewage ran through the street for weeks, creating a bad smell and a health hazard. While the neighborhood was located close to the island's main airport and airplanes took off nearby several times daily, residents did not perceive the ensuing noise as a nuisance.

Conclusion

Kingston and Willemstad, and their different neighborhoods, were shaped through distinct political, economic, social, and ecological processes.

Willemstad's more or less straightforward development as a commercial port town and later petro-industrial hub is associated with an increasingly diverse migrant population and a patchwork of socio-economically and demographically differentiated *barios*. Kingston was more directly connected to a hinterland of plantations and developed more through internal relations; it has a more schematic socio-spatial configuration, organized around a clearer distinction between a wealthier Uptown where Brown Jamaicans and ethnic minorities are overrepresented, and an impoverished Downtown inhabited primarily by Black Jamaicans. These distinct socio-spatial constellations, in combination with ecological factors (such as trade winds, rainfall, and the relief of the landscape) and infrastructure (from the oil refinery to the network of rainwater gullies), have shaped the extent to which urban environmental problems such as air pollution or contaminated gullies affect the larger city or only specific places and populations. In addition, the physical and socio-political positioning of neighborhoods within the urban landscapes of Willemstad and Kingston may also influence socio-ecological processes. In both cities, not only do neighborhoods differ in terms of class and ethno-racial makeup, but their physical location (in the old city center, on the harbor, or on the urban periphery in closer proximity to "wild" nature) may also affect residents' ecological experiences and perceptions, while their socio-political position may inform these groups' sense of agency in solving environmental problems.

While remaining attentive to these various inter-urban and intra-urban differences, we can identify common historical trajectories that were central to the formation of the Caribbean as *oikoumenê* and are still evident in the region's present-day cities, where the colonial past has shaped the built environment and continues to inform socio-spatial relations. In this book, I start from the assumption that there is an added value in analyzing the socio-ecological politics of Willemstad and Kingston within a broader, comparative Caribbean framework. Nonetheless, the extent to which these findings can be generalized for the broader Caribbean should not be overstated. In particular, Hispanic Caribbean cities, which reflect different trajectories of slavery, colonialism, and decolonization, and sometimes display more similarities to Latin American cities, developed differently from Dutch and British colonial cities such as Willemstad and Kingston. In addition, issues of urban size and scale make it difficult to fully compare these two relatively small cities with sprawling metropoles such as Havana, Santo Domingo, or Port-au-Prince. Mindful of these qualifications regarding the broader regional applicability of the findings,

I build on the discussion presented here in the next chapter by elaborating on socio-ecological parallels and differences within the region and in the specific cases of Willemstad and Kingston. Concentrating on both continuities and shifts within colonial environmental discourse and practice, I historicize the interrelated production of pollution and difference by situating the two cities' individual histories within broader imaginations of, and interventions in, Caribbean landscapes.

specific

3

COLONIAL LANDSCAPES OF PARADISE AND POLLUTION

Historically oriented anthropologists have done much to enrich
our understanding of the ways in which colonial practices and discourses continue to inform the present. In her diachronic approach
to violence in Jamaica, Deborah Thomas (2011) develops a "repara-
tions framework for thinking" that takes as its starting point the
interlocking of temporalities in order to understand more fully the
role of the past in the present. Such a "complexly cyclical engagement with history," she argues, involves developing "a sustained
conversation about history—and about the place of the past in the
present—in terms other than those of righteous blame or liberal
guilt" (Thomas 2011, 238). By attending to the persistence of specific politico-economic and ideological structures over time, this
approach helps refute essentialist explanations of violence that
rely on raced, classed, and gendered notions of Jamaican cultural
deviance. Ann Stoler (2008, 194) similarly argues for a complex
understanding of "the material and social afterlife of structures,
sensibilities, and things" that goes beyond vague invocations of
"colonial legacy" to ask *how* "imperial formations persist in their
material debris, in ruined landscapes and through the social ruination of people's lives." Stoler's work points us toward the enduring
materiality of imperial processes, emphasizing the zones of abandonment that remain in the wake of conquest and exploitation.

Building on these authors, I seek to understand Kingston and
Willemstad, and, more broadly, Jamaica and Curaçao, as landscapes
in which forms of politics and power endure materially and meta-
phorically, long after formal racialized exclusion has been brought
to an end. We might understand the socio-ecological relations that
took shape from the beginning of European colonialism as a type
of assemblage in which different material and discursive, human

and nonhuman elements come together. Some of these elements—specific tropes, narratives, landscapes, infrastructures, or government agencies—may persist over time and be discernibly reassembled in the context of late colonial public health interventions, or in postcolonial forms of environmentalism, while other elements may fade from view. I am interested in *how* colonialism still matters and which traces of empire are prone to reactivation. How have classed and racialized ideas of purity, pollution, and progress remained stable or taken on new meanings and expressions through time? How were colonial regimes' categories of difference and patterns of inequality produced through tropical and urban landscapes, and how have they been reproduced or trans-formed? How have these colonial processes been embedded not only in zones of abandonment, but also in those spaces that were singled out for colonial attention, for care and reform?

In this chapter I seek to lay the historical groundwork for understanding contemporary forms of environmental injustice, focusing on the critical role that socio-ecological relations play in the construction, maintenance, and transformation of both difference and inequality. I emphasize the extent to which constructions of difference rely on spatial processes of categorization. Understanding when and how difference translates to inequality necessitates an engagement with the social production of space, with the processes and power struggles through which spaces come to be used and imagined, trans-formed materially and represented discursively (Lefebvre 1991). These power struggles include conflicts over who controls access to, and use of, certain spaces, contestations that involve the segmentation of urban landscapes and the spatial separation of populations. The Caribbean natural and built envi-ronments, which are to a large extent products of the inequitable relations of power under colonialism, continue to shape contemporary social rela-tions: they enable certain types of encounters, interactions, and connections, while frustrating others.

The power structures of colonialism relied on both material and discur-sive spatial techniques. Material spatial techniques used in organizing society and governing populations involved disciplinary strategies such as isolation, confinement, segregation, expulsion, and surveillance. Such material inter-ventions structured processes of both domination and resistance: fortified enclaves, segregation, and the ordering and "cleaning" of unruly spaces were and are countered by various subversive appropriations and uses of collec-tive or individual spaces. In addition to material techniques, power operates through discursive techniques that establish accepted knowledge that distin-guishes between the normal and the abnormal (Foucault 1977, 1980). Such discursive interventions are also spatial: How do we know certain spaces? Whose narrative of what these spaces mean becomes dominant? Who gets to name our islands, our parishes, our streets; who is allowed to map them and place them under surveillance? Who is able to destabilize such dominant ways of knowing spaces, and how? Power and knowledge are intimately related in categorizations of good and bad areas, of clean and dirty spaces, of civilized and uncivilized zones—spatial categories onto which social difference and hierarchies are mapped. Within and through such moral geographies, discourses of distance, alterity, and danger serve to maintain the boundaries between spatialized group identities, and to naturalize and legitimate inequalities. These various ways of using and defining space to assert, uphold, or contest power relations were central to the practices and discourses of colonialism, and many of them can still be recognized in the contemporary Caribbean.

In this chapter, by focusing on intersecting material and discursive techniques, I examine which interventions into the built and natural environments, and which discourses and narratives of difference and inequality, have been important in shaping Jamaica and Curaçao. I focus first on the imperial discourses and practices that worked on and through Caribbean natural landscapes. I sketch the way these links among imperialism, nature, and landscape developed broadly from the earliest European encounters with the region into the nineteenth century and were mapped differently in the distinct ecological contexts of the two islands. Early colonial narratives and policies, which framed Caribbean island landscapes as instances of tropical paradise threatened by human intervention, were important in shaping what can be seen as a form of proto-environmentalism. Despite their centrality to colonial commerce and control, cities tended to play a minor role in these imaginative geographies. Contrasted with the tropicalized natural landscapes, the cities featured as sites of modernity and progress, even as they were also imagined as spaces of pollution and sin.

My second focus in this chapter is on locating antecedents to contemporary socio-ecological relations by exploring instances of colonial urban interventions in the nineteenth and twentieth centuries. Following the emancipation of the enslaved population and increasing urbanization, more political, scholarly, and literary attention was devoted to urban areas and their regulation and improvement. Across the globe, this period of liberal reform was characterized by heightened attention to dirt, filth, and pollution as urban problems, and by the development of measures to combat them that combined technical and administrative measures with moral and educational strategies. Focusing on two different episodes in the history of sanitary reform, this section discusses the urban policies and debates that emerged in the post-emancipation Caribbean. I examine the connections among class, skin color, space, and pollution through a discussion of sanitation policy related to a mid-nineteenth-century cholera epidemic in Jamaica and to the early-twentieth-century regulation of prostitution in Curaçao, tracing both parallels and divergences between the interventions of different colonial powers in two different historical periods.

The "discovery" of paradise

External representations have long marked the Caribbean as a space of nature rather than culture. As Michael Dash (1998, 29) writes, "Whether the prevalent trope is savage wildness or pristine innocence, the New World is overwhelmingly the realm of the natural. To even the most benign commentators, there is no culture or civilization worthy of mention." Over the centuries, scholarly, literary, and artistic representations accentuated and exaggerated the contrast between the lush, green Caribbean tropics and the civilized, temperate cityscapes of Europe and North America. Despite the fact that urban areas were developed soon after colonial conquest and settlement, cities were largely elided from both celebratory and derogatory descriptions of natural, tropical settings and supposedly pristine islands.

The region's framing as a realm of nature often carried negative connotations; the Caribbean was known as the Torrid Zone (see Figure 3.1), a wild, pathological space of death, danger, and disease that was especially dangerous to White Europeans (Khan 2010; Stepan 2001). Jamaica, in particular, has often been depicted as a wild, unruly space in which both climate and inhabitants may pose a threat to newcomers. Such representations of danger, abjection, and lawlessness were fed by staggering mortality rates (Curtin 1989), and by fears of slave uprisings and Maroon attacks on plantations. Contemporary reverberations of this specific dystopian imaginative geography are recognizable at the urban level in postcolonial depictions of the urban poor, gang wars, and drug traffickers. Balancing these negative representations of Caribbean islands, a powerful trope that has impacted more directly on environmental imaginations has been that of tropical paradise.[1]

European colonial sources projected images of paradise onto the Caribbean with great consistency. Early colonial reports on the area reveal the awe Europeans experienced on encountering the region's abundant and supposedly pristine natural landscapes. The early seventeenth century, as Charles

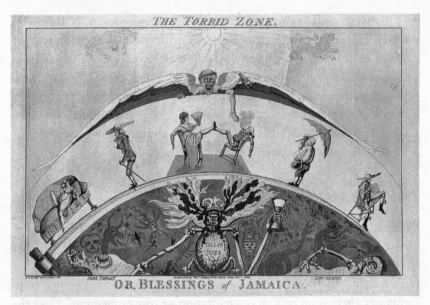

FIGURE 3.1 *The Torrid Zone, or Blessings of Jamaica.*
Courtesy of the Wellcome Trust.

Withers (1999, 70) notes, saw the prevailing "idea of paradise as a site within the 'New World,' and the idea of the contemporary New World *as* paradise, or, at least, having paradisal qualities now lost to Europe." In particular, the apparent abundance of natural resources—trees, fruits, animals—fed a pervasive association of the region with the biblical Garden of Eden. Caribbean islands were represented as cornucopian gardens, as sites of natural bounty where the inhabitants could live off the fat of the land (Grove 1995).

The polysemy of the master trope of paradise is evident in the range of ways in which the concept has been manifested discursively in the Caribbean over the last five centuries, signifying "notions of the primitive, innocence, savagery, and a lack of civilization, as well as of ignorance and nakedness, health and happiness, isolation from the rest of the world and humanity, timelessness, nature's beauty and abundance, life without labor, human beings' absolute freedom and domination over nature as God's stewards on Earth, and . . . wild pleasure, perpetual sunshine, and leisure" (Strachan 2002, 5). Recognizing many of these associations, Mimi Sheller (2003) traces three main strands in the visual and literary representations of Caribbean natural landscapes.

First, she locates in sixteenth- and seventeenth-century accounts of the region a utilitarian approach to natural products as potential commodities

that is nevertheless "informed by an imagery of tropical fecundity and excessive fruitfulness, which conjured up utopian fantasies of sustenance without
labour, even though this was manifestly at odds with the difficult experience
of survival" (Sheller 2003, 42). The wild abundance of nature was interpreted
as proof that the original inhabitants did not have the need, the desire, or
the capacity to "improve" these landscapes. In contrast, the European ambi-
tion and ability to master nature and make it profitable through agricultural intervention was taken as evidence of civilization, or even humanity
(Drayton 2000; Tobin 2011).

Early accounts of Jamaica evince this sense of wonder at the island's natural
abundance, starting in 1494, when Columbus and his crew first encountered
"Xaymaca," as Jamaica was called by its original Taino inhabitants. In the
centuries that followed, and after the Spanish ceded Jamaica to the English
in 1655, representations of the island as an Edenic, bounteous natural space,
waiting to be rendered productive and profitable by European intervention,
persisted. In contrast, Curaçao's semi-arid climate, which differs from that of
most of the other Caribbean islands, where higher levels of rainfall produce
more recognizably tropical scenes, and limited fecundity were seen as disap-
pointing. Yet Dutch colonial literature on Curaçao reveals a comparable fas-
cination with the natural landscape and the wealth of "new" and unknown
flora and fauna, sometimes concentrating on marine life in particular.

In contrast to these early accounts, eighteenth-century and early-
nineteenth-century images and texts tended to feature a picturesque
emphasis on cultivated landscapes, celebrating the plantation as a triumph
of European progress. This shift entailed "a greater sense of the social uses of
landscape, the power and mastery encoded in certain kinds of land use, and
an emotional investment in the constructive project of harnessing land to
generate capital" (Sheller 2003, 52). Caribbean landscapes, in these depictions, had been civilized by colonial planters, who had mastered tropical
nature and rendered it productive; such representations provided an implicit
justification for slavery. They contrasted the population of African descent
with European colonizers who were adept at rendering the fertile soil economically productive (through enslaved labor) and who built civilized cities. These racialized divisions supposed that non-Europeans were somehow
closer to nature: less capable of mastering nature and thus less human, or at
least less civilized. Both non-European bodies and natural landscapes were
seen as ripe for cultivation and productive management by Europeans; such
perspectives helped justify slavery and naturalize its brutal inequalities (cf.
Moore et al. 2003).

In Jamaica, where the plantation was the dominant institution, such imagery is evident in picturesque and pastoral estate views, such as the landscapes produced by George Robertson in the late eighteenth century, or by James Hakewill (Figure 3.2), Isaac Mendes Belisario, or Joseph Bartholomew Kidd in the early nineteenth century. In the years leading up to the abolition of slavery, Jefferson Dillman (2015, 172) argues, such peaceable landscapes portrayed "slave labor . . . as part of a great project of transformation of uncultivated land into a paradise of rural delight." They also served as aesthetic counterpoints to representations of the region as the Torrid Zone: "The picturesque West Indian landscape with its focus on the natural beauty and splendor of the islands worked in tandem with the pastoral to, ideally, mitigate any reservations one might have about the Caribbean as the site of virulent pathogens and a vicious slave system" (2015, 6). Kay Dian Kriz (2008) suggests that such visual representations continued to play an important role in "de-toxifying" Jamaica's landscape after full emancipation was achieved in 1838, undoing its reputation as unhealthy and immoral, and making it more appealing to White investors and immigrants. In Curaçao, where plantation agriculture was much less significant, Dutch colonists displayed a similar eagerness in exploiting the island's natural resources for the benefit of the motherland. In addition to salt mining, their commercial interest in mahogany, manzanilla,

FIGURE 3.2 Trinity Estate, St. Mary, plate from James Hakewill's *A Picturesque Tour of the Island of Jamaica*, 1820–1824.

and brazilwood led to rapid deforestation and decreased rainfall. Their attitude is illustrated in an observation of the island's coconut palms written
by the early-nineteenth-century author G. G. van Paddenburg that combines
religious imagery and a utilitarian approach: "The constant movements of the
top of the tree, the beauty of its soft green, sometimes fifteen-feet leaves pro-
voke admiration of, beyond its utility, this work of God's hand" (1819, 51).

Following the abolition of slavery and within the context of Romanticism,
the nineteenth century saw a renewed interest in Caribbean wilderness. In a
process of re-naturalization, the region was imagined once more as a "primeval, untouched site of luxurious profusion" (Sheller 2003, 60). In Jamaica,
this reassessment of wild nature in the late nineteenth century coincided
with the emergence of tourism. As one local official emphasized, the government aimed to attract North American tourists to the island over Florida on
the grounds that "scenery in Jamaica is diversified, picturesque, beautiful and
wild [and has] more valuable mineral springs and more natural curiosities"
(Taylor 1993, 61). In his illustrated travelogue *Untrodden Jamaica*, Herbert
T. Thomas (1890), an inspector for the Jamaica Constabulary, describes the
island's mountains, rivers, forests, and vegetation in the most romantic terms,
as in the following passage on his ascent to Blue Mountain Peak:

> And now the beauties of the forest were revealed to us. The path,
> the rocks, the trees, all were carpeted with the loveliest mosses and
> ferns. Mosses, clinging close and enfolding the tree-trunks with lov-
> ing clasp, and mosses drooping in feathery silken sprays of green. Tiny
> little creeping ferns with diminutive leaves, broad-leaved ferns bend-
> ing down their heads from the branches, and in the ravine on the left
> a verdant world of monster treeferns. Everywhere ferns, moss, orchids
> and parasites of every description in delicious, bewildering profusion.
> An hour there is worth a year of everyday life. (11)

In Curaçao, where the vegetation was less profuse, late-nineteenth-century
Romanticism expressed itself in interests in ornithology and marine biology.
The U.S. lieutenant Wirt Robinson (1895), on a trip to Curaçao and Colombia
shooting and collecting specimens of bird life, was not too impressed by the
island's landscape but waxed romantic in his description of the sea:

> I have never seen a more beautiful sight than the deep blue waters
> of the Caribbean Sea breaking in waves on the smooth beaches of
> Curaçao. As the water grew shallower, the blue changed in shade to the

color called peacock-blue, and this closer in became a light green. . . .
The water is wonderfully clear and we saw numbers of fish of different
kinds and sizes swimming about. (12, 15)

The German ornithologist Ernst Hartert (1893), visiting Curaçao, Aruba,
and Bonaire, disagreed with the "exaggerated reports of their heat and dry-
ness," finding that while "no tropical forest is found on the islands . . . trees
of different kinds abound." In light of negative stories about the island's climate, he recalls his "joy and astonishment when . . . I saw the picturesque
rocks of Curaçao before me, sparsely but thoroughly covered with the freshest
green" (290–291). He summarizes his trip in a decidedly romantic tone: "The
almost continuous sunshine, the beautiful clear atmosphere, the salubrious
and wonderfully warm temperature, never or seldom rising to an endur-
able heat, and the picturesque scenery gave me pleasures which can never be
forgotten" (293).

Visual culture scholars have pointed to the instrumental, agentive role
of landscape in projects of imperial power. W. J. T. Mitchell (2002), for
instance, argues that landscapes are implicated in the colonial project as
processes, rather than merely objects—verbs, rather than nouns. As a rep-
resentational practice, landscape is an instrument of cultural power that is
central in shaping social subjectivities and hierarchical relations. In her analysis of British visual and literary traditions in the late eighteenth and early
nineteenth centuries, Beth Fowkes Tobin (2004) shows the centrality of
tropical natural landscapes—imagined as both paradisiacal and in need of
intervention and management—in constructing a British imperial identity.
European concepts of progress and civilization were associated with the mastery of nature, with a strong emphasis on the transformation and cultivation
of landscapes. In the Caribbean, this aim was manifested principally through
the reshaping of "wilderness" in the form of plantations. These landscapes
operated through European technology and capital yet were possible only
through African slave labor. Contrasting themselves with indigenous and
later the Afro-Caribbean inhabitants, the Dutch and English, along with
other European colonial powers, took on themselves the task of unlocking
the unmined potential of nature in the New World.

The roots of the contemporary environmental movement can be traced
to such colonial encounters with what were seen as natural, undisturbed,
innocent Edens. Environmental awareness materialized in the context of
European expansion, with islands playing an important role in the development of this early environmentalism. As environmental historians such

as Richard Grove (1995, 1997) and Gregory Barton (2002) have demonstrated, ecological degradation resulting from colonial practices, combined with the image of the colonies as tropical Edens, gave rise to the emergence of European proto-environmentalism from the seventeenth century onward. Insular ecosystems display environmental degradation rapidly, and natural resource depletion, deforestation, soil erosion, and localized climate change were particularly evident in the Caribbean island colonies following the introduction of plantation agriculture in the seventeenth and eighteenth centuries (Watts 1987). The visibility of such degradation contributed to a sensitization to, and understanding of, human–environment interactions. A basic sort of environmental awareness developed following such interactions, as the demise of natural landscapes provoked the image of "paradise lost." Explorers, naturalists, and scientists, including the staff of botanical gardens, recognized the detrimental effects of agricultural and extractive policies and practices and took colonial governments to task, with varying levels of success.

Apart from direct confrontation with human-induced environmental change, these first environmental "activists" were also influenced by philosophical currents such as Romanticism (Tomalin 2004). The notion of discovering the Garden of Eden and the fear of losing it again has been a recurrent theme fueling conservation, extending from colonial times to the present (Grove 1995). As I point out in Chapter Six, this theme can also be discerned in the personal stories of professional environmentalists in contemporary Jamaica and Curaçao: expatriates or residents returning from extended stays abroad "discover" the natural beauty of these islands only to realize how fragile and imperiled this beauty is. Historically, such narratives centered on the relationship between European outsiders and Caribbean nature, excluding both non-European "locals" and Caribbean cities.[2] Colonial accounts generally depict the enslaved African population and their descendants as childlike creatures, incapable of managing their natural surroundings sensibly. They rarely recognize the ability of Afro-Caribbean populations to transform the landscape either productively or destructively (see Yarde 2012; cf. Li 2007).

Dirt, disease, and difference

As ideas of Caribbean landscapes as paradise developed and transformed as part of broader colonial discourses and interventions, pollution, dirt, and disease also emerged as important tropes within colonial regimes of representation and governmentality. In the late nineteenth and early twentieth centuries, sanitation and healthcare became increasingly central sites for the deployment of new forms of government, not least in cities. While colonial states continued to rely on disciplinary modes of government, based on techniques such as the segmentation and surveillance of urban space described in the previous chapter, they expanded their focus to include biopolitical modes of government aimed at the management of the welfare of populations (Paton 2004; Thomas 2011). The move toward biopolitics was tied to similar developments in nineteenth-century European cities, where, as Thomas Osborne and Nikolas Rose (1999, 742) note, the city emerged "as an ethicohygienic space, a particular way of understanding problems of disease and ill health and their moral consequences, to be acted upon spatially." This period saw the elaboration of the perceived relationship between character and milieu as a vicious cycle in which those of poor character degrade their surrounding milieu, while unfortunate milieux attract and degrade those of lesser character (Osborne and Rose 1999, 743).

This causality displays parallels with the environmental determinism of the race theories of the period, which mobilized nature and climate to produce the "fact" of racial difference and "innate" social hierarchies. This hemispheric form of determinism claimed that tropical and temperate climes had contrasting effects on their inhabitants, justifying the imperial endeavors and "civilizing mission" of the "temperate races" (Livingstone 1999; Sheller 2003). Indeed, the nineteenth-century belief in the pathological nature of urban places worked as a refraction and rescaling of earlier colonial notions of the Caribbean as the Torrid Zone. Fears of disease and degeneration in the metropolis and in the empire were entangled, with conceptions of European slums as pathogenic spaces closely linked to colonial constructions of the tropics as a corrupting, disease-ridden landscape (Edmond 2005; Bewell 1999). These moral geographies, in which disease often functioned as a metaphor for threats to the dominant social and political order, served to justify both restrictive interventions and strategic neglect.

The sanitary reform movement, which emerged in the context of industrialization and rapid urban expansion in Europe and North America, articulated the relationship between place and pathology clearly. The squalid conditions of the slums in which factory workers and their families lived emerged as a central urban concern, especially as cholera, typhoid, and other deadly diseases ravaged the cities. Following the disease etiology of the time, which pointed to the role of the environment in spreading illnesses, filthy and overcrowded urban environments came to be seen as health hazards rather than merely aesthetically displeasing spaces. In addition to the concept of "contagionism," which viewed disease as spread through human contact, so-called "miasmatic" theories located the cause of disease in specific unhealthy locations characterized by "foul air." This focus on environmental factors helped explain why the poor were hit hardest by diseases such as cholera, but it also reinforced the status quo by eliding structural political and economic factors. Only with the ascendance of microbiology and germ theory in the late nineteenth century did this emphasis on locale in conceptions of disease transmission shift, slowly, toward a focus on the role of pathogens (Anderson 2006).

Drawing on both contagionism and miasmatic theory, the sanitary reform movement sought to improve the living conditions of the urban poor, driven not only by concern for their well-being but also by the economic imperative of maintaining a healthy workforce. The humanitarian and economic impulses that shaped such campaigns were framed by broader nineteenth-century discourses of morality and uplift, with sanitary reformers seeking to instill civilization and order in the lives they were saving from disease and poverty. In addition to environmental factors, unsanitary and immoral behavior were seen by these reformers as encouraging ill health, and accordingly they advocated a combination of infrastructural improvements, legal and administrative measures, and moral and educational strategies to combat the problem.

Such reforms and underlying "ideologies of cleanliness" (Gandy 2004) extended to colonial cities, where fear of epidemics bolstered the consolidation of racialized urban space. Where class was the most important integer in European and North American cities, race played a more explicit role in colonial sanitary reform. Fear of infectious disease, not always grounded in medical fact, provided a rationale for the creation and maintenance of racialized space within urban planning (Goldberg 1993, 48; King 1990). Colonial Indian cities such as Madras, Bombay, and Calcutta, for instance, were developed in a more or less dualist fashion, differentiated into a "White Town" dominated by colonial elites and an indigenous "Black Town." Sanitary efforts concentrated on protecting the colonial sections from cholera and similar diseases, while the "native" sections were depicted as inherently dirty and diseased (Prashad 1994). Even after the decline of miasmatic theory, the conviction that diseases were produced by places and categories of people, rather than by bacteria, persisted. While extensive research has been conducted on African and Indian colonial urbanism, few scholars have considered how these imperial sanitarian ideologies were mapped out onto Caribbean cities, where the emancipation of the enslaved population colored many of the infrastructural, legal, and social interventions that were advocated and sometimes implemented by governments and charitable organizations.[3] Campaigns to eradicate diseases and cleanse cities of filth were often discriminatory in nature and reinforced existing social, racial, and spatial hierarchies and power structures.

Here, I offer a critical examination of discourse and reform in the fields of urban sanitation, hygiene, and public health in the context of two cases: the mid-nineteenth-century cholera epidemics in Jamaica and an early-twentieth-century moral panic surrounding prostitution in Curaçao. These cases emerged in distinct colonial and historical contexts. The Jamaican epidemic of the 1850s reflected racial anxieties specific to the post-emancipation period and a British empire marked by liberalism and Victorian culture. In contrast, the 1910s episode in Curaçao took shape in the context of Dutch attempts to reposition an economically unsustainable colony within a modernizing landscape of maritime commerce and to develop an "ethical politics" of colonialism. How was urban space implicated in attempts to inculcate the formerly enslaved with norms of social and physical propriety a few years or several decades after emancipation? To what extent did these reforms improve the well-being of the urban poor, and how did they serve the interests of local elites and the colonial power? I use these two distinct episodes in Caribbean urban history to explore how material and cultural pollution were entangled in different ways in policies aimed at producing specific types of raced, classed, and gendered urban order.

Cholera, cleanliness, and post-emancipation anxieties in Jamaica

In the post-emancipation Jamaica of the mid-nineteenth century, pervasive notions of Black abjection, in which race, hygiene, and civilization were conflated discursively, played a central role in establishing social and spatial order. The end of slavery and the destabilization of racialized social and economic hierarchies engendered new struggles between politicians and administrators in the European metropolis, local elites, and the formerly enslaved. Both British observers and White Jamaican elites were concerned with how to maintain colonial order in the wake of emancipation, and their preoccupation with sanitation and the related domains of morality, civilization, and industry can be seen in this light. The multiple cholera epidemics that afflicted the island in the decades after emancipation offer a productive site for teasing out these intersecting concerns. The severity of the 1850–1851 epidemic led the British Colonial Office to commission Gavin Milroy, an epidemiological specialist, to report on Jamaica's sanitary condition, resulting in *The Report on the Cholera in Jamaica and on the General Sanitary Condition and Wants of the Island* (Milroy 1854 [1852]). I use this document as a starting point for understanding sanitation as a locus in which anxieties concerning the future of post-emancipation Jamaica intersected with liberal sanitarian ideologies.

The epidemic ravaged Jamaica, and especially its urban areas, with about one-tenth of the population succumbing to the disease. In Kingston, around 5,000 people died, out of an estimated population of 40,000. The pathogenesis of cholera is currently well understood: the transmission route is "fecal–oral," and the disease spreads quickly when water sources come in contact with untreated sewage and become contaminated with the fecal matter of infected persons. To mid-nineteenth-century physicians operating without this present-day medical knowledge, the incidence and spread of cholera were still largely mysteries. In discussing the general sanitary condition of the island, Milroy remarked on the presence of foul water and the lack of drainage or sewers to remove it. He mentioned only in passing what must have been the direct cause of cholera transmission in Kingston: "It is no uncommon thing to find wells sunk in the immediate vicinity of huge unbricked privies, whose fluid contents readily permeate the loose soil" (Milroy 1854, 41).

Reflecting the miasmatic theories of his time, which pointed to "bad air" (*malaria*) as the cause of ill health, Milroy's disease etiology focused primarily on "exhalations," "emanations," and "effluvia." He identified effluvia from decomposing organic matter and human respiration as the two main sources of atmospheric impurity. The first source of miasma led Milroy to fulminate against the piles of decomposing vegetables and animal carcasses that lined the streets of Kingston, as well as the dung-heaps that were visible and could be smelled throughout town, but especially in the lower-class areas. The second source of miasma was "the breathing of a multitude of people in confined, ill-ventilated apartments." This observation explains the concern Milroy and his contemporaries shared regarding overcrowding: too many people inhaling and exhaling in a small space, without the benefits of good air (such as the sea-breeze), they were convinced, was bound to lead to disease. In its strong focus on local conditions, the cholera report also demonstrates a strong belief in environmental determinism—the effect of surroundings and specifically housing on character and behavior. Speaking of the "wretched hovels" on the outskirts of Spanish Town, Milroy (1854, 50) stated that "it is scarcely necessary to add that human beings in these circumstances are not only squalid and diseased, but vicious and depraved. The occupants are the vagrants of the town, living by occasional jobs, when they choose to exert themselves, or by thieving and other forms of crime. The ravages of the cholera here were dreadful." This example neatly demonstrates the direct causal relationship epidemiologists assumed to exist among disease, substandard housing, and moral deficiency (including laziness and a reluctance to exert oneself). In an 1851 letter to the governor of Jamaica, Milroy had already noted that "the intellectual and moral condition of the negro population has anything but advanced of late years—[which] is not a little owing to the wretched condition of the houses of the people."[4] Similarly, the grand jury of Kingston had written to the mayor in 1850 about the city's squalor and filth, entreating him to intervene specifically into the "hovels which form the residences of the great mass of our people," given that "we know nothing that tends so much to demoralize the people, and to promote and foster indolence and plunder, as these receptacles of filth and vice."[5] This emphasis on environmental factors is apparent throughout the report, which on several occasions also emphasizes the relationship between sexually immoral behavior and disease.

The report noted how few deaths there were "among the well-conditioned whites, and the mortality among the respectable brown population was also very small" (Milroy 1854, 62) but consistently ignored the structural causes that skewed morbidity and mortality so dramatically toward the impoverished Black population.[6] Instead, Milroy consistently resorted to blame-the-victim explanations, pointing to the "excessively filthy habits" and "disgustingly offensive" housing of those who suffered most. He did not focus on malnutrition and its possible effects,[7] much less on the political-economic structure that had resulted in the overcrowded, substandard housing he found in the parts of Kingston currently known as "Downtown." Beyond his focus on environmental factors and immoral sexual behavior, Milroy depicted the Black population as unwilling to pay for medical care and too lazy to work for the wages to afford proper treatment. In so doing, he implied that Jamaica's formerly enslaved population willfully chose to live a life of squalor and poverty.

The recommendations that the Milroy report made to address Jamaica's sanitary condition included passing public health legislation and introducing new forms of taxation and convict labor to make the development of medical infrastructure and waste removal financially viable. These recommendations were couched in terms that reflected post-emancipation anxieties regarding the availability of plantation labor and the attainable level of civilization of the free Black population. In a letter to the British undersecretary of state two years after the epidemic, C. Macaulay, assistant secretary of the Board of Health, suggested that "the waste of money value of labour in the West India colonies, from the barbarous habits of the population, and their low sanitary condition [was] enormous."[8] Sanitary reform, then, was seen as commendable, given its effects on worker health and the resulting economic benefits. Both Milroy and the Board of Health considered it unlikely that the local elites would address the sanitary condition satisfactorily, and they argued for active supervision on the part of the Colonial Office. Indeed, the most important sanitary improvements were not realized until Jamaica came under Crown colony rule following the 1865 Morant Bay Rebellion. Several decades later, the authorities implemented substantial sanitary reform in Kingston, constructing new sewage and drainage infrastructure and improving the city's streets and lanes (Ford and Finlay 1903, 440–441).

The hierarchical understandings of social and physical propriety, according to which the urban poor were weighed and found wanting, linger in present-day Kingston. The conflation of the poor Black population with polluted urban places often acts to legitimate the unequal distribution of environmental disadvantages in the form of blame-the-victim policies, institutionalizing the spatial concentration of material-symbolic pollution in specific places. Such political-ecological strategies were evident in the cities of Victorian Jamaica, where the persistent conflation of sanitation with morality and civilization reflected attempts to maintain racial hierarchies in an era of freedom while simultaneously securing (healthy) Black labor and with it the economic productivity of the colony. The historical association of dirty places with "unclean," morally deficient people continues to inform environmental and health inequalities in Kingston. Diseases such as gastroenteritis continue to disproportionately affect the residents of the same districts that Milroy and his contemporaries spoke of so disparagingly. As I note in the chapters that follow, there is still a tendency to explain environmental and public health outcomes through individual behavioral decisions or cultural factors rather than addressing the combined socio-economic, political, and spatial factors at work. Such parallels indicate the resurgence of processes of responsibilization, informed by moral discourses that conflate Downtown Kingston with dirt and deviance, always with a subtext of class and race.

Sex and sanitation in Curaçao

Some of the anxieties that surrounded proper urban and bodily conduct in mid-nineteenth-century Jamaica are also discernible in the moral panic that developed in Curaçao in the 1910s regarding Willemstad's "sanitary condition." The first years of the new century saw a growing Dutch governmental interest in improving urban sanitation both in the Netherlands and in its colonies. This Dutch biopolitical turn, which involved new legislation and significant interventions in housing and urban planning, took place significantly later than in Britain and its empire. While nineteenth-century Dutch politicians and elites had been largely averse to government welfarist interventions, viewing poverty as the natural or divine order of things, this began to change in the early twentieth century (van der Woud 2010). One indication of this shift was Queen Wilhelmina's announcement of a new "ethical policy" (*ethische politiek*) for the colonies—formulated mainly in relation to the Dutch East Indies, but also influential in the Dutch Caribbean—which outlined a biopolitical mission of welfare, civilization, and moral uplift (Alofs 2011). In Curaçao, these new politics coincided with a prolonged economic depression, which compelled the local government to search for new commercial and industrial opportunities. These combined political, moral, and economic imperatives formed the context for the case analyzed here.

Despite the island's fairly dire economic position at that point in time, Willemstad was a booming harbor town (Figure 3.3). The construction of the Panama Canal, which was to open in 1914, offered possibilities for the harbor to further strengthen its position within the global maritime network. The Dutch authorities were eager to make use of this opportunity, and in anticipation of the opening of the canal, a diplomatic envoy, the embassy secretary (*gezantssecretaris*) H. M. van Weede, traveled to the United States in late 1910 to investigate the possibilities.[9] Van Weede reported that a main concern with regard to the harbor's potential involved Willemstad's prostitutes. Apparently, reports of rampant venereal disease had begun to circulate, and it was rumored that this was causing foreign marine vessels to avoid Willemstad. Colonial officials and local elites feared that the reputation of the city's prostitutes as diseased and disorderly might threaten the harbor's competitiveness.

In July 1911, Theodorus Nuyens, the governor of Curaçao, appointed a Sanitary Committee made up of officials with medical, legal, commercial, and infrastructural expertise to investigate the matter and "whether it would be necessary or desirable that certain sanitary measures be taken here, especially with the objective of upholding the good reputation of the harbor of Curaçao abroad, and to study in particular what could be done to counter the spread of venereal disease."[10] In addition, he recommended that the committee consider carefully the measures that the U.S. colonial government had taken to

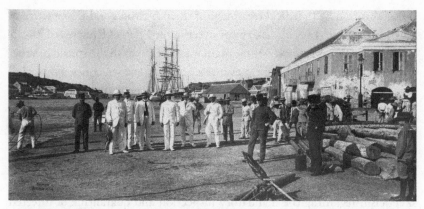

FIGURE 3.3 Dutch Minister of Water Management Jacob Kraus, Willemstad Harbor, around 1906.
Photograph by Soublette & Fils, KITLV Collection.

regulate prostitution in Puerto Rico and Panama. The governor connected prostitution and venereal disease to the city's broader sanitary conditions, tasking the committee with investigating more generally "what, in the realm of sanitation, might stand in the way of the development of Willemstad as a harbor for international traffic."[11] In March 1912, the committee issued its report, which focused primarily on "the prostitution question" and on the issue of urban public cleanliness (*stadsreiniging*), including the disposal of human waste.

The committee's report (Centrale Gezondheidsraad 1913), and the attendant colonial correspondence and public debate, reveal the intersection of the governance of sexual health with colonial hierarchies. In its linking of morality, public health, hygiene, and urban sanitation, the report's sanitarian ideology mapped out difference onto the urban landscape and onto raced and gendered bodies. As Mimi Sheller (2012, 242) notes, sexuality "is interactively elicited through encounters between bodies and sexual geographies, which include spaces of belonging and safety, ethnosexual borders and frontiers, and modes of normalizing, policing, and surveilling sexualized bodies and places." In their discussions of sex and sanitation, colonial officials repeatedly made associations between certain bodies and places, and disease and dirt. Ignoring structural inequalities, they generally drew on narratives of vice and uncivilized behavior to explain the association between Afro-Curaçaoans and polluted low-income areas.

Starting with the issue of "venereal" prostitutes, the Sanitary Committee began by explaining why previous measures—including the compulsory hospitalization and medical treatment of the prostitutes and the practice of driving them into the city's narrower streets after 7 p.m.—had proved unsuccessful. The report proposed three main measures to curb the spread of venereal disease, drawing on both preventive and curative strategies: post-coital "disinfection" of the prostitutes' clients onboard their ships; the establishment of a free, anonymous clinic for sexually transmittable diseases on land; and reducing temptation by providing sailors with lodging and alternative forms of "appropriate entertainment" far away from the prostitutes (Centrale Gezondheidsraad 1913, 38–41). Governor Nuyens, also advised by the island's government council (*raad van bestuur*), supported the committee's skepticism regarding the mandatory inspection and quarantine of infected prostitutes, given the high costs and limited benefits of such a strategy. In contrast to Puerto Rican and Dominican government officials, who blamed the spread of venereal disease on the women, the Sanitary Committee and other Dutch colonial officials pointed to the role of the men involved. Nuyens himself noted that "the number of venereal men here is probably much larger than that of venereal women. The measure [of enforced inspection and quarantine] would . . . only be successful, if one could also isolate the venereal men."[12]

Notwithstanding this relatively progressive attitude and preference for biopolitical over disciplinary strategies, the report reproduced moral geographies that were racialized and gendered at both the geopolitical and the urban scale. In discussing the pros and cons of regulation (*reglementeering*) versus prohibition, the committee cited experts who held that whereas the criminalization of sex work was desirable for Dutch cities and "civilized countries," tolerating and regulating the sector was more appropriate for the "colored populations of our colonies" and for countries whose culture was "still very low on the ladder" (Centrale Gezondheidsraad 1913, 34–35). The racialized character of conceptions of sexuality was also explicit in the discussion of child prostitution. The committee members considered Curaçaoan girls *manbaar*—"mannable," that is, sexually active—by the age of twelve (36), while Attorney General (*procureur-generaal*) Gorsira noted that the legal age limit was lower in Curaçao than in the Netherlands "with an eye to the earlier development of the girls."[13] The measures aimed at preventing sailors from visiting specific neighborhoods demonstrated the extent to which the committee conflated disease with women who lived and worked in specific urban areas. The acting minister of the navy, S. Colijn, also expressed his belief in the pathogenic effects of place, arguing in a letter to the minister of colonies "that this scourge can only be addressed by cleaning up the complex of sordid dark residences, indicated by the Commission, as quickly as is feasible, in the hope that the improved lighting that should accompany this, will diminish the prostitution, which has a penchant for dark neighborhoods."[14]

Moving on from this discussion of sex work, the sanitary report proceeded to discuss the problems surrounding solid waste and wastewater management in Willemstad. The committee members expressed concern about the inadequate removal of garbage and, more urgently, of human waste. Despite developments in medical science since the nineteenth century, a miasmatic disease etiology still informed the committee's discussion of health hazards. This concern with foul air came out, for instance, in their description of the litter that was dumped in pools throughout the island as resulting in both "miasmas and typhoid" (Centrale Gezondheidsraad 1913, 48). The committee's recommendations included the establishment of a separate department of urban sanitation: "Willemstad, with a probable future as world harbor, in our opinion requires a separately organized [sanitation] department, which is tasked with removing the products from human society, especially where these originate for the most part from the colored population," the committee members declared, also stressing the need for "the population be educated in sanitary respect" (46–47). Such recommendations connected race, space, and pollution to economic progress and visions of modernity. For Willemstad to become a properly modern city, a competitive hub in global naval and commercial networks, and a civilized space on the world map, the government had to get serious about sanitation. It was all the more urgent to make an effort in this regard, apparently, when the waste products of Afro-Curaçaoans were involved. Their garbage was somehow more threatening to the possibility of achieving the level of sanitary conditions that would coincide with Willemstad's status as a world harbor, and it was their sanitary education that needed to be pursued most pressingly.

These depictions of Afro-Curaçaoan locals as dirtier and less civilized than their European neighbors are mirrored in a moral analysis offered by Dr. P. C .T. Lens, the former head of Curaçao's military medical department. In a letter to the Dutch minister of colonies, Lens complained that Curaçaoans deposited garbage, feces, and urine around their houses and that they defecated in the open air. He advocated a stricter policing of sanitary legislation, as he found the Curaçaoan population to be "docile and sufficiently intelligent but morally weak."[15] In contrast, Governor Nuyens, in his response to the Sanitary Committee's report, took a rather different position. Less dismissive of local norms or mindful of the costs involved in implementing reform, Nuyens argued that Willemstad was much cleaner than many other cities and characterized the city's residents as "a bit spoiled in this regard. They scream of dirty streets so quickly, when elsewhere those would not be called dirty at all." He did, however, deflect Dr. Lens's general portrayal of the island onto low-income areas: "In the lesser areas there are parts here and there that are far from hygienic, because garbage is constantly dumped clandestinely."[16]

Low-income areas and impoverished Afro-Curaçaoans, then, bore the brunt of stigmatization in terms of dirt, disease, and vice. This was also apparent in the Sanitary Committee's consideration of substandard housing in Willemstad, which reflected the influence of environmental determinism. The committee members and various other colonial officials repeatedly connected dark and dirty residences to immoral behavior ranging from prostitution to violent crime. An area of Willemstad called the Murderer's Neighborhood (*Moordenaarsbuurt*) received recurring attention in this regard. The report described the neighborhood as consisting of slums and narrow alleys "where the sun lights the street only very rarely and where deep darkness reigns by moonlight." This gothic description preceded the recommendation that "sordid dark residences" be declared unfit for human habitation (Centrale Gezondheidsraad 1913, 51). The repeated emphasis on the problematic *dark* nature of these houses and neighborhoods, so similar to Minister Colijn's descriptions of the same areas, suggests another way that racialization crept into sanitary discourse through language.

The conjoined analysis of issues that may strike the twenty-first-century reader as highly divergent—prostitution, waste disposal, housing conditions—demonstrates the sanitary reformers' conflation of physical and moral pollution. These conflations were mapped most closely onto low-income areas and Afro-Curaçaoan female bodies, even though comparatively progressive voices, such as that of Governor Nuyens, pointed to men's role in spreading venereal disease and to the structural economic difficulties that thwarted comprehensive waste management. Colonial governmental discourse and interventions, such as those documented in the 1912 sanitation report, reflected and shaped moral geographies that continue to inform present-day understandings of urban space and environmentalism. As the following chapters suggest, the modern-day stigmatization of Willemstad's *barionan marginal*—which cannot be understood outside the classed and racialized nature of urban space—echoes historical representations of these neighborhoods as criminogenic locales in which urban poverty, environmental pollution, and immoral behavior are durably entangled.

Conclusion

A geographical refocusing of urban political ecology that attends to the experiences of cities in the global South involves elaborating the complexities of different colonial histories. This chapter has drawn on environmental humanities approaches that analyze colonial socio-ecological processes in relation to wild and agricultural landscapes, extending such analyses to understand how analogous processes might have worked through urban landscapes. The long colonial era in the Caribbean, stretching from the late fifteenth century to the mid-twentieth century in Jamaica, and arguably into the present in Curaçao, has left enduring traces on both natural and urban landscapes. The various material interventions into these landscapes—from the plantations that rendered wild nature productive to the sanitary reforms that sought to order dirty and diseased bodies in urban space—cannot be understood outside of the imaginative geographies, the discursive mapping of difference in and through space, that accompanied them. Politicians, reformers, and scholars drew repeatedly on representations of Edenic islands and pathogenic urban milieux in ways that generally reinforced social hierarchies and facilitated political-economic interests related to plantation agriculture and maritime commerce. These representations have not necessarily faded in importance as the regional economic focus has shifted to tourism.

Widely shared spatial imaginaries have normalized interventions in Caribbean natural and urban environments. Island nature as tropical paradise is one such well-known spatial imaginary. The polluted, impoverished ghetto is another. Neither of these spatial imaginaries is fully separable from imperial projects of racial hierarchy and economic exploitation. Productivity, paradise, and pathology are tropes that have been invoked across the centuries to legitimate colonial endeavors from plantation slavery to urban planning. Zones of dangerous, seductive natural and cultural "wildness" have been mapped in relation to projects of modernization and civilization onto different landscapes in different ways across the centuries. At both the island and the urban levels, moral and medical mappings of difference have often worked to spatially reinscribe race, class, and gender hierarchies. The specific manifestations of these geographies and hierarchies reflect the different political, moral, and economic preoccupations of different periods, from Victorian anxieties over the regulation and self-regulation of free Black labor in the years following emancipation in Jamaica to an "ethical" Dutch colonial concern with regional competitiveness and urban modernity in early-twentieth-century Curaçao.

In the twenty-first century, representations of tropical paradise and urban blight continue to inform both everyday socio-spatial relations and urban and environmental policies in ways that are specific to the preoccupations and priorities of this period in time. As has been documented extensively, the colonially derived trope of tropical paradise still figures prominently in contemporary tourism policy and practice (Sheller 2003; Thompson 2006). In Chapter Six, I discuss how it also influences the policies and practices of professional environmentalists. I extend this work on Caribbean tropicality to consider imaginaries of urban space as well, suggesting that racialized historical narratives of urban pollution and purification continue to inform present-day discussions of physical and social decay in marginalized urban areas in Jamaica and Curaçao. These urban spatial imaginaries are also implicated in producing and naturalizing patterns of inequality, including differential exposure to the material realities of garbage, sewage, and air pollution. Politicians, policymakers, and NGOs continue to mobilize colonially derived discourses of dirt, disease, and difference to justify interventions into—or, conversely, neglect of—certain urban areas.

4

Through my husband, who worked in Jamaica's heritage sector, I became acquainted with a wealthy White Jamaican couple who would occasionally invite us to brunch and dinner parties at their country estate or their Uptown Kingston residence. The wife was both astonished and amused by my fieldwork in Downtown Kingston, and particularly in Riverton. She repeatedly encouraged me to describe to other guests how I spent time on and around the garbage dump, and took evident pleasure in hearing me recount how I would hitch rides on garbage trucks to the nearby transport hub of Three Miles. The guests, most of whom were also White or Brown Jamaicans, would also react with surprise at my evident transgression of the imagined borders of where a White-identified woman could go. Why would a respectable person want to go to such a place? How would she negotiate the dirt and danger? While in most countries, of course, trips to the garbage dump might well elicit similar surprise, these incidents mark some of the ways in which raced, classed, and gendered identifications are entangled with urban space.

Although Riverton is certainly extreme in terms of pollution, this type of reaction to my presence in Downtown Kingston more broadly was not an exception. In fact, I encountered similar reactions of astonishment and amusement in both Riverton and Rae Town. On various occasions, inner-city residents would ask me, "Aren't you afraid to come down here?" Patrolling police officers pulled over to ask me whether I was lost and needed help. Similarly, many Curaçaoans also considered my presence in Willemstad's "marginal" *barios* to be very unusual. A friend in Wishi/Marchena told me that initially residents had thought I must be a missionary. Jehovah's Witnesses and Mormons were the only White people who would enter the neighborhood on foot, and my behavior—walking around with a bag full of papers, entering people's yards to engage in long conversations—seemed to confirm their suspicions. While I never experienced any safety-related problems during fieldwork in either Wishi/Marchena or Seru Fortuna, wealthier Curaçaoans would warn me: "Never go there alone! Never wear jewelry or take your cell phone with you when you go there—those people are dangerous!"

In both Kingston and Willemstad, urban space is fragmented along intersectional fault lines of race, class, and gender and anchored by strong normative ideas about who can and should access which parts of the city. This urban fragmentation reflects historically shaped geographies of exclusion, but it is also shaped and reshaped in everyday ways by contemporary perceptions and social uses of city spaces. Colonially derived urban hierarchies both persist and are prone to destabilization—some residents reproduce older associations between social positioning and urban geographies in the stories they tell about their city and through their everyday movements as they negotiate the urban landscape, while others contest these associations. Raced, classed, and gendered social positioning is expressed, reinforced, and subverted through urban narratives and spatial strategies.

Anthropologists have traditionally been concerned with the ways that social difference along lines of gender, ethnicity, and class is expressed through and inscribed on the body. Historically, much of this work studied forms of bodily adornment and modification, from fashion and jewelry to hairstyles and tattoos. In recent decades, research has focused on the performativity of social identities, pointing to the work involved in constructing gendered and sexual categories (Butler 1990, 1993). Caribbean feminist scholars have emphasized the ways in which these categorizations always intersect with ethnicity, race, and class (see, e.g., Barrow 1998; Mohammed 2002). I propose that increased attention to the spatial aspects of bodily adornment, modification, and performance can enrich our appreciation of how power works on and through the body. Embodied practices and performances both reflect and reinforce the meanings of the spatial contexts in which they take place. Bringing work on self-disciplining, self-styling, and the body into more direct dialogue with critical geographical research, this chapter seeks to focus our attention on emplaced bodies. Studying the complex ways in which bodies are always emplaced, both within the broader urban landscape and within micro-places, can help us understand how urban fragmentation and segregation become naturalized.

The socio-spatially differentiated ways in which social life is regulated across the urban landscape can be understood through the concept of "everyday spatial regimes" (Jaffe and de Koning 2016). These regimes are varying sets of norms, rules, and social identifications that work to organize public space by shaping our ideas and norms about comportment, propriety, and who belongs where. Varying across the urban landscape, these regimes organize how specific people and behavior are interpreted and ascribed social identities: the spatial context will determine whether, for instance, an unaccompanied young woman is assumed to be a prostitute or a middle-class professional (cf. Secor 2002). This spatial ordering of how we recognize and ascribe social identities enables certain interactions and inhibits others. Working from this concept, I want to explore how such regimes intersect with what we might term "everyday bodily regimes." By this I mean not only the different sets of norms and ideas about bodies that guide our reading of markers such as skin color, hairstyle, or clothing, but also "regimes" in the sense of everyday routines, mundane yet political practices of self-styling through bodily care and comportment. By emphasizing the spatiality of such bodily regimes, I seek to highlight their role in producing bodies that fit "naturally" into certain environments, and to emphasize how a lack of fit between bodies and spatial context can produce an acutely physical sense of discomfort.

This chapter, then, explores these intersecting regimes by analyzing how residents of Kingston and Willemstad use and imagine urban space, both through their movements around the city and through their differentiations of the urban landscape and of various forms of mobility. I focus on the emplacement of bodies to understand the everyday reproduction and contestation of inequality, segregation, and exclusion. The chapter starts with a discussion of the intersectionality and co-production of race, class, gender, and space, focusing on how different identity markers can be mutually constitutive and how intersecting forms of privilege are distributed in the two cities. The next two sections consider the role of fear and social distancing in urban fragmentation in Kingston and Willemstad, focusing on residents' everyday urban narratives and spatial strategies. The final section connects these urban and neighborhood-level processes to the idea of emplaced bodies, discussing how micro-level processes can both reproduce and subvert dominant spatial and bodily regimes.

Intersectional fault lines

In both Jamaica and Curaçao, as throughout the Caribbean region more broadly, there has been a strong historical relationship between social class and skin color. On both islands, slavery produced a more or less three-tiered social hierarchy, with European Whites occupying the higher strata, enslaved African Blacks the lower strata, and mixed-descent Browns in between. This structure of stratification was of course always complicated by exceptions and by other immigrant groups, including Chinese, Lebanese, Jews, Portuguese, and Indians, who did not fit the schematic division. Indeed, historians such as Mimi Sheller (2012, 136) have emphasized the inattention of post-independence nationalist historiography to the "fault lines ... that cross-cut presumed racial categories with complex patterns of ethnic identification, landholding, family formation, and class identity." More schematic conceptions of racial categories and their relation to class also obscure the gradual increase in possibilities for social mobility that followed the nineteenth-century abolition of slavery and the acceleration of this process through twentieth-century political autonomy and migration (Thomas 2004). However, throughout the Caribbean, class power and prestige still remain associated with race—or skin color, with distinctions often framed in terms of "complexion." In Jamaica, where the population of White Jamaicans has become extremely small, the differentiation is now mostly between Brown and Black Jamaicans. In Curaçao this distinction in skin color and descent tends to be expressed in terms of *koló skur* and *koló kla*, dark-skinned and light-skinned, rather than as Black and Brown.

This differentiation between Blacks and Browns, or between *koló skur* and *koló kla*, is not based on skin color or phenotype alone. As the Latin American expression goes, "Money whitens." Skin color can be "mediated" through education and middle-class consumption patterns. A darker-skinned individual wearing an expensive suit and speaking Dutch rather than Papiamentu, or "proper English" rather than Jamaican Creole, may be classified as Brown. Similarly, a light-skinned person displaying adornments and behavior considered lower class may still be read as Black. These raced and classed forms of adornment and behavior are also strongly gendered, with strong norms guiding "appropriate" feminine and masculine attire and conduct. Class, race, and gender, then, are co-produced in simultaneous, intersecting processes that reflect everyday bodily regimes, a point I return to in more detail later.

The flexible co-production of race and class extends to space. Like many other postcolonial cities, the socio-spatial hierarchies that characterize Kingston and Willemstad reflect the legacy of colonialism and, in the case of the Caribbean, slavery. In my fieldwork I encountered a widespread perception of ethno-racial segregation that was not entirely supported by demographic data. Regarding Kingston, for instance, an analysis of census data by Colin Clarke (2006) indicates that the city's residential segregation along lines of skin color decreased significantly during the twentieth century. Nonetheless, I found that the relationship between color, class, and space remained prominent in how many residents from a range of social backgrounds narrated Kingston. Such narratives tended to map a combination of class and color onto a largely bipolar socio-spatial structure (see Verrest and Jaffe 2012).

During my research, I found that Uptown and Downtown Kingston were broadly understood as, respectively, Brown and Black spaces. As outlined in Chapter Two, this division developed in the second half of the twentieth century. The historically impoverished areas of West Kingston, those hit hardest during the cholera epidemic described in Chapter Three, continued to bear the stigma of poverty and pollution, but even formerly elite areas have become known as ghettos. A description by Omar, a fisherman from Rae Town, of his neighborhood's historical development indicates the racialization of such shifts in class. "Rae Town is a nice community," he told me. "It used to be pure Jews living here, Colored people. Me as a Black man could not come. *Nega* [Black] people got what was left after the Colored people moved up into the hills." Up in the hills remains the place for middle-class Jamaicans to reside, even those who identify as Black. As Soldier, another Rae Town fisherman, declared, "Every community have a couple people come out good. But if you start to earn some money they move Uptown. They make a little money, you have to go up. People get jealous, you have to go up." Social mobility, then, required a move Uptown.

Demographic and urban geographical shifts have challenged this historically constructed dichotomy somewhat. While Jamaica's lower socioeconomic strata have remained largely Black, the wealthier classes and the places they frequent have become increasingly diversified (Clarke 2006a). This dynamic was reflected in a growing sense of Kingston's Uptown areas as mixed, rather than Brown per se. Many Kingstonians still saw Downtown, Blackness and poverty as coterminous, but over the years I encountered an increasing recognition of Uptown as a more ethno-racially mixed space, which included a Black bourgeoisie. Notwithstanding these changing dynamics, to a large extent the production of difference in Kingston continued to be articulated through bipolar oppositions between Brown and Black, rich and poor, Uptown and Downtown. As Charles Carnegie (2014, 74) argues, "even though the geographic and social markers of the Uptown/ Downtown divide have always been inexact and have varied over time ... they nonetheless retain powerful metaphorical force: meaningfully secured through acts (and perceived acts) of transgression." The urban isomorphism of lines of class and skin color is established linguistically when geographical designations—Downtown, or "inner city"—become adjectives that are taken to self-evidently mean lower class and Black. These dichotomous frames work as everyday spatial regimes that shape differential readings of bodies across the urban landscape.

In Willemstad, where low-income and high-income neighborhoods are interspersed across the urban landscape, I encountered less symmetrical correlations among class, color, and space. Paralleling processes of decolonization in Jamaica, in the twentieth century, new pathways to social mobility opened up for darker-skinned Curaçaoans. Through education, migration to the Netherlands, and the "Antilleanization" of the civil service, the visible presence of wealthier, educated Afro-Curaçaoans increased significantly, even as the minority of White Curaçaoans maintained their elite position. Formerly homogeneously White neighborhoods such as Emmastad or Julianadorp gradually became more ethno-racially diverse, although new forms of racial enclaving have emerged in recent years with the rapid development of gated communities dominated by White Dutch expats.

Beyond the impact of social mobility, the diversity of the migrants who came to Curaçao in the twentieth and twenty-first centuries disrupted established ethno-racial hierarchies. In the mid-twentieth century, the arrival of impoverished light-skinned migrants from Portugal and Madeira, and of darker-skinned Afro-Surinamese who found relatively advantageous employment as skilled laborers within the oil refinery, began to complicate the schematic association of a darker skin color with a disadvantaged class position. In recent decades, the co-production of class and color has been challenged further, and perhaps more dramatically, by the presence of many light-skinned Latin American migrants. These immigrants, many of whom are undocumented, often work under relatively exploitative labor conditions and tend to reside in low-income *barios*. These processes are often gendered; Latina women, in particular, are associated with sex work and suffer significant stigmatization (Ministry of Social Development, Labor and Welfare [SOAW] 2014). In comparison to these migrants, the Dutch passport that *koló skur* Curaçaoans possess tends to be a stronger factor in the construction of social status than their skin color.

Projecting a bipolar division has also been less tenable in Willemstad than in Kingston because of the former's spatial development. Much more so than Kingston, Willemstad has developed into a heterogeneous agglomeration of neighborhoods that vary in historical background, ethnicity, income level, and infrastructure quality. The urban planning instigated by Shell, which differentiated neighborhoods according to migrant origin—White Dutch, Portuguese, Surinamese—did cement associations between space and ethno-racial belonging, but in a multipolar rather than dichotomous fashion. While the dynamics have changed over time, specific neighborhoods are still associated with different ethnic groups, such as Kanga or Buena Vista with Jamaicans, and Souax with Dominicans and Colombians.

While racialized patterns of differentiation played a role in their discussions of Willemstad's different neighborhoods, most of the residents I spoke to in Wishi/Marchena and Seru Fortuna tended to go beyond skin color to refer to specific ethnic groups as they distinguished between different *barios*. They associated the wealthier *barios*—the *lujo* (luxurious) or *riku* (rich) areas—with White Dutch (*makambas*), Jews, and East Indian (*hindu*) businessmen, as well as with *koló kla* Curaçaoans. In contrast, they characterized the so-called *marginal* neighborhoods as the home of *koló skur* Curaçaoans and of Latin American and Caribbean immigrants. Especially in Wishi/Marchena, which has a long history of migration, residents had a negative impression of all types of foreigners, speaking disapprovingly of Dominican, Haitian, Colombian, and Jamaican immigrants, and of wealthy European Dutch expatriates.

Urban narratives of fear and exclusion

Throughout the Caribbean, colonially derived hierarchies of class, color, gender, and space have become destabilized. Precisely because these hierarchies have become less stable—and because the categories of class and race are never fixed—different strategies have been needed to maintain structures of urban privilege, and new tactics have emerged by which these structures are challenged and subverted. The stories people tell each other about their city and its different parts can be understood as discursive interventions into socio-spatial hierarchies. Such urban narratives both reproduce and subvert these hierarchies, not only justifying but also questioning the segmentation of urban space and spatial separations of people.

Anthropological inquiries into the exclusionary effects of the socio-cultural production of urban space have tended to focus more closely on the discourses and practices of middle classes and elites. Teresa Caldeira's (2000) classic work on São Paulo, for instance, studied the retreat of the upper and middle classes into fortified enclaves: privatized spaces of residence, work, consumption, and leisure. This retreat is linked to increased insecurity, but also to the pervasive "talk of crime." Drawing on research in Managua, Dennis Rodgers (2004) has built on this work, pointing to the rise of the fortified networks that are created when such enclaves are connected by an exclusive transport infrastructure. Where fortified enclaves lead to increased urban fragmentation and segregation, fortified networks signal the disembedding of an entire layer of elite space from the urban fabric. Charles Carnegie (2014) analyzes such processes for Kingston, describing how the city's postcolonial elites have restricted their circuits of movements in a retreat from formerly cross-class spaces and institutions. He recognizes this shift as occurring also at the smaller scale of the house, symbolized by the loss of the verandah, as elites have moved "from a domestic architecture more open to the outdoors and to the street, where ample verandahs served as important spaces for socializing, to an architectural ethos now more closed-off, centered on interiorized sociability, lived within gated communities, and with verandahs attenuated or altogether absent" (2014, 64). However, non-elite discourses and practices also impact on urban fragmentation, as I found during my research in Kingston and Willemstad, which involved spending considerable time discussing the differentiation of urban space with residents of the low-income neighborhoods of Riverton, Rae Town, Wishi/Marchena, and Seru Fortuna.[1]

Kingston's Uptown citizens considered Riverton and Rae Town to be dangerous ghettos, while elite Curaçaoans regarded Wishi/Marchena and Seru Fortuna as criminal havens. On both islands, the residents of these neighborhoods also described the broader urban landscape as characterized by social distance and danger. Histories of intentional ethnic, class, and political segregation, combined with current conditions of violence and fear, were evident in residents' portrayals of their cities as fragmented, divided into accessible and safe parts and no-go areas plagued by problems. Despite short physical distances between different communities, many inner-city residents seemed to have developed a limited mobility that was to some extent self-imposed. Many people I spoke to were truly familiar with only a limited range of places and felt uncomfortable or unsafe outside of those areas.

While I approached both cities as coherent urban areas, in these local constructions Kingston and Willemstad emerged as archipelagoes of loosely connected neighborhood islands, whose residents had far less than unrestricted access to each other's territory. Barry Chevannes (2001, 133) has called

Kingston "an overlapping congeries of communities," and to a large extent this typifies Willemstad as well. The concept of a cohesive urban entity—a "Kingston metropolitan area" or "greater Willemstad"—seemed to be largely absent. I rarely observed feelings of ownership for, or identification with, the urban area as a whole. What planners would define spatially as a unified urban entity did not appear to function as such in the minds of most residents. Rather, they experienced and narrated the municipality as a number of separate communities or *barios*, loosely connected but often lacking in physical and symbolic interaction. Although many of my interlocutors expressed a strong identification both with their neighborhood and with the nation, they identified much less readily with the city as a whole. People rarely spoke of themselves as "Kingstonians" or "from Willemstad." Rather, they identified themselves as coming from one neighborhood community, or as Jamaicans and Curaçaoans; their identifications were focused on either smaller or larger levels of scale than the urban.

Awareness of segregation along class, ethnic, and political lines came out clearly in residents' urban narratives. In addition, fear of violence was an important factor in differentiations of urban space in both Kingston and Willemstad. While both cities have suffered from high rates of violent crime, Kingston in particular has been plagued by exceedingly high homicide rates, resulting in geographies characterized by fear of violence. I repeatedly encountered representations of Kingston as a crazy-quilt where patches of peace, cool, and calm alternated with no-go zones raging with urban warfare. Fear of violence segregates and isolates both rich and poor citizens. David Howard (2005, 98) notes that "whether [Kingston's] differences are visible or verbal, one of the most divisive forces is that of fear, separating and dividing people into their imagined citadels of safety. . . . Anything or anyone outside the norm, in an uptown suburb or downtown neighbourhood, elicits cause for concern or outright anxiety."

Riverton and Rae Town residents spoke repeatedly of the area stigmatization they experienced on the basis of such geographies of fear. As Shelly-Ann, a young woman from the neighborhood, explained, "Riverton is nice, but if you tell them at work you from Riverton you don't have a chance. People outta road [from outside Riverton] think we evil and all that." The stigma attached to residence in these communities complicated the task of finding work, unless an individual lied about his or her address, and Riverton residents told me that some schools would not take students from the area, based on its reputation. Residents from both Riverton and Rae Town did, however, use comparable schemata to differentiate between Kingston's neighborhoods, describing certain areas with low crime rates as peaceful and "free and safe," while other areas were characterized as "war zones" and the people who lived there as "messed up and wicked." They characterized other Downtown neighborhoods such as Tivoli Gardens and Trench Town as "gunmen town," characterized by "cussing and fighting" or, worse, killings and "pure gunshot."

Differentiations on the basis of safety connected to the Uptown–Downtown divide. Many inner-city residents spoke of Uptown communities with admiration, praising them as safe, clean, cool, and organized "residential areas" where "top of the top people" lived in pretty houses. In contrast, fewer people voiced resentment of Uptown, expressing feelings of exclusion. On the whole, most people I spoke to referred to Downtown Kingston, the half of the city where they resided, in negative terms. They described Downtown as characterized by "war," sweltering heat, crowded streets, and zones that were inaccessible to strangers. Downtown was the part of the city where poor Black people and "ghetto youth" resided. Many people did make smaller differentiations within this Uptown–Downtown dichotomy, distinguishing between different types of ghetto on account of their level of violence, infrastructural development, or location. Hence residents described August Town, a low-income neighborhood on Kingston's northeastern fringe, as a "cool hill ghetto" or a "more nature ghetto" in contrast to Trench Town, a true "inner-city ghetto," or Tivoli Gardens, a "developed ghetto."

In Willemstad, crime also featured prominently in discourses on the city. Seru Fortuna had one of the island's worst reputations for crime, and residents complained about the negative effects area stigmatization had on their lives. Though shootings, stabbings, and drug deals were not uncommon occurrences, most residents seemed to be more concerned with the area's reputation than with their personal safety. They explained to me that they knew where they could and could not go, or that they were safe because they were known and respected in the neighborhood. However, living in the area made it harder to find work: "If you apply for a job and you write your address on the application form you know you won't get the job," residents would tell me. "They don't want people from here." In addition, because of the area's reputation, mini-buses, the main form of transport for those without a private vehicle, would often refuse to take passengers there at night, limiting residents' mobility. Yet many residents of Seru Fortuna and Wishi/Marchena were similarly fearful of other low-income neighborhoods. They described Koraal Specht, a neighborhood where the island's main prison as well as a large public housing complex are located, as "like Dallas, with gunfights," a violent place where drug dealers ruled the streets. Other areas, such as Scharloo, in the old city center, were portrayed as overrun by drug addicts, prostitutes, and foreigners. As in Kingston, residents associated violence, crime, and dilapidation most closely with poor neighborhoods and poor people. However, in contrast to Kingston, their descriptions of wealthier *barios* were rarely positive. Elite neighborhoods such as Mahaai or Emmastad were seen as spaces with less *ambiente* (atmosphere) than their own *humilde* (humble) neighborhoods, and many people perceived rich people as arrogant and racist.

One day I was sitting on a bench in Seru Fortuna near the community center, talking to Mario, a *koló skur* man in his mid-thirties. He had just told me that he felt rather different from others in the *bario*, because he had a higher level of education: he had completed the HAVO level of secondary school, which has more academic content and is considered more prestigious than the LBO level, which has a stronger vocational focus. It was true that many of the residents I had interviewed in Curaçao had not gone beyond an LBO-level education, and Mario distinguished himself from them with a certain pride. In Curaçao, as in Jamaica, increased educational opportunities from the middle of the twentieth century on have facilitated social mobility for many darker-skinned, working-class citizens. As Mario and I began to discuss Willemstad and the differences between its various neighborhoods, the corners of his mouth drooped. Speaking of the wealthy *bario* of Mahaai, he told me: "I can't get in there." He was not referring to being able to afford a residence there, but to actually entering the neighborhood on foot. While I had been to Mahaai a number of times to visit a colleague's relatives and had noticed that many of the houses had gates and watch dogs, it was not a gated community, nor had I seen any kind of guards in evidence. Yet Mario explained to me, "Its a very protected *bario*. If I walk in there on foot, with my [dark] skin color, someone would be sure to call the police within five minutes." When I asked whether he had visited Mahaai and experienced this treatment, he told me he hadn't, but this was really just the way things were. His understanding of the hierarchies that structure access to the wealthier parts of Willemstad, then, connected skin color and specific forms of mobility to patterns of fear.

These representations of different parts of the city are colored by the geographies of fear that emerge in the context of urban violence, geographies that connect to spatial and ethno-racial othering. Inner-city residents challenged the ways in which racist and classist practices of exclusion restricted their mobility. Specifically, they contested the processes of area stigmatization by which their own neighborhoods were misrepresented and their opportunities for social mobility impaired. Yet in other, more subtle, ways their own urban narratives reproduced patterns of social distancing, sometimes by replicating dominant socio-spatial discourse, and sometimes by deflecting it onto other areas or social groups.

Self-representation and social distancing

The ways in which residents of stigmatized areas relate to their urban surroundings can be analyzed as a form of agency. Urban space shapes and is shaped by social behavior, through processes in which spatial practices are established and spatial meanings are assigned and negotiated. Place sustains social difference and hierarchies, "both by routinizing daily rounds in ways that exclude and segregate categories of people, and by embodying in visible and tangible ways the cultural meanings variously ascribed to them" (Gieryn 2000, 474). Notwithstanding structural constraints, some of which are embedded in urban geography, the urban poor are agents capable of strategically "using space," by, for instance, establishing place-related identifications, building spatially defined social networks, and developing economically functional forms of spatially circumscribed interaction and movement (Gotham and Brumley 2002). Kingston and Willemstad's inner-city residents used space in a multifaceted way and to various ends, primarily to counter stigma, negotiate contexts of urban violence, and create a spatial basis for social and material support.

A number of studies have found that residents of stigmatized communities can internalize prejudices and hold negative attitudes toward their own places of residence (e.g., Blokland 2008; Wacquant 2007). However, the opposite reaction is also possible: I found that rather than engaging in self-stigma, both Jamaican and Curaçaoan residents tended to collectively develop positive neighborhood narratives that can be understood as oppositional place images (Gupta and Ferguson 1992). This discursive strategy of rejecting stigma through place-based narratives of unity and support was bolstered by collective material and social interventions into the neighborhood environment. Residents sought to redress widely held ideas about their neighborhood by organizing *bario* days and by caring for community spaces, for instance by engaging in beautification efforts. Residents rhetorically constructed their own neighborhood as a safe space within a violent, unwelcoming city by contrasting it favorably with other urban places. In so doing they posited themselves as respectable citizens unfairly subjected to stigma. This use of space, the assigning of meaning and value, the owning and disowning of urban places, serves to order and understand the larger city while claiming and redeeming a place-based social identity.

Like other *marginal* neighborhoods in Curaçao, both Wishi/Marchena and Seru Fortuna made concerted efforts to improve their reputation by organizing a *dia di bario*, a neighborhood day on which outsiders were invited to visit and enjoy musical performances, food, and children's games. In Seru Fortuna, which is located farther from the center of Willemstad, this day did not attract many visitors, but in Wishi/Marchena the strategy appeared to be working. The *dia di bario* I visited there was well attended and featured performances by some of the island's most famous musical acts. Vendors sold food and drinks, while the *bario* organization ran a stand selling t-shirts decorated with the neighborhood's name in large letters and a stylized image of a hill and the oil refinery, the area's two main geographical features. Following significant lobbying efforts, another major accomplishment in the effort to improve Wishi/Marchena's reputation had been the successful alteration of the route of the annual Carnival parade, one of Curaçao's biggest events, so that revelers now passed through the community. Residents held up the fact that the parade and revelers were willing to come to Wishi/Marchena as evidence that this was a safe, low-violence area, and that the area's stigmatization was misplaced.

In the Jamaican neighborhoods of Riverton and Rae Town, many residents heatedly rejected the negative reputation that plagued their neighborhood. While they generally emphasized the need for development—more and better employment, housing, and educational opportunities, and improvements in environmental services and infrastructure—they would claim the neighborhood as a space to be proud of. Riverton's peripheral location as the municipal dumpsite had certain benefits, as Mosiah, a Rasta farmer from the community, explained: "Riverton is a blessed community. In other inner-city communities you can't raise pigs, you can't raise cows, or get a little plot of land." Indeed, visiting his plot of farmland was like entering a small green oasis, away from the smell and dust of the landfill that dominated the neighborhood. Even those residents whose livelihoods involved "hustling" on the dump—collecting recyclables for resale—were proud of the neighborhood; Johnny, for instance, described Riverton to me as "the number one ghetto, a top of the top ghetto." Rae Town residents praised their neighborhood's location on the harbor, with the fishing beach as a breezy spot to cool off. In particular, many residents spoke with pride of "Ole Hits," the Sunday night reggae dance the neighborhood was known for. In addition to providing income to many locals, the dance also attracted Uptown visitors and Japanese tourists. Similar to the role of the Carnival parade in Wishi/Marchena, this presence of outsiders confirmed to residents that Rae Town was a safe, respectable place.

Of course, some of these positive portrayals can be read as strategic narratives, part of struggles to control representation. Outsider researchers such as anthropologists are potential resources in reshaping a stigmatized neighborhood's reputation. At one point, I met a group of University of the West Indies (UWI) geography students doing a housing survey in Rae Town. Their survey included a question about how many toilets the interviewee's house had. This question was rather intrusive and potentially embarrassing, as many people in the neighborhood lived in tenement yards where several households shared one toilet. Rather than report this humble situation to light-skinned, middle-class students, I heard Janice, a young woman from the area, tell them breezily, "Oh, my house has three toilets." Daniel Goldstein (2004) has pointed to the ways in which residents of low-income marginalized urban areas in Bolivia both resent and desire outside attention, balancing intrusive government and NGO efforts to produce legibility by using encounters with these outsiders to influence representations of their neighborhood. Residents have various reasons to represent their neighborhood's social and economic situation as either better or worse than it actually is. They fear that any information they pass on to possibly influential researchers on informal economic activities or levels of crime may lead to increased taxation or repression, but they also seek to portray their neighborhood in ways that might encourage positive government or NGO interventions and lead to an improved reputation.

Obviously such considerations will color residents' representations. However, the pride and comfort I perceived residents as feeling went beyond verbal assertions. In both Riverton and Rae Town, the strong identification residents felt with their own community was evident in their behavior. Janice, for instance, left Rae Town to live with her mother in the nearby town of Portmore, in a lower-middle-class neighborhood with "real houses." However, a year later she returned to Rae Town, which she felt was more sociable and lively. She explained that while Portmore was a more developed place to live, it was very boring, as everyone stayed inside their houses and nobody talked to each other; her move back to the inner city confirmed her attachment to Rae Town. Residents also demonstrated their emotional and material commitment to these stigmatized spaces through material interventions. No matter how dilapidated the private residences and yard spaces, these domestic environments featured colorfully painted walls, carefully tended plants, or decorations such as plastic flowers and porcelain knickknacks. Similarly, residents expressed their positive feelings toward their surroundings in collective, public spaces such as the street, where murals and whitewashed tires or cement containers filled with plants were proof of micro-scale beautification efforts (see Figure 4.1).

The creation of such spatial markers is part of a larger process of creating urban meaning. As Christien Klaufus (2012) notes in her research on urban Ecuador, interventions in the domestic built environment can be read as performances that seek to communicate social prestige and well-being. Her work on architecture shows that residents of neighborhoods on the peripheries of Ecuadorian cities actively use the appearance of their homes to counter area stigmatization, incorporating international and upper-class architectural references. More broadly, throughout cities across the world, people draw on urban markers, from gates to graffiti to garbage, to distinguish between urban segments and to guide their mobility. Mario Luis Small (2004, 102) speaks of the "ecology of group differentiation," by which an area's spatial features become inextricably associated with class or ethnic features. This process reinforces differences between residents and nonresidents and spatializes boundary work, the construction of group differentiation and mutual exclusion that I encountered in Kingston and Willemstad. By physically creating

FIGURE 4.1 Beautification efforts in Rae Town

elements in their built environment, and assigning meaning to those created by others, residents both write and read urban spatial texts.

Despite the negative standing of their "ghetto" neighborhoods, Rae Town and Riverton residents obviously felt safe and at home in them, with both men and women walking the streets freely at all hours. Many residents explained their feelings of security by mentioning that the murder rate was very low, as well as by referring to their feelings of ownership: these were places they knew and loved, they were *their* places, and therefore nothing could happen to them there. A relatively low murder rate did not imply an absence of crime or violence. One day, while I was having a drink with a few residents in Rae Town, a woman from the neighborhood was caught stealing a bunch of bananas in the adjacent, slightly wealthier Manley Meadows, only to be stabbed by the security guard on duty so badly that "them no know if she a go make it," that is, they were not sure she would survive. This was widely condemned as an excessive reaction on the part of the guard, and in revenge he was attacked—kicked and stabbed—by a group of women, friends and sisters of the woman he had wounded. While this incident indicated the speed with which conflicts could become violent, the fact that the woman's stabbing was revenged so quickly can also be read as indicative of the closeness of the community. Especially in Rae Town, many residents were "born and raise" in the community. They hung out together, outside or in each other's yards, and they generally felt similar to one another, because, as Janice put it, "me and them grow up together."

Beyond the countering of stigma through positive neighborhood narratives, another reaction to territorial discrimination that I encountered was a rejection of the stigma through what Loïc Wacquant (2007, 68) calls "lateral denigration and mutual distanciation." In Seru Fortuna and Riverton in particular, residents would apply internal differentiation to the neighborhood, categorizing the larger space into "micro-locales" and applying "micro hierarchies" (Wacquant 1993): "*This* street is fine, but be careful as soon as you turn the corner." In Seru Fortuna, such micro-hierarchies played out within Seru Papaya, the section of Seru Fortuna where more recent residents lived in public housing, in contrast to the families who had been living in "Old Seru Fortuna" for several generations and owned their houses and the land they were built on. The newer residents felt that their street or block was safe and occupied by good people, but that this did not hold for the entire *bario*. Maria, one of these more recent residents, warned me: "Miss, you know you must always be very careful elsewhere in this *bario*." She continued, however, by checking this assertion: "But I am sure you have noticed that this street is very nice, haven't you?" While such strategies of internal differentiation and distancing can have a negative effect on interpersonal trust and solidarity, they can also increase social ties and spatial bonds within the smaller spatial sub-units of the street, the block, or the corner.

The same mechanism writ large can be identified within the larger space of Downtown Kingston or *marginal* Willemstad. While residents in all four of the neighborhoods where I worked were keen to put their own area's reputation into perspective, they often expressed fear and aversion with respect to other "bad" areas. In Curaçao, people from Wishi/Marchena saw Seru Fortuna as a problematic, violent *bario*. Richenel, a young man from Wishi/Marchena, described Seru Fortuna as "a dangerous *bario* with gunfights and rapes. ... You can't walk there, it's scary." Similarly, Seru Fortuna residents described Wishi/Marchena as a very aggressive *bario* with nothing but problems, though they conceded that it had improved in recent years. In Jamaica, people in Rae Town spoke with pity and disgust of Riverton, describing its residents as crazy people who ate off the dump. Through such deflections of stigma, residents of marginalized neighborhoods resort to a form of sociospatial distancing that strengthens local ties but reproduces urban hierarchies of place.

Emplaced bodies

The discursive and material forms of place-making and social distancing described previously are part of how residents of Kingston and Willemstad negotiate their neighborhood and the larger urban landscape. These place-based negotiations of status intersect with embodied forms of social positioning and self-presentation in everyday spatial and bodily regimes. In both cities, the racialization or ethnic labeling of urban space means that as bodies move, their ethno-racial designations shift. During the fifteen years that I have been working in Kingston, I have repeatedly been called Chinese. The first time I took notice was when a group of schoolchildren boarded the public bus I was riding. Once they spotted me, they started jumping up and down, pointing at me and shouting, "Chinee! Chinee!" excitedly. Being referred to as "Miss Chin," another common designation for Chinese women, also became a common occurrence. While my mother is of mixed Dutch and Indonesian descent, I had rarely been "recognized" as Asian outside of Jamaica and was initially confused as to why I was being identified as such. Such remarks made me aware of the apparently ambiguous character of my ethnicity. Walking across the Parade, near Downtown Kingston's central market, a passerby shouted at me, "Whitey or Browning? Which one, tell me nuh!" Another time, while driving through West Kingston, three different people shouted, "Whitey," "Browning," and "Miss Chin" at me as I passed by, all within the space of a minute.[2] At a certain point I realized that these interpretations of my appearance were related to my location in the city. I would be called Chinese or Brown far more frequently in places where White people were not presumed to dwell: on public transport, on sidewalks, and, more broadly, in Downtown Kingston and its so-called ghettos. Here, the most common groups of non-African descent are Chinese, who own the numerous wholesales and corner shops, followed by Lebanese. More generally, my designation as White, which was taken for granted in Uptown Kingston, was called into question as I moved into other spaces.

This variable racialized reading of my body points to the importance of everyday spatial regimes. Ethno-racial designations are not just formed on the basis of skin color or classed markers such as dress and speech; the spatial context is also highly significant in the interpretation of people's physical markings. Similar to my becoming identified as Chinese more readily when in Downtown Kingston, a light-skinned person who lives in a Downtown "ghetto" will be more likely to be read as Black than a person of similar complexion living Uptown—and vice versa, a person with a supposedly Black complexion may become Browner by moving from Downtown to Uptown. Gina Ulysse (2007) emphasizes the ways in which these spatial mappings of color and class are always gendered through dichotomous notions that contrast socially privileged White and Brown "ladies" who live Uptown with working-class Black "women" who live Downtown. She focuses on the role of informal commercial importers, who transgress these boundaries to refashion themselves as "Downtown ladies." Similarly, drawing on research on women's informal work, Winnifred Brown-Glaude (2011) points to Kingston's enduring if increasingly contested social and spatial order that locates women differently according to class and color.

However, the co-production of race, class, gender, and space goes beyond these Uptown–Downtown, *bario lujo–bario humilde* urban divides. Diane Austin-Broos (1994) has pointed out how, for Jamaica, the class–color dualism corresponds with another spatial differentiation, that between inside and outside. Brown, middle-class, or elite Jamaicans are associated with "inside" life: they work inside buildings such as offices; they socialize inside; they shop inside supermarkets and shopping malls; their offspring are "inside," legitimate children. Black, lower-class Jamaicans, in contrast, are associated with outside work in the open air (whether as street vendors or manual laborers); they socialize in the space of the street; they shop in open-air markets; and their children are often "outside," illegitimate. This spatial differentiation works in a remarkably similar fashion in Curaçao. In the popular imagination, lower-class Afro-Curaçaoans socialize and consume in outside spaces, while men have *byside* relationships and children. In contrast, *hende haltu*, "high people," are expected to display more closed, "inside" types of behavior and relationships. This similarity came out in a discussion I had with Lorena, a long-time resident of Wishi/Marchena. She described wealthier Willemstad neighborhoods such as Mahaai to me as "pretty, big houses but they're all closed up [*será*], they're separate, isolated." In contrast, she described Willemstad's poorer areas as "normal" and open.

Increasingly, however, the spatiality of race, class, and gender is not only related to the distinctions between inside and outside. Extending Austin-Broos's work, we might analyze contemporary Caribbean social positioning fruitfully by focusing on the distinction between bounded and open spaces. Making this analytical distinction points to the micro-spatial strategies that are central to everyday bodily regimes. Beyond the social situatedness of bodies within the larger urban landscape, different forms of emplacement at the micro level also shape their categorization and, correspondingly, become important sites for self-styling. In both Kingston and Willemstad, boundedness and openness are characterized by different sets of norms and ideas, structuring different possibilities for embodied and emplaced forms of social positioning. A higher position in the color–class hierarchy is associated with a life spent mostly within bounded spaces: a car with its windows up and its doors locked; a sealed-off, air-conditioned office with a security guard at the entrance; a house with a grille and a fence; or a gated community.

This boundedness ties to the notion of everyday bodily regimes. To perform a higher social status, these bodies, and in particular female bodies, *need* to be spatially bounded to maintain their social status. Apart from security concerns, practical issues related to climate inform the emphasis on bounded spaces. In both Jamaica and Curaçao, looking professional often involves wearing suits, button-down shirts, pantyhose, and other outfits that tend to be uncomfortably hot if worn outdoors, and this dress code is maintained much more strictly than in the European countries that originally introduced it as a set of colonial norms. These professional dress requirements mean that the windows and doors of most office buildings are sealed shut, so that air-conditioning systems can maintain a sufficiently low temperature.

This chill also serves to mark social boundaries, to condition the climatic fit between "professional" bodies and spaces. The frigid temperature at which the air conditioning is set in many offices makes visitors dressed in outdoor attire—those people whose self-styling does not fit the bounded locale—feel physically uncomfortable and out of place. Conversely, people who have styled their bodies to conform to these bounded bodily regimes may feel physical discomfort in less bounded, outside spaces. For women in particular, to dwell in opener spaces means exposing one's body and one's social status to pollution, a point I also return to in the next chapter.

Mobilities are another crucial aspect of the intersecting everyday bodily and spatial regimes (cf. Cresswell 2006; Sheller and Urry 2006). Different sets of ideas and norms determine the "proper" form of transport for various social categories, with the various forms of public and private transport representing mobile micro-locales that can shield or expose men's and women's bodies as they traverse the city. The ascription of color–class identities relies not only on where you are in the city, but also on how you move through it. Black/poor people are those who share route taxis, take the public bus, or, worst of all, walk. Brown/rich people are those who travel by air-conditioned private car, increasingly SUVs—a defensive form of mobility that locks off its passengers from the street, cushioning them from potholes and literally placing them above pedestrians. As Gina Ulysse observes, "Walking on the street not only brings [a "lady"] into a public arena, but also results in the unladylike conditions of being dusty and sweaty. Contact with the hot sun not only induces perspiration, but also damages and darkens sensitive white or light skin. Hence ladies use private cars with air conditioning" (2007, 43). However, walking or even cycling can be part of the performance of more privileged social identities if it takes place in elite urban areas or outside the city for exercise or recreational purposes. In both Kingston and Willemstad, women in particular increasingly have begun to walk or jog to stay fit, if only in certain circumscribed areas.

In my first six years of visiting Kingston, I traveled through the city almost exclusively on public transport. During fieldwork, I would stay with a host family in a peri-urban community to the northeast of the city. To reach Riverton and Rae Town, I would first take a shared minibus or route taxi down to the commercial hub of Papine. There I would catch one of the large Jamaica Urban Transport Corporation (JUTC) buses and transfer to another bus to reach my destination. A one-way trip from home to my research neighborhood would often take an hour and a half, especially in rush hour traffic. On the whole I did not mind this commute; I was rarely in a hurry, and the city's public transport system proved an important site for observing and participating in Kingstonians' interactions in public spaces. Moreover, I did not have a driver's license, and given my limited budget I did not consider taking private taxis a viable option. When I moved to Jamaica in 2006 to take up a position as a lecturer at the University of the West Indies, several colleagues offered advice on how to settle in and make my way around, and much of this advice was related to transport. One colleague advised me: "Make sure you get a big car. You can't have a little car. Those little Smart cars they have in Europe? That can never work in Jamaica, you need a *big* car." Another suggested I take down the name of a man who would wash my car for me in the faculty parking lot—"Everybody uses him." When I told university colleagues that I was used to getting around by bus, they would react with amusement or, more often, concern. A female colleague admitted that she had never in her life taken a bus. At one point, when she was younger, she had found herself standing at a bus stop, waiting for her father to pick her up. Before he arrived, however, friends of her parents who happened to be driving past spotted her standing there and pulled over: "You're not taking the *bus*, are you?" They were only willing to leave her standing there once she had reassured them she had no intention of taking public transport and would soon be picked up by car. Such expressions of concern, dismay, or amusement in response to "inappropriate" modes of mobility are central in solidifying the association between particular social identifications and particular spatial practices.

In Curaçao, I also traveled around mostly by public transport. While middle-class locals would rarely take a minibus, much less the larger state-run buses, public transport was less stigmatized than in Jamaica, perhaps because tourists and Dutch interns would occasionally use this mode of travel. During one stay, I shared a house and a car with a colleague who had many relatives in Curaçao. At one point, we drove her light-skinned, middle-class aunt Tanchi to the airport. As the car was a cheap model without air conditioning, we usually drove with the windows open. Disappointed at the lack of comfort, Tanchi still insisted we roll the windows up, not only to avoid the smell of the oil refinery as we drove past it, but also to prevent her carefully straightened hair from becoming frizzy and tangled. Her investment in being a middle-class *koló kla* Curaçaoan woman, which had become apparent to me in other conversations and remarks, suggested a reading of her discomfort with traveling in our car in terms of gender, class, and color. A closed-off mode of transport was central to the maintenance of her social position. Similarly, Tanchi insisted on watching Curaçao's annual Carnival from her home in an elite suburb, where it was cool and quiet, rather than joining in the action on the streets of central Willemstad. Her emphatically asserted decision *not* to participate in what is arguably Curaçao's most important festive event—a time of year during which class, ethno-racial, and sexual boundaries are temporarily suspended—underlined the significance she placed on maintaining a specific, bounded form of physical integrity.

Like residential and professional location, urban mobilities mediate classed, gendered, and racialized identifications. They structure our understanding of where others fit within urban hierarchies and offer opportunities for styling our own bodies to display a desired social status or match a specific environment. Whether these practices are carried out in an SUV in Kingston or a Carnival parade in Willemstad, they can produce physical sensations of discomfort or dislocation when we venture across socio-spatial borders. As Greg Noble (2005) argues, feeling comfortable in public space is directly connected to the acknowledgement of belonging there, of having a right to claim a part of urban space. By encouraging conformity to everyday spatial and bodily regimes, and deterring transgression from them, such embodied sensations of comfort and discomfort are a critical factor in the construction and legitimization of social hierarchies.

Conclusion

Urban inequalities are reproduced through the discursive construction and social use of space. The spatial stories and strategies that residents develop in cities characterized by fear of crime and violence often exacerbate the urban fragmentation produced through histories of colonial segregation. In Jamaica and Curaçao, the historical co-production of race, class, gender, and space continues to inform city-dwellers' notions of where they and others are supposed to live, work, and play. Individuals' experiences of a city are influenced by how they are positioned within the broader urban landscape, a positioning that relies heavily on interpretations of physical features, bodily adornment, and comportment. Widely shared socio-spatial norms delineate which types of users and forms of behavior are regarded as appropriate, and which are considered to be illegitimate. The ability or inability of differently positioned individuals to conform to such norms can produce distinctly physical and psychological experiences of discomfort. These normative associations among people, places, and behavior are reproduced in everyday micro-level narratives and mobilities. Understanding how urban privilege is obtained or maintained requires attention to emplaced and embodied micro-politics. Being or becoming a respectable, middle-class Brown or *koló kla* man or woman involves an embodied fluency in specific social spaces, from the office to the supermarket to the restaurant. For women in particular, maintaining a "professional" appearance that is still significantly influenced by Eurocentric ideals of hair and beauty involves restricting oneself to bounded, air-conditioned buildings and cars. More generally, an elite social position is predicated on physical distance from, or insulation against, the dirty and violent spaces of the urban poor.

Across lines of color and class, however, urban residents engage in processes of social distancing and place-making in a context of general insecurity. Both the visible barriers of the gated communities of the rich and the more subtle boundaries isolating low-income areas limit intra-urban mobility and interaction. Many of my lighter-skinned, middle-class friends and colleagues in Jamaica and Curaçao were fearful to venture beyond their "safe," socio-economically circumscribed spaces of work, home, and leisure, scared by narratives of crime that depicted low-income, racialized neighborhoods as loci of danger and desperation. In the face of these processes of area stigmatization, in which poorer and "Blacker" neighborhoods were branded as deviant and dangerous, residents of low-income areas displayed a strong sense of place attachment to their own neighborhoods, demonstrating a shared emotional connection to the space of their Downtown or *marginal* communities.

Although intra-community tensions were occasionally discernible, these residents tended to express loyalty to and pride in their neighborhood. The majority of those I spoke to in the areas where I did most of my research had developed a strong place-based identity and relied on the neighborhood for social and material support. Simultaneously, they were hesitant to move around the rest of the city, feeling afraid or unwelcome outside their own area, and reproducing narratives about other groups, neighborhoods, and communities that were based on stereotypes and media reports rather than on their own experience. The discursive and material construction of safe, defensible spaces offers order and logic in chaotic and threatening urban surroundings, but limits movement to different places and interaction with different people. The imagining and social use of space in inner-city Caribbean neighborhoods challenged the area stigmatization produced by existing hierarchies of socio-spatial value. Yet the strategies of socio-spatial distancing and the lateral deflection of stigma also reinforced patterns of urban exclusion and fragmentation in comparable ways to middle-class and elite practices of maintaining distinction.

5 URBAN NATURALISMS

The spatiality of urban inequalities comes out clearly in the distribution of urban environmental problems. The intersections of race, class, and space discussed in the previous chapter provide a background to understanding the uneven spatial concentration of pollution in Willemstad and Kingston. While the standard of living is generally higher in Curaçao than in Jamaica, I found in both cities that environmental pollution related to garbage, sewage, and airborne emissions was concentrated disproportionately in low-income neighborhoods, where the majority of residents were categorized as Black or *koló skur*. In the "ghettos" of Downtown Kingston, Black Jamaicans had significantly less access to proper sewage and waste disposal services than their wealthier, Browner counterparts in Uptown neighborhoods. They were also disproportionately exposed to hazardous industrial activities. In Willemstad, the former Shell refinery known as the Isla, located in the middle of Curaçao's harbor, was by far the main source of pollution. Because of the dominant northeasterly trade wind, the refinery's emissions have always blown in one direction. The neighborhoods that received most of this pollution were the "marginal" *barios*, where most residents were *koló skur* Afro-Curaçaoans and immigrants.

In both cities, I encountered the intertwining of material and symbolic concepts of pollution, with many residents associating the low-income Afro-Caribbean urban population with dirty places and substandard environmental infrastructure and housing. I suggest that popular conflations of environmental pollution and social pathologies serve to justify urban inequalities. Many Jamaicans and Curaçaoans—of different socio-economic and ethno-racial backgrounds—engage in the reproduction of racialized and classed narratives about dirty places. Within such narratives, not only is the pollution of these urban places often seen as resulting from the behavior of the people who live there, but these neighborhoods are also often understood as shaping the people who live in them. In Willemstad and Kingston, as in cities elsewhere, such popular conceptions of environmental determinism—which echo historical beliefs about the influence of milieu on character (Osbourne and Rose 1999)—hold that good neighborhoods produce better citizens than do bad neighborhoods, not only through the social environment but specifically through the biophysical and built environment.

In this chapter, I analyze such narratives to develop a cultural political approach to environmental injustice. I focus more closely on the material semiotics of pollution, drawing on insights from political ecology and urban theory to tease out the connections between environmental injustice and the cultural production of difference through urban space. To connect these two fields, I develop the concept of "urban naturalisms" to indicate the process through which social hierarchies and the unequal distribution of urban environmental problems are naturalized, focusing on the use of the trope of pollution. I explore how Jamaican and Curaçaoan narratives that attribute social pathologies to residents of low-income, contaminated neighborhoods also serve as frameworks for the allocation of environmental causality and blame.

Such explanatory frames, which elide political economic factors, portray stigmatized areas as "a malign womb within the city rather than the result of urban forces long concealed by the perdurance of its myth representation" (McDonogh 2003, 268). By parsing blame-the-poor narratives that rely on conflations of people, places, and pollution, I aim to demonstrate their potential to provide a discursive justification for environmental inequalities. These narratives, which can make it seem only natural that those neighborhoods where "nasty" people live are the dirtiest, have material effects. They can affect the location of physical and social interventions and influence the uneven allocation of economic resources across urban space, resulting in material differences in urban cleanliness that may then feed back into the original stigmatizing narratives.

The chapter starts with a discussion of work that has theorized the uneven distribution of environmental problems in relation to racism and classism. I draw on these approaches to show that environmental injustice, such as the unequal exposure of residents in Kingston and Willemstad to pollutants, does not always result from malicious intent. Rather, it often emerges in complex ways, as part of the historical development of urban landscapes that are saturated with classed and racialized meaning. Next, I go into more detail on the concept of urban naturalisms, illustrating how pollution works to naturalize environmental inequalities. Analyzing media narratives, online discussions, and everyday conversations I had throughout the two cities, I sketch the close entanglement of categories of social and biophysical pollution. I then show how residents of polluted neighborhoods, such as those where I did research, deal with socio-ecological stigmatization. Drawing more directly on my ethnographic research, I suggest that these residents use various spatial and discursive tactics to counter this stigmatization, simultaneously rejecting, deflecting, and reproducing urban naturalisms.

Race, class, and environmental injustice

In both Kingston and Willemstad, urban pollution is concentrated in poorer neighborhoods with larger proportions of Black or *koló skur* residents. The middle and upper classes and historically privileged ethnic groups are not confronted with the same levels of garbage, sewage, and air pollution that other residents encounter in their day-to-day lives. To what extent can this form of environmental injustice be understood as environmental racism? Racism is often understood in a narrow normative sense that restricts racist practice to overt individual actions in which malicious intent is evident. Various environmental justice scholars and activists have sought to point out the ways in which racism operates not only, or not so much, through deliberate, conscious acts of discrimination, but rather through less overt and less evident structures of ideology and political economy (Pulido 1996; Pellow 2005). Drawing on this perspective, Robert Bullard (1994, 451) defines environmental racism as "any policy, practice, or directive that differentially affects or disadvantages (whether intended or unintended) individuals, groups, or communities based on race or color."

Debates surrounding environmental racism often center on the siting of environmental hazards, such as dumpsites or toxic industries, in particular areas. In the United States, such hazards are sited disproportionately in non-White working-class communities, particularly African American and Latino neighborhoods. In a number of cases, evidence has been found of the intentional targeting of ethnic and low-income communities for the siting of such facilities. In other instances, the injustice is not so much in an initial discriminatory intent on the part of those deciding where to locate such facilities as in the longer-term outcome of these processes. This is evident in so-called "minority move-in" cases, in which specific ethno-racial groups move into already-polluted neighborhoods. Rather than seeing this situation as the outcome of supposedly race-neutral market dynamics, such cases show how housing and labor markets reinforce racism when race and class are entangled. As David Pellow (2005, 156–157) emphasizes, "even when institutions (governments, corporations, and agencies) make decisions that appear to be race neutral in their intent, they often produce racially unequal impacts." The root causes of racialized environmental injustice, then, often lie in institutional racism: the discrimination that follows from the policies and practices of public and private institutions, rather than from the actions of specific prejudiced individuals.

Move-in arguments remain popular in attempts to displace industry or government responsibility for community exposure to pollution. In the case of Curaçao, Shell officials have argued that the oil company was never responsible for pollution in Wishi/Marchena because the neighborhood only developed in the 1930s, after the refinery was established, and the area's inhabitants moved there voluntarily. This argument obscures the refinery's major role in urban development and the fact that the first Wishi/Marchena residents were predominantly low-paid Afro-Curaçaoan refinery workers, who (unlike higher-paid immigrants from the Netherlands, Portugal, and Suriname) were not provided with company housing in unpolluted areas.

In addition to emphasizing structural forms of racism, critical geographers have drawn attention to the spatiality of racism and the need to take a relational approach to understanding this spatial dimension. As Laura Pulido (2000, 13) argues,

> Because racism is understood as a discrete act that *may* be spatially expressed, it is not seen as a sociospatial relation both constitutive of the city and produced by it. As a result, the spatiality of racism is not understood, particularly the relationship *between places*. Yet pollution concentrations are inevitably the product of relationships between distinct places, including industrial zones, affluent suburbs, working-class suburbs, and downtown areas, all of which are racialized.

In U.S. cities such as Los Angeles, Pulido explains, the historically developed relationships between middle-class White suburbs and low-income non-White inner-city areas—and the associated differences in land values and political clout—are central to understanding why pollution becomes concentrated in certain urban places and not in others.

Like environmental racism, environmental classism (which has received less explicit attention in the literature) works through structural and spatial processes—through ideological structures, labor and housing markets, and the political economy of place—rather than only through intentional malicious practices. In Jamaica, the dumpsite at Riverton existed prior to the establishment of the informal settlement. The first squatters who "chose" to build their homes there in the 1960s—and similarly, many of the squatters who built their dwellings on the edges of Kingston's gullies and other environmentally hazardous sites—were displaced from other parts of the city by political violence instigated by Jamaica's main political parties. Rather than an intended outcome, the exposure of these residents to environmental harm was a side effect of the political tribalism that reshaped relationships between Kingston's low-income neighborhoods in the decades following independence. In addition, the dump's location as part of an industrial strip on the southwestern edge of the city—far from Uptown residences, but not far from working-class housing developments and other squatter settlements—was not coincidental. As Pulido (2000, 20) underlines, we should study individual polluting facilities as part of industrial zones, which do not develop in isolation from, but in relation to, other places, from elite suburbs and commercial areas to inner-city neighborhoods: "All of these places represent specific class relations that are functionally linked. At the same time, all these places are racialized, and racism works in particular ways in their formation and evolution."

Given the entanglement of race and class in the Caribbean, as in many other places, it would appear fruitful to pursue an intersectional analysis of their role in environmental injustice. The complex interactions of race/color, class, and urban space in postcolonial Jamaica and Curaçao suggest that an understanding of environmental racism and classism can contribute to our understanding of urban environmental inequalities. In using the terms "racism" and "classism," it is not my intention to single out specific individuals or groups in either Jamaica or Curaçao as personally involved in deliberately discriminatory practices. Rather, I hope to establish how historically developed classed and racialized meanings of the urban landscape work to justify and normalize environmental injustice. I seek to connect the classed and racialized forms of urban place-making described in the previous chapter with the socio-spatially unequal distribution of environmental hazards. I do this by focusing on the concept of "urban naturalisms": the equation of specific urban populations with specific types of spaces.

Urban naturalisms

The urban naturalisms that render environmental injustice normal rely on cultural constructions of pollution. Following Mary Douglas's (2002) seminal work on dirt and danger, such cultural constructs are generally analyzed as concepts that underpin the social order. Dirt, as "matter out of place," marks any kind of disorder and in so doing highlights what is seen as normal, orderly, and innocent. Concepts of symbolic pollution do boundary work—that is, they serve to create and maintain social categories, to mark and protect the difference between what is safe and what is dangerous, what is acceptable and what is unacceptable. The relationship between order and pollution works in the opposite direction as well: the production of difference and boundaries creates dirt. As John Scanlan (2005, 182) notes, "every act of differentiation produces garbage."

The cultural framing of bodies as pollutants, as disposable waste—human refuse, vermin, scabs, or trash—is a common tool in the production of social hierarchies and in struggles over space and place between groups differentiated on the basis of, for instance, ethnicity, class, gender, or religion. Charles W. Mills (2001) uses the term "black trash" to indicate the historically established ideological framework that associates people of African descent with dirt and a lack of (or threat to) civilization. Mills argues that although "the problem of waste disposal is usually posed as an environmental challenge for an undifferentiated, raceless 'human' population," this is a misleading framing; in the United States, "blacks *themselves* have been thought of as disposable, an excrescence in the body politic, and thus part of the [environmental] problem" (2001, 73, 74).

In the Caribbean, lower-class Afro-Caribbean bodies are most likely to be classified as dirty and dangerous. Historically, they have been depicted as symbolic threats to the social order of the civilized cities. Within these racialized and classed constructions, their "unruly" bodies represent a new type of "natural man": a form of savage nature that threatens the modernity and civilization of the city through its presence. This concept of unclean and contagious non-White bodies has its roots in slavery and post-emancipation colonial urbanization. Krista Thompson (2006, 113) gives the example of a late-nineteenth-century White traveler to the Bahamian city of Nassau, who feared that the winds blowing toward his hotel would carry disease from Black neighborhoods "over the hill." In colonies where the abolition of slavery was followed by large-scale immigration of indentured laborers from British India, pollution was also projected onto the Indo-Caribbean population. In late-nineteenth- and early-twentieth-century Georgetown, Guyana, for instance, there were strong discursive associations between dirt and Indo-Guyanese labor. Urban livelihoods dominated by Indo-Guyanese, such as street-level sanitation work and itinerant milk vending, were associated with corruption, contamination, and disease (De Barros 2002).[1]

These historical processes have worked to produce urban landscapes that can be understood as infused by a "racial ecology [that] determines which populations are viewed as 'fit' for particular environments and specific places" (Pellow 2005, 149). The association of a category of dirty, dangerous bodies with "bad" areas of the city, those plagued by violent crime, drug trade, and general disorder, is most evident in the concept of the "concrete jungle."[2] These wild places—the inner city, the ghetto, the *bario marginal*— are more readily classified as dirty places because of the polluting, "unhygienic," or "antisocial" poor people who live there. Working in the United States, Robert R. Higgins similarly traces the connections between historically rooted conceptions of African Americans as social pollutants and the disproportionate environmental pollution of minority communities: he sees the relationship between social and environmental pollution as productive of what he terms "appropriately polluted space" (Higgins 1994). Bodies that are seen as polluted produce polluted places, which come to be understood as the "natural" locations for such bodies.

Such representations are depressingly common in the Caribbean media (and in Europe and North America). They are also implicit in many Curaçaoan and Jamaican environmental policies and campaigns, which often frame the urban poor as socio-ecological threats rather than as victims. In Curaçao and Jamaica, the places and people seen as dirty tend to be exposed disproportionately to environmental hazards such as industrial pollution, open sewers, and uncollected garbage. Blame-the-victim narratives draw eagerly on the idea that places are dirty not because garbage is not collected there, but because they house dirty people. For example, the gullies that form the drainage systems of Kingston, and that run through Rae Town, often flood as a result of the garbage that piles up in them. Only the poorest of the poor live close to a gully (Figure 5.1). A columnist writing in the *Jamaica Observer* blamed the flooding of the houses bordering on the clogged gullies on the residents' own improper waste management: "Nobody is accountable for the nastiness which they contribute. The worst part is the politicians seeking office who give these people the impression that somehow the state is responsible for much of the breakdown that the people themselves cause."[3] The use of words such as "nastiness" bracket together environmental pollution and social pathology.

FIGURE 5.1 Informal dwellings built on a gully, Kingston

Such associations between dirty places and dirty people, and the related allocations of blame to the more vulnerable groups of society, were evident in an environmental sociology course I taught at the University of the West Indies in Jamaica in 2007. During a lecture devoted to the topic of informal settlements in Jamaica, several students expressed their disgust at squatters. They characterized them as dirty criminals who were to blame for environmental degradation such as polluted gullies because of their illegal, ecologically negligent behavior. Despite a guest lecturer whose research focused on the topic and a long, heated debate on the various structural causes that have resulted in the phenomenon of squatting in marginal urban areas, a number of students reproduced exactly the same narrative of blame and disgust in their written exams. Another example of specific urban figures that are the target of pollution talk is informal vendors, who are often singled out in a comparable fashion. In her research on women's informal work in Kingston, Winnifred Brown-Glaude points to widespread perceptions of vendors or "higglers" as pollutants, especially if they venture into Uptown areas: "Social pathologies ... are mapped onto the black poor female bodies of higglers, who are figured as contaminants" (2011, 157). She also stresses the relation between these women's social status and the unsanitary conditions of the markets where they work: "Socially polluting higglers are both symbolically and spatially put in place by being relegated to the filthy places of the city—their physical environs, in effect, reflected how they were generally perceived and valued" (154).

In Curaçao, similar ideas circulate, especially among Dutch expats—who tend to be overwhelmingly White—and other privileged groups. On the Dutch-language Curaçaoan news site versgeperst.com,[4] Dutch journalist Elisa Koek posted a series of articles on the garbage, littering, and illegal dumping that characterize not only neighborhoods such as Wishi/Marchena and Seru Fortuna but also the island more broadly. The comments under these articles, which appeared to be mainly from Dutch expats who had lived on the island long enough to feel they had a stake in it, reinforced the association between dirt, marginal *barios*, and Afro-Curaçaoans. Under one article on the problem of litter produced by *trùk di pan* (mobile snack bars) in the entertainment district of Saliña, for example, one commenter calling him- or herself "Obi" wrote, "That part of Saliña is an eyesore. Every time I drive by there I feel like I'm in a slum. The stores and buildings look awful, there's hardly any streetlights and it's dirty!" Another commenter, "Linda van Dalen," explained that "people in Curaçao don't know better, at least most of them, because it was already written in the history books about Curaçao that the inhabitants of Curaçao made one big garbage dump out of their little island! They don't care that they throw trash on the street, they don't care that they throw trash in their own yard, never mind the street! That mentality is ingrained, but how to get them to change that, eh???" An individual called "Mientje" added: "Well, this has been the case for yeeeears, most Curaçaoans are porkos [pigs]. They shout and scream when it's THEIR island but they don't have any respect for their island. There's trash everywhere. . ... People, get off your ass and start loving your island so you don't throw garbage!!!!"[5]

Other articles spawned similar comments, asserting that Curaçaoans were historically dirty, calling them pigs, and suggesting that education was the only solution. A commenter writing under the name "DaSilva" (a surname suggesting that the author was a Curaçaoan of Portuguese or Jewish descent) argued that "Afro-Curaçaoan culture brings a few very wonderful things (music, relaxation, laissez-faire, etc.) but very many excesses of that culture are outright degrading to humans, animals and nature. . ... By the way most of the cleanups and such are not organized by Afro-Curaçaoans but by others."[6] Such comments reinforce conceptions of *koló skur* Curaçaoans and their "slums" as innately dirty and imply that only "others"—White Dutch *makambas* or *koló kla* Curaçaoans—are willing and able to clean up the place.

The persistent association of culturally dirty bodies and social groups with specific places conflates race, poverty, space, and social pathology.

Jamaica's nineteenth-century cholera epidemic and Curaçao's early-twentieth-century prostitution policy demonstrate the longer histories of such discourse. Urban residents collectively construct moral geographies involving the "locating of impropriety," shared constructions of place-behavior that often support the dominant urban order and the position of elites in it (Dixon et al. 2006). These moral geographies enable the stigmatization of specific urban areas in which assumptions of place-based deviance intersect with class and ethno-racial hierarchies. Loïc Wacquant describes this type of area stigmatization as "a *blemish of place* . . . super-imposed on the already existing stigmata traditionally associated with poverty and ethnic origin . . . to which it is closely linked but not reducible" (2008, 67). More privileged populations often see the places where marginalized social groups live, work, and spend their leisure time (which are often the places to which they have been relegated) as patches of urban blight in otherwise modern landscapes. Especially in the context of tourism, these urban areas and the people who live there tend to be regarded as highly unpicturesque and as places that need to be segregated and hidden away from the urban spatial "norm."[7] The "ghettos" formed by these divisions and exclusions become known as aggregates of poverty and deviance, and are depicted as sources of potential contamination to other, untainted urban areas.

The pollutants that threaten urban order can take on a wide range of forms that vary depending on the context. Dominant spatial regimes determine whether littering, urinating, smoking, spitting, loud music, and graffiti are or are not constructed as symbolic markers that threaten the urban order. Both stigmatized urban areas themselves and their "characteristic" features are constructed as forms of visual pollution. In Jamaica and Curaçao visual signifiers such as zinc fences, ramshackle housing, or men hanging around on the street (in Papiamentu, *sinta pa nada*, sitting for nothing) indicate disorderly deviations from the supposed norm. References to bad smells, emanating from uncollected garbage, open sewers, polluting industry, or cooking, compound this sense of disturbance of the urban landscape. Noise pollution features as well, whether it be the "filthy language" or the music associated with these "bad" areas, such as dancehall in Kingston. In Willemstad, the association of loud reggaeton and bachata music with Dominican immigrants, and "loose women" in particular, aggravates their reception as sonic irritants.

As places, people, and specific features and behaviors come to be conflated with pollution and pathology, the material consequences of these representations crystallize. A proliferation of garbage works as a symbolic message, an urban marker used to distinguish urban socio-spatial segments. The urban "text" of a dirty person, house, street, or neighborhood is read as a signifier of laziness, moral dissolution, and a lack of virtue. Occupations related to the practical business of waste removal, which carry a near-universal stigma, have a similar outcome of guilt by association. A feedback loop reproduces the social differentiation involved: "dirty" jobs associated with the removal of waste are assigned to low-status groups, and the association of individuals who hold these jobs with pollution inhibits their chances of achieving social mobility through more highly valued forms of employment. In Jamaica, this was especially evident in the opprobrium suffered by residents of Riverton who worked as "scavengers" involved in informal recycling activities on the landfill. While many residents viewed the presence of waste pragmatically, as a potential resource, they were also acutely aware of the disdain and pity that their involvement in informal recycling evoked among other Kingstonians.

Symbolic pollution also becomes materialized and institutionalized through the actions of government agencies, such as when they consciously or unconsciously view these neighborhoods as housing the undeserving poor and concentrate on providing services and infrastructure to populations seen as more deserving. Examples of this preferencing of populations include concentrating garbage collection services in commercial areas rather than in (low-income) residential neighborhoods and the tendency to delay response to fires on Riverton's dump until the noxious smoke begins to affect wealthier areas of the city. In addition to this type of deliberate or inadvertent neglect, the material manifestations of these conflations also emerge in the context of benevolent paternalism. Fragano Ledgister (2012) recounts a controversy in 1970s Jamaica surrounding the opening of a training school for auto mechanics that was donated by the West German government. The People's National Party (PNP) politician D. K. Duncan gave a speech at the opening in which he allegedly deemed the school too clean and too orderly and suggested it needed to be "de-sanitized" to suit the needs of his Black working-class constituents. While Duncan's statements may have been intentionally misinterpreted by his political opponents, the controversy underscores both the societal plausibility of the conflation of race, class, and "unsanitary" urban spaces, and the contested character of this conflation. The speech resurfaced decades later in the context of a controversial article by *Gleaner* columnist Dawn Ritch, who referenced the earlier scandal to berate the PNP's Black nationalism as having produced a "Jamaican cultural identity of dirt and blackness, African struggle, tams, barefoot, and Jesus Sandals."[8] Across the decades, these instances show how associations between dirt and Blackness become political fodder and serve to maintain or deny privilege. Taken together, discursive traditions and a broad range of policy decisions have reinforced the "natural" association of poor Afro-Caribbean populations with polluted ghettos, and have normalized persistent environmental inequalities.

When areas associated with particular groups are polluted, it is often because the inhabitants have limited access to environmental services and infrastructure. In addition, their underprivileged position means they are more likely to be the recipients of environmental hazards through their disproportionate exposure to industrial and traffic-related air pollution, proximity to waste disposal sites, or employment in the most polluted and hazardous urban workplaces. Meanwhile, they tend to enjoy less access to "good" nature such as clean water and air. Well-maintained green spaces are often located in the more orderly, wealthier parts of the city, or are policed to exclude offending persons. Stigmatization of the poor may function to legitimize the physical deterioration of their living and working environments. In a causal inversion, dominant discourse often portrays these individuals' "nastiness" and concomitant social inferiority as the cause of their poverty, rather than framing their unsanitary living and working conditions as a result of a weak socio-economic position.

In Curaçao and Jamaica, those places and people commonly seen as dirty—including areas such as Wishi/Marchena, Seru Fortuna, Riverton, Rae Town, and their residents—tend to suffer disproportionate exposure to environmental hazards such as industrial pollution, gullies overflowing with garbage and sewage, and uncollected litter. An important reason for neighborhood pollution is that socially disadvantaged people do not receive environmental services or have access to infrastructure such as solid waste collection and adequate sewage systems. Neighborhood poverty often entails a lower level of the political and financial clout necessary to obtain publicly or privately provided environmental services (such as gully cleaning in Jamaica) or to fend off polluting industries (such as the oil refinery in Curaçao). Michael Thompson (1979, 35) emphasizes the distortion of causality in explanations of urban squalor, arguing that "slums are socially determined. ... Such physical, physiological, and economic considerations as poor living standards, lack of services and amenities, poor health, dampness, inadequate light, inadequate cooking facilities, overcrowding, high fire risk, whilst real enough are essentially the by-products of a concealed social process. They are the effects, not the cause." However, the urban naturalism that legitimizes environmental inequalities obscures these underlying social, political, and economic processes.

Countering urban naturalisms

The trope of pollution can be deployed to serve contradictory interests. It can reinforce the existing urban social and spatial order, as detailed previously, but it can also serve as a site from which to contest the same power structure. Those people whose bodies and neighborhoods are targeted first as being polluting deal with this stigmatization in various ways, simultaneously rejecting, deflecting, and reproducing it. The residents with whom I worked in marginalized neighborhoods in Kingston and Willemstad had developed various strategies to engage with the trope and counter the urban naturalism as it was applied to them.

One form of engagement rejects all the pollution-related stereotypes associated with poverty and racial classifications by emphasizing cleanliness and order. Irrespective of the gender of their inhabitants, no matter how small or dilapidated the houses I entered, almost without exception they would be kept painstakingly clean and neat, with well-kept pieces of furniture—in particular, dressing tables and whatnots—and carefully maintained decorations such as plastic flowers, decorative calendars, and school photographs. I found that a similarly strong emphasis was placed on personal hygiene and dress. Even in the absence of running water or private sanitary facilities (as was often the case in Riverton and, to a lesser extent, Rae Town), the narrated norm was to bathe more than once a day. The use of talcum powder, cologne, and deodorant was strongly advocated. Both men and women placed a high value on neat grooming and well-kempt hair and nails. In their own yards many people dressed quite casually, but to go out in public dressed "sloppily" was strongly frowned upon. I was initially not always conscious of my own appearance in this regard and was gently reprimanded if, for instance, a bra strap was visible or a button on my shirt was missing. If individuals looked disheveled or did not smell clean, this would be remarked upon in pointed comments or gossip. This importance placed on a clean house and body can be understood as countering historical narratives that categorize the Afro-Caribbean poor as dirty or unkempt.

An alternative engagement with the dominant discourse of pollution is to invert it, with what Loïc Wacquant (2007) calls "dishonored groups" wielding the label of pollution against those who would classify them as dirty.

In both Jamaica and Curaçao, it was commonly held that White people were dirty and smelled bad, in part because their standards of personal hygiene were seen as insufficiently stringent. In Jamaica, this generalized mapping of unpleasant odors onto White bodies connected to perceptions of unsavory White eating habits and the idea that White people ate "nasty" things that were prepared improperly or unhygienically. Afro-Curaçaoans spoke regularly with disdain of *makamba stinki*—smelly White Dutch. While this designation has a specific bodily connotation, it also refers to ideas of the Dutch as morally suspect. In Jamaica, the lack of morality on the part of corrupt politicians was classified as "dirty," and, more generally, the Rastafari phrase "dutty Babylon" branded the oppressive power structure as polluted. Such designations reverse colonially derived hierarchies of cleanliness and morality.

A third strategy also involves the deflection or projection of pollution toward other groups, but in a way that tends to reproduce the urban naturalism. Broadly speaking, residents in the neighborhoods where I worked rejected stereotypes of dirt and crime in relation to their own neighborhood. Many people would, however, apply the same marginalizing labels to other poor neighborhoods that did house "nasty" people. In Curaçao, one of the first questions people would ask in trying to evaluate a person's status was "*Di ki bario e ta?*" (From which neighborhood is he or she?), reinforcing the idea that a person's worth is determined by their urban location. As a relatively prosperous non-independent island, Curaçao has a large immigrant population that also bears the brunt of othering narratives of pollution. The term *ingles stinki* was used to denote "smelly" immigrants from the Anglophone Caribbean, mainly from smaller islands such as St. Lucia and St. Kitts. However, many Curaçaoans perceived the large number of recent Latino immigrants, mainly from the Dominican Republic, Colombia, and Venezuela, as a more pressing threat to the social order. Latino women were branded as prostitutes, and more broadly I encountered a fear, expressed in the media and everyday discourse, that this group of immigrants was "taking over the island," arrogantly refusing to adopt Curaçaoan values and learn Papiamentu (Allen 2003).

In Jamaica, where immigration is much more limited, such deflections of polluting discourse onto newcomers were much less prevalent. However, in recent decades, Haitian refugees have occasionally landed on the island's north coast when their boats have drifted off course, and there has been a significant strand of media and everyday discourse that pathologizes Haitians as dirty and diseased. In a UWI course on Caribbean sociology I taught in

2007, a discussion of Haitian immigrants within the region unearthed similar articulations of social aversion expressed through a language of physical pollution. One Bahamian student insisted that others would understand how problematic Haitian immigration was "if you could see how they live! It's just so dirty!"

Finally, another form of inversion that I encountered in Jamaican popular culture was the embrace of polluted labels, specifically that of the gully. The gullies that form Kingston's drainage system often flood as a result of the garbage that piles up in them, and to live next to a gully is an indication of dire poverty. However, from around 2007 a series of dancehall songs began to celebrate "the gully," using the term to designate Kingston's most marginalized areas. Songs such as "Gullyside" by Movado, "Gully Sit'n" by Assassin, and "Gully Creeper" by Elephant Man transformed this space of environmental pollution into a badge of honor and a metaphor for belonging. Movado, a popular dancehall artiste, began to sport the nickname "Gully God," which fans proceeded to spray-paint on walls throughout Downtown Kingston. This adoption of a "dirty" moniker echoed the tendency of 1990s dancehall star Shabba Ranks to introduce himself as "big, bad, dutty, stinking Shabba," proudly claiming badness and dirt before anyone else could accuse him of these attributes. In Riverton, local musicians and producers started a record label called "Swamp City," highlighting the area's boggy, dirty environment rather than downplaying it. The stereotypes and stigma attached to these polluted spaces become neutralized through such popular culture appropriations: the gully or the swamp are resignified as positive spaces and become imaginative sites in which a largely masculine, class-based identity can be grounded.

Conclusion

In Jamaica and Curaçao, environmental pollution in the form of uncollected garbage, unprocessed sewage, or toxic airborne emissions intersects with symbolic forms of pollution. In what I have termed "urban naturalisms," pollution acts as a trope that organizes understandings of classed and racialized bodies in relation to urban space, reproducing socio-spatial hierarchies and justifying the unequal distribution of environmental problems. The socioecological practices and discourses that shape the production and justification of environmental injustice do not always emphasize the dimensions of race and class in explicit ways, nor are these practices and discourses necessarily intentionally discriminatory. While bold commentators may make explicit links between the urban poor, Blackness, and pollution in newspaper columns or anonymous Internet forums, in many contexts these connections are implicit.

The naturalization of environmental inequalities builds on historically developed patterns of urban development within which cityscapes became clearly differentiated along lines of race/color and class, and in which low-income Afro-Caribbean persons and their environments were portrayed as threats to health, security, and modernity. Where in the past such depictions often served to legitimize repressive measures against the non-European urban poor, as discussed in Chapter Three, in the contemporary Caribbean the trope of pollution is often wielded in more paternalistic ways, with calls for increased education to address perceived social and ecological deviance. In other instances, as I argue in the next chapter, the naturalized association of poverty and pollution diverts professional environmentalist attention from problems that are concentrated in inner-city areas. While the co-production of material and symbolic pollution still works to reproduce and justify unequal social relations, residents of inner-city communities and "marginal" *barios* also make use of discourses of pollution in critiques or subversions of the dominant order. These interventions are more effective, however, in the realm of cultural politics than in that of political ecology.

6

UPTOWN ENVIRONMENTALISM

Far away from what we knew to be civilization, the . . . class of some thirty
environmentally conscious students carefully prodded up the muddy
slopes of the Blue and John Crow Mountains. What we saw and heard was
nothing short of faultless perfection, the sweet sounds of the innocent birds
echoed alongside the soft patter of the refreshing raindrops, it was simply
paradisiacal.

—*Field trip report, University of the West Indies sociology student*

This rather poetic description, which echoes the excerpt in
Chapter Three from Herbert Thomas's nineteenth-century report
of his ascent to Blue Mountain Peak, is taken from a field trip
report written by a student as part of an environmental studies
course I taught at the University of the West Indies in Jamaica. In
March 2007, the class went on a field trip to a national park run
by a prominent environmental NGO (ENGO) in co-management
with government agencies. Only one of the students had previously visited the park, which was located some forty minutes by
bus from Kingston. We were met by the head of the NGO and
received a guided hike along one of the nature trails, followed by a
talk on the management of the park. During the walk, the NGO
director pointed out various species endemic to Jamaica, as well as
the "exotic" (i.e., exogenous) species that were encroaching on the
park. She spoke with some vehemence about these species, which
included ferns and wild ginger, and of how the park management
was trying to halt their invasion by ripping them out. Eradicating
these invasive species would allow the endemic species to flour-
ish, as they would no longer have to compete for water and light
with the exotics. During the director's formal lecture, my students,
whom I had prepared for the field trip through a lecture and readings on conservation, asked a number of critical questions regarding the level of community participation in the park. The NGO
director admitted that their efforts in this regard, while constant, were not always successful. She suggested, however, that the

transfer of management responsibilities to the community might not always be appropriate in the case of the Caribbean because of the poor relationship local people had with nature.

Both the excerpt from the student's field trip report and the NGO director's remarks point to the significance of concepts of purity and paradise in professional Caribbean environmentalism. These concepts inform a perspective in which nature is something "far away from civilization," and in which keeping it "simply paradisiacal" requires constant purification efforts. While many environmental professionals see community participation in these efforts as desirable (see, e.g., Otuokon and Chai 2009), they hold a dim view of nonprofessional attitudes toward, and relationships with, nature. This chapter presents a critical examination of the prioritization of "green" issues in Caribbean environmental policy and practice. In Jamaica and Curaçao, and more broadly throughout the Caribbean, the policy and practices of governmental and nongovernmental environmental professionals have tended to have a green agenda focus on nature conservation, while also emphasizing sustainable tourism and, more recently, climate change.

I situate this green prioritization among environmental professionals— and the general inattention to urban pollution—as related to specific interests and orientations that reflect the socio-spatial divisions of Kingston and Willemstad. Where the next chapter discusses in more detail the grassroots or vernacular forms of environmentalism I encountered among low-income urban residents in Jamaica and Curaçao, this chapter focuses predominantly on the environmental discourse and practice associated with Uptown professional stakeholders. There are various factors that explain this middle-class and elite concern with conservation. Financial considerations play an important role in shaping green conservationist priorities, which are influenced by the economic significance that tourism has for national governments and business elites, and by the funding priorities of stakeholders based in Europe and North America.

Beyond economic incentives, I argue that the green character of professional environmentalism is informed by socially situated experiences and by spatial imaginaries of the Caribbean and its cities. Uptown environmentalism demonstrates a specific understanding of what constitutes an environmental problem. At the regional and island levels, green forms of environmentalism reflect a continued commitment to an image of the Caribbean as a realm of nature. At the urban level, green environmentalism shows a marked lack of attention to problems of pollution that are concentrated in inner-city areas, a neglect that can be partially explained by the urban naturalisms described in the previous chapter. Following an examination of the green priorities of environmental professionals at the government and ENGO levels, I discuss the ways that these professionals' socio-economic and ethno-racial positioning colors their environmentalism. The bourgeois character of professional environmentalism filters through in ENGO discourse and practice, which is often paternalistic and anti-urban in character. One expression of this dedication to a "natural" Caribbean is what I call "disurbia," the desire for a world, or an island, without cities. These imaginaries and experiences—of urban space and of the island Caribbean—continue to inform Uptown environmentalism and its general neglect of urban pollution. The colonial roots of these imaginaries, as well as the Uptown position of many contemporary environmentalists, point toward the salience of understanding Caribbean environmentalisms within an environmental justice frame.

Green priorities, green money

Professional environmental discourse and practice in Jamaica and Curaçao are predominantly "green," and the precedence this type of environmental problem receives is evident in governmental policy (see Vomil/Mina 1998, 1999, 2000, 2001, 2004; Natural Resource Conservation Agency [NRCA] 1997; National Environment and Planning Agency [NEPA] 1999, 2002, 2006, 2011) and ENGO campaigns and websites. The majority of professional efforts target green agenda conservation issues, such as biodiversity and endangered species protection, the marine environment and especially coral reefs, and forestry and watershed management. This green prioritization by Jamaican and Curaçaoan organizations reflects the situation among environmental organizations in the broader Caribbean (Jácome 2006). Governmental agencies such as Curaçao's Environmental Service (*Milieudienst*) and Jamaica's National Environment and Planning Agency (NEPA) do attempt to address "brown" issues related to wastewater, energy, waste management, and air pollution. However, financial interests in state-owned utilities, industry, and environmental services often complicate decisive government action.

An example of the way that green priorities are reflected in government budget allocations is found in the *Nature and Environment Policy Plan 2004–2007* of the Netherlands Antilles, the political structure within which Curaçao operated until 2010 (Vomil/Mina 2004). The evaluation report of this policy showed that the original plan allocated a combined 30 percent of its budget to the priority area of biodiversity conservation and management, and a combined 15 percent to waste and wastewater management, oil and the environment, and sustainable energy. In terms of projects that were actually realized, however, 62 percent of funding went toward biodiversity, and only 5 percent toward waste, wastewater, oil, and energy (USONA 2008, A4). Similarly, Jamaica's *National Environmental Action Plan 2006–2009* (NEPA 2006), the government's triennial strategic plan for addressing environmental and physical planning issues, devoted a scant number of pages to waste and wastewater management compared to those dedicated to conservation, protected areas, watershed management, and the marine environment.

Even more so than governmental agencies, most Curaçaoan and Jamaican NGOs have tended to focus on the less "dirty," more attractive issues. As Marilène, a European woman running a Curaçaoan environmental center, explained to me, her organization maintained a "sweet, positive" image: it focused on educational activities involving women and children and aimed to raise consciousness first by focusing on nature and "cute animals." Once a certain level of consciousness had been achieved, she planned to address less attractive issues such as garbage and sustainable energy. This emphasis on environmental education and cultivating an appreciation of nature proved to be quite common. Another Curaçaoan environmental group that was affiliated with one of the island's largest banks organized picnics and nature hikes that included short garbage clean-ups along the way, such as the one described in the Introduction. The mainly female organizers told me that they "try to combine clean-ups with fun things." While the picnics admittedly had a short-term effect, and resulted in an abundance of Styrofoam and plastic waste through the use of disposable food and drink containers, the group believed such activities had a long-term effect because they "increase the appreciation of nature."

Underlying this green environmental focus, which has the effect of eliding urban environmental problems, are various financial motivations. The focus on the green issues of diminishing biodiversity, deforestation, and degradation of the marine environment reflects the importance of tourism to governments and business elites. A range of stakeholders have a vested interest in the image of the Caribbean as natural paradise. Historical tropicalizing representations of the Caribbean as natural and unspoiled, outlined in Chapter Three, are of continued relevance in environmental policy through their relation both to the tourist economy and to the priorities of global conservation groups. Politicians, policymakers, and NGOs in and outside of the region often represent the Caribbean as a range of natural landscapes that urgently need to be conserved, both as crucial resources for tourism and as intrinsically valuable high-biodiversity ecosystems. Perceived as the motor for development on most islands, Caribbean tourism is connected to a longing for tropical abundance and "pure," unspoiled nature. As Sheller (2004, 3) notes: "Caribbean tourism is vested in the branding and marketing of Paradise." This tourist-oriented version of Caribbean paradise promotes an image of exotic, fecund natural landscapes waiting for visitors to come and revel in them. Travel narratives from earlier centuries, through their invocations of Eden and references to verdant tropical beauty, have fed into a "cycle of expectation" that continues to attract tourists and shape their experiences (Nelson 2007).

Secluded white beaches, romantically swaying palms, and mysterious underwater worlds are what sell these destinations to tourists, a branding that inhibits representations of the Caribbean that focus more on the region's cultural or intellectual wealth and less on natural resources. Jamaica's *Master Plan for Sustainable Tourism Development* recognizes this basis of the industry in the natural, noting that "the Jamaican tourism industry relies on the preservation of the environment. The environment is its product and any loss of water quality or beach erosion, loss of habitat and deforestation represent direct threats to its sustainable development" (Commonwealth Secretariat 2002, 201). Similarly, in Curaçao, where tourists are attracted by the coastal and marine environment, the most recent update to the *Tourism Development Plan* acknowledges that "natural sea and land-based resources must be protected to maintain Curaçao's largely unspoilt inland and coastal environment whilst maximising its appeal to tourists" (Curaçao Tourist Board [CTB] 2005, 30).

In addition to these tourism-related concerns, the Caribbean prioritization of green environmental problems is promoted forcefully by international stakeholders, models, and financial resources. As Tighe Geoghegan notes, "Most conservation initiatives in the region ... have largely been shaped by forces and influences from the outside, particularly Western Europe and North America" (2009, 113; see also Jaffe 2009, 324). The narratives of transnational ENGOs, in particular, reaffirm historical and tourism-related representations of the Caribbean as a space of exceptional natural beauty and value, the purportedly unspoiled character of which is under threat. Conservation International, for instance, has designated the Caribbean islands as "biodiversity hotspots" whose diverse ecosystems and endemic species are in urgent need of protection. The Dutch Caribbean Nature Alliance (DCNA) draws on the familiar rhetoric of purity when it asserts that "the pristine nature of the Dutch Caribbean contains the richest biodiversity in the Kingdom of the Netherlands."[1] Centuries of plantation agriculture based on exotic, non-native species such as sugar and bananas, in addition to decades of industrial activity, mining, and tourism, have meant that there are very few, if any, pristine Caribbean ecosystems. Nonetheless, an emphasis on Caribbean natural purity—reminiscent of colonial tropes of paradise found and paradise lost—colors international conservationist discourse.

As has been well documented across the globe, transnational conservation organizations often promote a vision of an imperiled nature in need of protection from poor local people. This skeptical attitude toward low-income populations and local knowledge and practice is also evident in the Caribbean (Geoghegan 2009, 118–121). I encountered this attitude among expatriate as well as local environmentalists in both Jamaica and Curaçao. The Jamaican NGO director in charge of the national park who pointed toward the poor relationship Caribbean people had with the environment was one example. Similarly, Tom, a Dutch intern at a major Curaçaoan ENGO run by a White Dutch expat, described his organization's goal to me as "getting the local population to realize that nature should be respected and not regarded as a garbage can" and spoke more generally of the "bad mentality" of a section of the population.

Much environmental thought and discourse is disseminated through international, but Northern-dominated, bilateral and multilateral fora. Utilizing financial and political strategies, donor countries and international financial institutions exert "green" pressure on Caribbean governments and ENGOs. Donor countries, international financial institutions, and transnational ENGOs contribute to the diffusion and imposition of green discourse and practice. In Curaçao, the Dutch influence on both ENGOs and governmental organizations is striking. While officially Curaçao enjoys full internal autonomy, the island government is heavily influenced by the Dutch government through earmarked development aid, a strong presence of Dutch "technical support" in the civil service, and, arguably, the presence of Dutch cultural norms among Curaçaoan professionals educated in the Netherlands. Among nongovernmental environmental organizations, many leaders and members are White Dutch, while nearly all NGOs are to some extent dependent on Dutch development aid. In Curaçao, where the small size of the population limits the possibility of fundraising through membership dues or local campaigns, environmental organizations are highly dependent on external funds from the Dutch government and international ENGOs. The conservation-oriented Dutch Caribbean Nature Alliance, for instance, which describes itself as a "true grassroots organization" (DCNA 2013, 4), derives its income almost exclusively from the Dutch Ministry of the Interior and the Dutch state-controlled lottery.[2]

Aid or loan conditionality is another conduit for the transfer of global North environmental priorities. The United States, for instance, offered Jamaica a debt-for-nature swap that involved establishing the Environmental Foundation of Jamaica (EFJ). This foundation, which promotes and spon- sors sustainable development activities through the distribution of govern- ment funds previously earmarked for foreign debt relief, has disbursed some of its largest project grants to conservation-oriented ENGOs (EFJ 2005). In Jamaica, the best-funded organizations are indisputably those with access to international funding, whether bilateral, multilateral, or nongovernmental. As Patricia Lundy found for Jamaica, the consequences of ENGOs' depen- dence on foreign funding and government connections are that "the activities of environmental groups have been curtailed and certain pressing environ- mental problems have been avoided. Most notably, environmental groups have actively avoided challenging powerful business interests and govern- ment over industrial pollution" (1999, 98).

Beyond financial incentives and disincentives, the green priorities of gov- ernment and NGO environmental professionals are also shaped more sub- tly by forms of expert environmental knowledge that circulate globally and nationally within an ecological epistemic community. Such communities are knowledge-based networks whose members are linked by specific technical (environmental) expertise and who also share a set of normative and prin- cipled beliefs, causal beliefs, discursive practices, and policy projects. These networks influence policy through the diffusion of technical knowledge, norms, values, and specific terminology (Haas 1992; George 2009). Within these communities, Karin Knorr Cetina points to epistemic culture as "those amalgams of arrangements and mechanisms—bonded through affinity, necessity, and historical coincidence—which, in a given field, make up *how we know what we know*" (1999, 1). Jamaican and Curaçaoan environmental professionals within governmental and nongovernmental organizations are often themselves part of a global ecological epistemic community and are cer- tainly influenced by the epistemic culture these knowledge-based networks disseminate nationally and internationally. In addition, the cosmopolitan elites and foreigners that are prominent within Caribbean professional envi- ronmental communities tend to have enjoyed higher education outside the region, and their concern is fed by the (scientific) environmentalism current in Europe and North America.

Epistemic networks and cultures influence how professional environmentalists *know* what constitutes an urgent environmental problem, as well as its causes and possible strategies to solve it. In the transnational environmentalist sphere, "global environmental problems are presented as being *a priori* of a different order, and thus marginalize many other environmental concerns that might affect many people or eco-systems much more directly" (Hajer 1995, 11). Perhaps unwittingly, Caribbean governments and NGOs—under external financial and ideological pressure—reproduce this hegemonic discourse, which prioritizes environmental problems with a global rather than local dimension and emphasizes ecological rather than social vulnerability. Consequently, there is more money and more attention for "global" green agenda issues related to conservation, biodiversity, and, more recently, climate change, than there is for "local" brown agenda issues related more immediately to social vulnerability, such as waste management and air pollution.

Elite environmentalism and conservationist condescension

The globally oriented, green environmental discourse that dominates Jamaican and Curaçaoan environmentalism is very much a phenomenon of the elite and sections of the middle class. Working in Jamaica in the 1990s, Patricia Lundy (1999) found membership in environmental groups to be overwhelmingly well educated and middle class, with ENGO activities reflecting the concerns and priorities of local elites, thus inadvertently reinforcing inequality in social relations (see also Carrier 2003). Lundy (1999, 92–93) notes the significant influence of three groups within the environmental movement: expatriates, who "were often prominent members of environmental groups and had on many occasions initiated their formation"; Jamaicans returning to the island after having lived abroad; and individuals involved in the tourist trade. I found these circumstances to be largely unchanged a decade later and encountered a similar situation in Curaçao, with an even more pronounced presence of White Dutch environmentalists. Many NGO members and high-level government officials lived in a Curaçao that was quite distant from the reality of the popular *barios*. On both islands, the environmental movement that I encountered was largely a middle-class and upper-class phenomenon. Its leaders and members were well-intentioned individuals who worked hard to overcome the many obstacles they saw to conserving nature and achieving a more sustainable society, but overall they tended to occupy specific classed and racialized positions within two islands that are largely divided along these lines.

More than government professionals, ENGO leaders and members were socio-economically and ethno-racially distinct from the majority of the urban population in Kingston and Willemstad. Most environmentalists were locals or foreigners from relatively privileged backgrounds who had been educated in western Europe or North America. In Jamaica, many environmental organizations were headed by either upper-middle-class White or Brown Jamaicans, or foreigners, often expatriate Americans. On visiting an environmentalist meeting aimed at preventing mining activities in Jamaica's Cockpit Country, a White Jamaican friend of mine joked that "if anyone wanted to get rid of Jamaica's White population, they should just plant a bomb at these environmental meetings." In Curaçao, the number of Afro-Curaçaoans active in the environmental movement was fairly limited, particularly within the leadership of organizations; White Curaçaoans and Dutch émigrés tended to dominate as members and leaders.

The ENGOs' environmental message was both informed by and interpreted through this social positioning. Displaying affinity with conservation and other green issues appeared to be an increasingly important element in practices of elite and middle-class distinction (see Jaffe 2010). ENGO membership, nature hikes, and support of national parks functioned as forms of cultural capital, similar to appreciation of the arts, for instance. In contrast, an interest in garbage and sewage rarely conferred similar cachet. Social hierarchies also came out in the rather condescending attitude toward less privileged citizens or "the community" that I discerned among many environmental professionals. The president of one ENGO described how "many in Jamaica do not have an appreciation of nature—they do not comprehend the relevance of lizards, insects and plants (except in the light of economic gain) and *have to be assisted to 'see'* the wealth and beauty of our island" (Levy 1996, 25, emphasis added). In Curaçao, one of the more successful ENGOs, led by a White Dutchman, had as its slogan *konosé bo isla*, "know your island." Interestingly, the use of vernacular Papiamentu in this motto contrasted with the organization's general orientation toward the Dutch language. More strikingly, the fact that the majority of the local population was depicted as insufficiently knowledgeable—or appreciative—of its own island reflected a paternalistic sentiment similar to that expressed by the Jamaican ENGO president.

Some ENGO leaders expressed concern over the lack of grassroots representation in the environmental movement. During a 2004 conference held in Amsterdam on nature and the environment in the Netherlands Antilles, Lloyd, the head of one of Curaçao's older ENGOs, gave a speech in which he asserted that a major problem for nature organizations was that they were insufficiently rooted in the local society. He expressed his concern about the "Dutch clique" that dominated environmental action on the island. The inability of environmentalists to reach the local population, he argued, had implications for the "ownership" of environmental issues, potentially leading Curaçaoans to think, "It belongs to those Dutch people, doesn't it?" Within this context, specific issues were established as environmental problems by outsiders, who then proposed solutions to problems they had "discovered." This association of a category of problems with one group of people could result in the majority of the population perceiving "the environment" as an exclusionary White Dutch (*makamba*) sphere. Lloyd urged environmental groups to reconsider their reliance on foreign environmental professionals who had limited knowledge of the local, non-elite population, and encouraged them to connect more directly to Curaçaoan experiences and interpretations. His critical and self-reflexive insistence on attending to grassroots priorities was a relatively rare position within Curaçao's environmental scene. Nevertheless, he also expressed the opinion that environmental issues should be linked to the "social emancipation" of Curaçaoans, whom he felt were insufficiently connected to their own island and were not proud of their own country, culture, or people. This viewpoint echoed a commonly held professional environmentalist belief, which I encountered repeatedly over the years, that less privileged "locals" suffered an ecologically detrimental disconnect from their natural environment—a detachment that emancipation or education could remedy.

The tendency toward condescension displayed by many environmental professionals was evident in the heavy emphasis they placed on environmental education. Both governmental and nongovernmental organizations stressed the importance of changing environmental attitudes and values through education campaigns and school curricula. Therese Ferguson and Elizabeth Thomas-Hope (2006) suggest in this regard that, in the Jamaican case as elsewhere, environmental education may serve to reproduce hegemonic environmental values, specifically those values that are dominant within global discourse on sustainable development. Indeed, the focus on education in environmental programs implies a certain disregard for grassroots environmental priorities and worldviews—a disregard that, as Lloyd suggested, can inhibit ownership of environmental issues. Rather than addressing the environmental problems that affected the residents of Kingston or Willemstad in their everyday surroundings, educational campaigns often concentrated on relatively "distant" global concerns such as climate change and biodiversity. On assuming leadership of Jamaica's National Environmental Education Committee (NEEC), for instance, the committee chair declared that "my personal interest . . . is to penetrate inner-city communities with EESD [environmental education for sustainable development], especially those along the Kingston Harbour," adding that climate change would take priority among other issues in environmental education.[3] It is not self-evident why it was urgent to penetrate these inner-city communities rather than communities of, say, Uptown SUV drivers, whose contribution to climate change is probably larger.

A related skew was evident in the Jamaican environmental awareness–raising programs and mangrove-replanting schemes that were developed in low-income neighborhoods along Kingston Harbor and in coastal communities. These activities, organized by NEPA, have been aimed at educating supposedly environmentally unaware fishermen, including those in Rae Town, on such issues as mangrove ecosystems and fish stocks. Yet the same agency has simultaneously conducted environmental impact assessments and subsequently granted the requisite permits for massively destructive corporate coastal developments, especially in the tourism industry, that have a much larger impact on the marine environment. This kind of discrepancy in the way environmental policy is executed sends a message to low-income citizens. As fishermen in Negril concluded when a new all-inclusive hotel was suddenly built on the same fish nursery from which they had been barred: "One rule for the rich and one rule for the poor" (Garner 2009, 148).

At times, environmental professionals on both islands would make explicit reference to social divisions in terms of class, ethno-racial positioning, or urban geography. Marilène, the head of the Curaçaoan ENGO introduced previously, recognized the stratified nature of the island where she worked, explaining to me that "Curaçao is two worlds, the upper and the lower classes." To her, the divide was apparent in the level of environmental awareness she discerned in the different groups of children her organization worked with: "One group of children is outspoken and interested, the other really thinks that nature is dirty and that iguanas are dirty animals." The latter group of Curaçaoan children, whom she perceived as insufficiently interested in and appreciative of nature, occupy a similar position to that held by those Jamaican inner-city communities that need to be penetrated with environmental education. The tendency to identify lower-class, inner-city residents as a particular priority group who need to change their attitudes toward green issues such as conservation and climate change can be identified as a general trend in Caribbean environmentalism. Compared to middle-class and elite suburbanites on both islands, this lower-class urban target group tends to be Black or *koló skur*, reflecting the legacy of slavery and centuries of institutionalized racism. As I have argued in the previous chapters, these ethno-racial categories, co-produced with categories of class and urban space, are relevant to the production and reception of environmental discourse and practice.

The relevance of these categories is especially evident in encounters between relatively privileged environmental professionals and less privileged people and places. In 2004, I worked with one of the very few Jamaican ENGOs that concentrated on urban issues to organize a stakeholder discussion forum on the topic of "A Low-Cost Waste Management Solution for the Rae Town Fishing Beach, Kingston Harbour." This forum, which was organized in the headquarters of NEPA, brought Rae Town residents into conversation with Uptown representatives of governmental agencies, NGOs, and businesses concerned with the state of the harbor. The residents were lobbying for the construction of a concrete debris trap in the local gully, which would allow water to pass through while preventing garbage from flowing into the harbor. In addition to its environmental benefits, the community members also supported this rather expensive option (with an estimated budget of J$19 million) on the basis of the local employment opportunities they hoped its construction would provide. Following presentations by Mavis, a Rae Town community member, and by a consultant engineer, a NEPA representative presented an alternative garbage collection option. This option, which at J$2 million would be much cheaper, consisted of the placement of an entrapment fence in the harbor, which would allow garbage to wash up on the fishing beach, where it could be collected and removed.

What struck me during the forum were the social dynamics. The two-hour forum was a rare opportunity for Uptown and Downtown residents to enter into a sustained conversation on urban and environmental issues. The place of the meeting was also symbolic in this regard, given NEPA's location in the area of Crossroads, which was commonly understood as the border between the social worlds of Uptown and Downtown. However, this interaction highlighted rather than mitigated the social distance between the different parties. I had attended a preparatory meeting held in Rae Town at the fishing beach, where residents had been extremely eloquent and adamant in expressing their opinions and desires. However, in the formal context of a government boardroom and faced with a large group of Uptown representatives, their demeanor changed noticeably.

Mavis, the woman from Rae Town who gave the first talk on the community's experience of environmental problems and the strategies to resolve
them they envisioned, became extremely flustered and had difficulty fin-
ishing her presentation. The other residents also appeared to feel much less
comfortable expressing their opinions to this audience and in this formal
English- rather than Jamaican-Creole-speaking environment.

In contrast, the various government, NGO, and business representatives
appeared much more comfortable. Their behavior struck me as an expression
of their social positioning, as a conscious or unconscious manifestation of
their class and color privilege. For one, the NEPA representative who proposed building an entrapment fence in the harbor had attended the meetings
in Rae Town. He knew that the residents strongly opposed this solution—
not only because of its limited benefits in terms of employment, but also
because the garbage washing up on the beach would look bad, smell bad,
and attract mosquitoes. Nonetheless, he had apparently decided to disregard
their wishes and presented his own plan without consulting them or giving
advance notice, a move that caused considerable resentment among the Rae
Town residents. More generally, the other Uptown professionals behaved in
a rather patronizing manner. They took a moment to commend the residents
for their initiative in identifying solutions to a pressing environmental problem but then proceeded to discuss various other causes and solutions among
themselves, largely ignoring the residents. Despite the optimism and good-
will with which most of the participants came to the meeting, both Uptown
and Downtown residents quickly slid into the hierarchical social roles they
were accustomed to assuming in cross-class interactions.

The meeting was followed by a small flurry of e-mails, but ultimately
neither proposal for preventing garbage from flowing into the harbor was
adopted. One of the e-mails that was sent around to the professionals, however, provides a striking illustration of how urban socio-spatial difference
informs environmental priorities. An NGO leader who had been present at
the meeting had decided to take a look at the state of the gullies in question
and had driven to Rae Town to photograph the Paradise Street and Margaret
Street gullies. She sent around the photographs to the mailing list, expressing
her shock and dismay at their disgusting state and emphasizing that she had
not realized that the situation was so dire. The photographs she had taken
showed that the gullies were indeed clogged with piles of rotting garbage.
My initial reaction was disbelief that the NGO representative had never been
aware of the actual state of the gullies, which run throughout Kingston and

are almost always full of rubbish; anyone walking past them can see and smell their pollution.

I realized, however, that the NGO leader's e-mail in fact pointed to the significance of a sensory, aesthetic experience of pollution and, in relation to this, the importance of divergent urban mobilities. In addition to the role played by epistemic culture, a certain physical intimacy borne out of embodied experiences shapes how we come to "know" environmental problems. Citizens who live in more privileged urban areas may have a cognitive awareness that brown agenda problems affect their city, but their lack of physical exposure to these issues limits their affective engagement with them. Seeing or smelling garbage and sewage, smelling sulfuric industrial emissions, and feeling them on your skin and in your lungs—these embodied experiences of urban pollution produce a sensory effect. Uptown environmentalists' lack of exposure to pollution was not only a matter of residential or professional location in cleaner parts of the city, as some of them might visit government offices in less privileged areas. Their more bounded forms of mobility—driving around in air-conditioned cars with the windows up, rather than traveling on foot or by bus—also shielded them from the physical sensation of pollution. In so doing, these mobilities made certain environmental issues less visible and less perceptible than others. Inevitably, such differences in emplacement and mobilities shape perceptions of the urgency of urban pollution.

While the socio-spatial positioning of professional environmentalists worked to filter what they themselves perceived as problems, their ethnoracial positioning as environmentalist "messengers" also influenced how others interpreted their message. Ethnic stereotyping can be such that publics may assume they know an individual's story without having to listen to their actual words. In Curaçao, one of the more locally oriented ENGOs was headed by Lloyd, who is of Indo-Surinamese descent. Like many Curaçaoans, his roots lie elsewhere in the Caribbean. His parents moved from Suriname to Curaçao when he was young, attracted by the employment opportunities generated by the oil refinery. While Lloyd is culturally and emotionally rooted in Curaçao, he is at times misrecognized on the basis of what is seen as his "un-Curaçaoan" (i.e., not Afro-Curaçaoan) name and appearance. He told me how once, at an environmental meeting in a neighborhood that was more *popular* (of the people), a man came up to him and said: "Finally I know who you are! I've always seen you on television, but I never paid attention. . .. I never knew you were an environmentalist. I always thought, that *hindu* [Indian] must be on TV to promote his store."

Similar processes of racialized recognition and misrecognition are at work in Jamaica, as a minor media tiff illustrated. In 2011, the *Jamaica Observer* published a front-page article reporting on a controversy involving the development of the Blue Lagoon. This lagoon is a major tourist attraction in the parish of Portland and was one of the first officially recognized nature preservation sites in Jamaica. A local resort owner had gained a license from NEPA to develop the beach adjoining his hotel property. The Jamaica Environment Trust (JET), one of the island's more prominent ENGOs, expressed its concern regarding both the granting of the license and breaches of the terms of the license by the developer, including the removal of trees and attempts to construct an artificial beach. In the *Observer* article, the developer's spokesman defended him against these accusations by implying that JET, which was headed by Diana McCaulay, a White Jamaican, had a hidden agenda. "The truth be told, there is also a racial (component), whether you believe it or not," he told the *Observer* reporter. "The man who owns the property is black and these people don't believe that a little black boy from Port Antonio should own that property." He went on to argue that "the fact of the matter is that these people don't want no black people 'round the lagoon."[4]

Following the *Observer* publication, a number of well-known Jamaican activists and intellectuals sent letters to the editor complaining about the prominence the newspaper had given to these racialized allegations. It was perhaps not coincidental that two of the three writers were White or Brown Jamaicans. They urged the newspaper to apologize, arguing that the article and its headline gave support to a "baseless slur" against JET and McCaulay, and that the *Observer* was "suggest[ing] that there are racism issues related to concern for our environment." The third author concluded that "the editor was pursuing sales rather than fair play" but also provided a more complex analysis of the issue, suggesting that

> except for Rastafari, enough of us as black Jamaicans have not seen it fit
> to address what a truly sustainable future looks like. Instead, we have
> bought into a notion of "development" which cannot happen without
> a lot of concrete being poured, or re-arranging nature's design. As a
> result, the defence of the natural environment gets represented as the
> preserve of white Jamaicans, "foreigners" (read more white people) and
> members of the brown elite who are caricatured as having no apprecia-
> tion of "poor people's" needs (or worse . . . as having no desire for "poor
> black people" to get ahead).[5]

While identifying as one of "us black Jamaicans," the author confirmed the existence of different classed and racialized perspectives on the environment, contrasting the majority of the population's focus on unsustainable "development" with the defense of nature by White and Brown elites and expatriates. If the developer's racialized defense reflected a rather opportunistic logic, it was one that resonated with popular understandings of Jamaican environmentalists as classed, racialized, and anti-development. Indeed, in a follow-up article in the *Washington Post*, a Blue Lagoon fisherman and tour guide told the journalist that "I can tell you that when a black man tries something, the white man tries to keep him down. And that's exactly what's happening here."[6]

Disurbia and other colonial echoes

The apparent popularity of the idea that environmentalists "try to keep down poor Black people" may be fed by professional assumptions about the broader population. The profusion of governmental and nongovernmental campaigns and programs aimed at awareness raising and environmental education imply that environmental problems result largely from a lack of environmental awareness on the part of the population. During meetings and conferences, and in interviews and informal conversations, professional environmentalists often depicted the majority of Jamaicans and Curaçaoans as unaware or problematic. Caribbean environmental organizations reflect a much broader global conservationist tendency to see the "local" population as incapable of sustainable resource management. Despite increasing acknowledgement of the importance of participatory strategies in the management of protected areas, civil society participation and co-management approaches often still involve NGOs staffed by educated professionals rather than by low-income users. Few twenty-first-century organizations will formally endorse the preservationist ideal of unpeopled nature that characterized early environmentalism. Nonetheless, related ideas of purity are still discernible in top-down conservationist strategies that portray poor people and their lack of knowledge as the cause of environmental degradation.

Not everyone is so disparaging with regard to the role of locals. However, from its earliest inception, environmentalism as a movement has struggled with defining the role of humans in relation to nature. I asked Esther, a Jamaican filmmaker who had produced a very critical documentary on the environmental effects of tourism, whether she had grown up with a lot of exposure to nature and whether her environmental concern had developed from that experience. She told me that her family had gone on occasional trips out of the city, but that she would not really pinpoint that as the cause of her later interest. Rather, as she grew older, she said, "I just came to realize that I loved nature more than I loved people." Esther's work stood out from that of many ENGOs in its explicit condemnation of the environmental injustice associated with Caribbean tourism, especially the negative effects of the industry on the livelihoods of fisherfolk and small local entrepreneurs. Yet when she explained her environmental concern as deriving from a greater love of nature than of people, this was suggestive of a broader tendency toward what has been called misanthropic environmentalism (see, e.g., Bookchin 1994 on deep ecology; and Buell 1995, 388 on Thoreau).

Greg Garrard (2012) has extended this idea of misanthropy in environmentalism to explore a form of environmental imagination he calls "disanthropy," a desire to see the world without people. Building on this idea, I would like to suggest the existence of something I will call "disurbia": an imagining of the world, and in this case the Caribbean, without cities. Cities in general have played an ambiguous if not negative role in environmentalism. For the United States, Andrew Light (2001, 19) has noted that "hating the city, or at least ignoring it, is a fact of life in environmental circles which is only now being challenged, though largely from outside of the main environmental movement." This statement, while incisive, implies that ignoring the city is less problematic than hating it. Rather, I would argue that, while the two acts are similar and intertwined, ignoring the urban can have at least as significant an effect as explicit antipathy. Disurbia is not so much a strand of anti-urbanism as a kind of environmental imagination that actively elides cities and consequently disregards urban environmental problems. These anti-urban sentiments and "disurban" imaginaries reproduce the modern ontological dualism that sets "nature" apart from and in opposition to "the city" (Kaika 2005). The roots of mainstream U.S. and European nonurban environmentalism have been traced to historical movements such as Romanticism and pastoralism, which emerged in response to rapid urbanization and industrialization in the nineteenth and twentieth centuries (Cronon 1996). In the Caribbean, the dismissal or even elision of cities must be historicized differently, along the lines of the discussion in Chapter Three on the enduring representations of the region as a realm of nature.

While most governmental and nongovernmental environmental organizations in Jamaica and Curaçao were based in urban areas, their overwhelming concern with green issues incorporated a certain city-free image of the Caribbean. Professional environmentalist discourse implied that "natural" landscapes, while endangered, were representative of these islands, while cities and their residents were almost aberrations that disturbed the natural order of things. Such environmentalist visions merge with the tourism industry's representations of non-urban landscapes. In addition, it is hard to ignore the parallels between conservationist and colonial imaginaries. The construction of the present-day concerns of Uptown professional environmentalists in Jamaica and Curaçao echo colonial practices and ideas. In his work on colonial proto-environmentalism, Richard Grove (1995) shows how constructions of "tropical paradise," in combination with a growing awareness of the ecological damage effected by colonial rule, mobilized European concerns over the demise of natural landscapes. In a very different historical era, we can still recognize the phenomenon of outsiders and powerful elite actors organizing to combat visible degradation, as well as the resurfacing of discernible themes of encounter and revelation in the stories of various professional environmentalists in twenty-first-century Jamaica and Curaçao. These individuals' narratives of how they became involved in environmental activism are reminiscent of the politics of environmental salvage that Felix Driver (2004, 3) refers to in the context of tropicality.

On both islands, there were ENGOs that had been founded by educated Jamaicans or Curaçaoans who had spent years abroad in the United States or the Netherlands and rediscovered the natural beauty of their islands on their return, only to become aware that these fragile island ecosystems were rapidly deteriorating. Similarly, there were several Jamaican and Curaçaoan ENGOs that had been established by European and North American expatriates who had come as tourists and been overwhelmed by the beauty of the natural environment. Following an initial enchantment with the pristine state or abundance of nature, compared to that of their native countries, they subsequently organized to protect it from the destruction they saw it facing locally (see also Carrier 2003). More than one of these foreigners had moved to the Caribbean to set up a diving school or to become otherwise engaged in nature-based tourism. Through their extended engagement with the sea, these individuals had come to realize how quickly the coral reef and marine life more generally were degrading and decided to establish an organization to save the reef. While framed by different local and geopolitical contexts, the shock and concern that these foreigners experienced at the neglect and abuse of Caribbean nature, and their efforts to protect it, resemble the sentiments and actions of colonial European proto-environmentalists.

The emphasis on education and the condescending attitudes noted previously also suggest the ways in which colonial historical trajectories inform contemporary environmentalism in Curaçao and Jamaica. Within a structure of discursively maintained power and an expert-oriented epistemology of development (Ramphall 1997), Caribbean environmental professionals have the authority to portray residents as uneducated, polluting city-dwellers who must be led to conscious patterns of thought and behavior by way of environmental education programs. In her work on development and environmental conservation projects in Indonesia, Tania Li (2007) traces structural continuities between colonial and postcolonial renditions of what she calls "the will to improve." She argues that the hierarchical position of "trustees" vis-à-vis their "wards" has remained the same through these two eras, and that the techniques of improvement that they draw on are similar, although these uneven relations are now explained and justified through claims to scientific and expert knowledge rather than through reference to racial ideologies. The relationships between Caribbean Uptown environmentalists and their various "wards" suggest a similar analysis. However, as Li (2007, 9) also points out, the will to improve "can be taken at its word": the activities of sustainable development experts or environmentalists are not necessarily driven by a hidden agenda or the desire for domination or economic gain. It is not my objective to imply that the environmental professionals I encountered in Curaçao and Jamaica are primarily driven by something other than a sincere concern for the natural environment, or that they are conscious proponents of colonially derived hierarchies. Nonetheless, I seek to point out the undesirable effects that their environmental emphases and elisions may have on other lives and landscapes.

Poverty, pollution, and environmental justice

Environmental justice activists in the United States have critiqued mainstream conservationist environmentalism, noting that ENGOs' boards as well as their broader membership are overwhelmingly White and middle class. They argue that the absence of ethno-racial minorities and working-class constituencies has meant that these groups' environmental concerns—urban pollution and its unequal distribution within cities—have been ignored and excluded (Taylor 2000; Adamson et al. 2002; Sandler and Pezzullo 2007). Andrew Light (2001, 27) submits this position forcefully when he argues that one of the biggest shames of environmentalism is that those who benefit most from ghettoization, from poverty, from unequal distribution of wealth and entitlements, from pollution, and from social unrest, are served by an environmental movement which apparently dismisses the inner city and its residents as much as these agents of oppression do.

While North American environmentalism has a distinct historical trajectory from that of the Caribbean, a similar analysis can be given of the dominant form of professional environmentalism in Jamaica and Curaçao and its socioeconomic and racialized reverberations. Melissa Checker (2008, 391), in a discussion of the parallels between the environmental struggles of African Americans and those of African-descended people in Latin America and the Caribbean, notes that "conservation and regulation measures established by international environmental movements frequently backfire on people of color."

Studies of environmental movements have often made distinctions between forms of environmental activism in the global South and those in the global North. Influential authors in this regard have been Ramachandra Guha and José Martinez-Alier (1998), who contrast "First World environmentalism" with the "environmentalism of the poor," or the "full stomach" with the "empty belly" variety. Such contrasts imply that the environmental movements of the South are "essentially actions by the marginalized poor to protect their environmental means of livelihood and sustenance" (Dwivedi 2001, 15). More recently, however, this geopolitical dichotomy has been complicated by increased attention to environmental injustice within, rather than only between, nations. In particular, the role of the Indian middle class and elites in environmental activism has become the focus of critical research (see, e.g., Mawdsley 2004; Arabindoo 2011). In her work on "bourgeois environmentalism," Amita Baviskar (2003) analyses the propensity of India's urban middle and upper classes toward a consumption-oriented, aesthetically driven environmentalism. This is an ideology, she holds, that rejects the basic concerns of the urban poor, targets slums and squatters as environmentally harmful, and reshapes the urban landscape toward the interests of privileged residents.

In Jamaica and Curaçao, Uptown environmentalism is not necessarily implicated in the displacement of low-income residents. There are somewhat comparable Caribbean examples, such as the eviction of squatters or the removal of informal sidewalk vendors from Downtown Kingston, and the displacement of low-income immigrants by recent gentrification processes in

Willemstad. However, environmentalists are hardly ever directly involved in these contestations over urban space. In contrast to bourgeois environmentalists in Indian cities, whose focus is on urban parks and water management, the green conservationist focus of Caribbean Uptown environmentalism is almost entirely extra-urban or disurban. This results not so much in the displacement of people as in the displacement of environmental attention, as brown urban issues associated with low-income neighborhoods become less visible or are cast as less urgent. The lack of attention to problems that are concentrated in inner-city areas cannot be seen as separate from the class and ethnic position of the majority of environmental professionals, or from the urban geographies of Kingston and Willemstad, where residence and mobilities are still largely organized along lines of class and ethnicity or skin color. At the most basic level, the middle and upper classes and historically privileged ethnic groups of these two cities are simply not confronted with the same levels of garbage, sewage, and air pollution as other residents are in their day-to-day lives. At another level, the lack of attention to such urban environmental issues trivializes the realities and priorities of "the other half." The neglect of urban pollution should, then, be considered within an environmental justice framework.

An emphasis on environmental justice is especially important because Caribbean environmentalists draw on comparable framings of environmental causality and culpability to those propagated by bourgeois environmentalists in Indian cities. Blame-the-poor narratives, which are often implicitly racialized, seep through into environmental policies and campaigns that frame low-income Jamaicans and Curaçaoans as the target of educational interventions. Poor people are seen primarily as the cause of environmental problems, rather than as their victims. With limited access to political and economic resources, the urban poor suffer the ill effects of environmental problems even as they are blamed for their prevalence.

Poverty and urban environmental issues are related in various, and not necessarily straightforward, ways. While urban environmental degradation and hazards do contribute to poverty, the activities and lifestyles of the urban poor are generally not implicated directly in causing environmental problems. Rather, macroeconomic conditions impede environmental management as municipal and national governments suffer a shortage of resources. Yet inadequate and inefficient governance is an important mediator in this regard, which is apparent in the environmental degradation associated with unplanned urban expansion and the environmental injustice produced by environmental policies that disregard issues of equity.

As David Satterthwaite (2003, 76) argues, "the environmental problems that low-income groups face are often more related to inadequate
provision of infrastructure and services, lack of any rule of law, discrimination, and lack of political influence than to a lack of income." He notes
that many studies have neglected the contribution of middle- and upper-
class urban residents to environmental degradation, resulting in inappropriate, punitive policies that tend to target the poor, such as the clearing
of slum settlements or the obstruction of informal livelihood strategies.
The strong professional focus on environmental education and awareness
raising in the Caribbean, which are targeted especially at poor people,
similarly implies that environmental problems result largely from a lack
of environmental awareness and knowledge on the part of low-income
populations. Other explanatory frames are imaginable: structural causes
of environmental degradation could, for instance, be located in an unsustainable development model that encourages largely unregulated foreign
and local corporate investments or, alternatively, in a system of unequal
environmental service provision in which residents of poor urban areas
have significantly less access to proper sewage and waste disposal services
than their wealthier counterparts.

Conclusion

Environmental narratives and imaginaries—articulated in governmental
policies, NGO campaigns, and the everyday stories we tell about dirty places
and dirty people—legitimize particular social groups and forms of interventions while delegitimizing and constraining others. The "green" character
of professional environmentalism is interwoven with specific classed and
ethno-racial constellations, and is indicative of globally hegemonic forms of
environmentalism. When specific social groups have the privilege of defining what constitutes an environmental problem and the best way to solve
it, this benefits some stakeholders and disadvantages others. The residential
and professional spaces within which policymakers and activists dwell influence the priorities they give to different environmental issues, with negative
effects on the spaces and people excluded by those environmental priorities.
This chapter has pointed to the class and ethno-racial biases that characterize
mainstream Uptown environmentalism in Jamaica and Curaçao, problema-
tizing its dominant "green" focus and the attendant neglect of issues related
to urban pollution.

The intersections of class, color, and urban geography in the Caribbean, and the associated unequal distribution of resources and power, have been well studied. The expression and reproduction of these inequalities through the environment—through urban environmental injustice, both in the distribution of pollution and in the uneven representation in environmental decision-making—have been discussed much less. In Caribbean protected-area management and conservation projects, critical research has begun to document the conflicts of knowledge and power that reflect and reinforce the social and spatial situatedness of those involved (e.g., Garner 2009; Geoghegan 2009; Sletto 2005). Such conflicts tend to be overlooked in urban areas, as if local knowledge were an exclusively rural phenomenon. Professional environmentalism often fails to incorporate or reflect the knowledge, worldviews, and concerns held by the sizeable urban population living in Kingston's "ghettos" or Willemstad's low-income *barios*. In the next chapter, I continue to examine this discursive disconnect by elaborating on "Downtown" understandings and articulations of environment and nature.

7 DOWNTOWN ENVIRONMENTALISM

*Poor people fed up how yu system sheg up / Well every day the ghetto youths
dead up / Mi ask the leader / Him a di arranger / Fi mek poor people surround
by danger / Fly and the roach and giant mosquita / Sewage water weh fill wid
pure bacteria / Unno ever tek a look dung inna di Riverton area / Bactu, and
Seaview, Waterhouse, Kintyre / Long time the MP him nuh come near yah / And
the nedda one weh claim seh she a councillor / Rob seventy-five percent and gi
wi quarter / conquer the land nuh waan fi gi wi a acre / Disconnect mi light an
chop off mi water / To the Kings of Kings, well mi know them shall answer*

Poor people are fed up with how your system is messed up / Every day ghetto
youths die / I ask the leader / He is the one responsible for the fact /
That poor people are surrounded by danger / Flies and roaches and giant
mosquitoes / Sewage water filled with bacteria / Have you ever taken a look
down in Riverton / Bactu and Seaview, Waterhouse, Kintyre[1] / The MP[2] hasn't
come here in a long time / And the other woman who says she is a councilor /
They steal 75 percent and give us a quarter / Conquer the land but don't want
to give us an acre / Disconnect my electricity and my water / I know they will
have to answer to God

—*"Fed Up," Bounty Killer*

In his song "Fed Up," Jamaican dancehall artist Bounty Killer
implicates political leaders as responsible for the neglect of residents
of Kingston's "ghetto" neighborhoods, where poverty goes hand in
hand with risks to life and health caused by violence and a polluted
environment. This environment does not include swallow-tailed
butterflies, mangroves, or manatees. Rather, its wildlife consists
of flies, roaches, and mosquitoes, which thrive in the unsanitary
conditions. These lyrics, which connect dirt and danger to poverty and politics, represent an element of what I term "Downtown
environmentalism." I use this term to indicate the loose cluster-
ing of perspectives on environmental issues and human–nature
relations that I encountered within Kingston and Willemstad's
spaces of social and material marginalization. In contrast to the
Uptown environmentalism I described in the previous chapter,

these perspectives were not articulated or mobilized in the context of any type of organized activism.

Uptown, professional environmentalists often assumed that lower-class Caribbean people had a poor relationship with nature, and their policies and practices implied that environmental problems resulted largely from a lack of popular environmental awareness. Many middle-class and elite NGO actors felt that the majority of Jamaicans and Curaçaoans held attitudes toward the natural environment that were problematic, that they were disconnected from their natural surroundings, and that they needed to learn how to appreciate nature. These Uptown views, which were especially evident in the strong emphasis many organizations placed on environmental education, tended to be based more on general impressions of low-income populations than on actual research into existing forms of environmental knowledge, values, and behavior. In contrast, in doing my own research I was interested to learn what environmental imaginaries and narratives circulated among inner-city residents, and whether they gave credence to dominant culturalist explanations of environmental degradation. What are the environmental priorities in these urban neighborhoods, and how can we understand them in relation to the socio-spatial inequalities that characterize Kingston and Willemstad?

In this chapter, I sketch the contours of an emergent discourse on environmental injustice in these cities that prioritizes brown agenda environmental problems such as garbage, sewage, flooding, and air pollution, and emphasizes the power structures that underlie the disproportionate exposure of low-income Afro-Caribbean urban populations to these problems.

The complex combination of constructions of nature and the environment, which I identify as "Downtown environmentalism," is tied to the spatial context of urban marginalized areas, but also informed by historically shaped Afro-Caribbean religious beliefs and by colonially rooted narratives of moral hygiene and progress, defined as the domination of wild nature. The first two sections of this chapter explore residents' interpretations of pollution as connected to social, economic, and political issues, and their ambivalent attitudes toward human–nature relations, connecting them to specific place-based environmental subjectivities. The next section focuses on critical perceptions of urban political ecology, in which low-income Curaçaoans and Jamaicans connect ecological vulnerabilities to their social and political marginalization, although such framings co-exist with culturalist blame-the-victim discourses. I end with a consideration of the lack of organized environmental activism in Caribbean inner-city neighborhoods in a section that concentrates on the relationship between Wishi/Marchena residents and "the Shell."

Portraits of pollution

In the "concrete jungles" of Downtown Kingston and *marginal* Willemstad, the main environmental problems that residents prioritized were "brown" issues related to pollution. Beyond this different prioritization, I found that residents' approach to environmental issues diverged from that of professional environmentalists in two ways. Where professional, Uptown environmentalists (perhaps necessarily) bracketed "the environment" as a separate sphere, the majority of residents of low-income areas approached environmental problems as inseparable from other urban problems that plagued their neighborhoods. They associated air pollution, inadequate sanitation, and solid waste management with social and economic concerns such as health, poverty, social disintegration, and violence and crime. In addition, and following from this more holistic approach, I encountered a politicized understanding of socio-ecological concerns—articulated much more forcefully by some residents than by others—in terms of socio-spatial injustice.

I drew on photo elicitation (see Harper 2002) to gain insight into residents' perceptions of different urban, rural, and industrial landscapes, using photos that depicted scenes of mangroves, cacti, and other tropical vegetation; garbage dumps; litter in urban and rural settings; the oil refinery and polluted gullies; and beaches and bays. Using this method, I found that solid waste management in particular was a main concern in all four research neighborhoods, including Riverton, where the presence of garbage was noticeable at all times because of its proximity to the dump. I encountered a broad range of emotional, aesthetic, medical, and ecological objections to litter and garbage across the four neighborhoods. While viewing the pictures of garbage, many interviewees expressed their dismay vocally or turned away from the photographs in disgust.

In Curaçao, the inadequacy of solid waste management was visible in the piles of litter found throughout the entire island, from construction materials and garden waste to plastic bags, beer cans, and dead dogs. Wishi/Marchena and Seru Fortuna residents associated urban scenes of garbage with social decline and the relative status of *barios* within the city's socio-spatial hierarchy. As in many other cities across the world, garbage was taken as an easy visual indicator of an area's social standing, of its respectability. In commenting on these photographs to me, residents often connected the presence of litter and informal dumpsites to crime, drugs, and prostitution. One picture depicted an empty lot full of garbage in the central *bario* of Scharloo, near Fleur de Marie, a section known for housing Dominican prostitutes. While no people were visible in this photograph, it elicited multiple disapproving references to sex work. Such associations of garbage with prostitution not only invoke the archetypical polluted category of the sex worker but also directly echo the early-twentieth-century colonial debates, discussed in Chapter Three, which repeatedly bracketed "the prostitution question" with "urban public cleanliness" under the rubric of sanitation. In addition to sex workers, residents' discussions of "dirty" Scharloo also involved disapproving mentions of the number of *choller* (homeless drug addicts) who could be found there.

More broadly, Wishi/Marchena and Seru Fortuna residents associated a *mal nomber* (bad reputation) with polluted urban landscapes. Mirroring the deflection of pollution onto other marginalized groups, they sometimes blamed solid waste management issues on migrants, particularly Dominicans. A more complex association among garbage, air pollution, migration, and reputation emerged in Wishi/Marchena, which had changed significantly following the departure of "real Curaçaoans" (*yu di Kòrsou*) to better neighborhoods or to the Netherlands. Certain houses had been abandoned when the owners moved out and had become garbage-filled crackhouses. Others were now occupied by Dominican migrants; the presence of the oil refinery meant that houses in this neighborhood were cheap and rents were low, a pull factor for recent immigrants with modest means. Such multi-causal associations also connected to the linguistic conflation many Papiamentu speakers made between *medio ambiente* (environment) and *ambiente* (atmosphere, fun). When I asked Daisy, a Seru Fortuna housewife in her forties, to tell me whether her neighborhood had any environmental problems, she answered: "The *ambiente* is not very good, nobody wants to come visit because they're scared. Everybody is frightened because of the shootings."

More than low-income Curaçaoans, Riverton and Rae Town residents emphasized the extent to which garbage presented a health hazard as the cause of rats, roaches, and disease. In Riverton, residents told me horror stories of people dying or becoming crippled after coming in contact with medical waste while searching for recyclables on the dump. In addition, they linked air pollution from the landfill to the prevalence of asthma and other respiratory diseases. In Rae Town, where garbage-clogged gullies flooded following heavy rain, residents worried about the drains' smell and pathogenic qualities, as well as the danger they posed to people living on their banks. The state of the gullies showed the clear connections Rae Town residents made between the different issues that affected their neighborhood. They blamed the clogging on "bad-minded," nasty people who threw garbage into them but also emphasized that many inner-city residents did not have access to proper garbage collection and had little choice but to use the gullies for waste disposal (see also Chevannes and Gayle 1998). Some residents did not have access to flush toilets and had to resort to dumping bags of feces in the gullies. Even outside of the rainy season, when the gullies would flood, these channels' polluted state presented a health risk to Rae Town children, who played in them. The fact that children played in the gullies was also associated with the absence of safe and clean play spaces, and sometimes with parents' financial inability to send their children to school.

More than in Curaçao, Riverton and Rae Town residents associated litter and illegal dumping directly with crime and violence. Looking at an image of a derelict building in Downtown Kingston, Greg, a carpenter from Riverton in his mid-thirties, told me: "These places need refurbish, build back, beautify the city. This is a safe haven for criminals." An earlier qualitative study conducted among Jamaican lower-income youth in the context of an environmental education campaign also found that violence was integral to understandings of "the environment," with all definitions of "good environment" referring to peace and unity. The majority of the respondents within that study defined the word "environment" as "what they saw in their surroundings: their community, people and their behavior (including 'war'), the state of the infrastructure, living conditions, flowering plants, painted and decorated corners, buildings, trees and animals" (Hope Enterprises 1999, 20). Similarly, in a study by David Dodman (2004), low-income focus groups in Kingston identified the top-ten "environmental problems" in their city as unemployment, water, toilets, housing, garbage, lack of education, pollution, war/violence, electricity, and sewage. The findings of these studies correspond with those of my own: clearly, the urban poor did not see environmental problems as separate or even distinct from violence, deficient infrastructure, and socioeconomic disadvantage.

In both Kingston and Willemstad, images of industrial pollution elicited more divergent responses than garbage did. In Downtown Kingston, residents tended to take a positive view of factories and oil refineries as visual expressions of jobs and development. Jamaicans such as Pops, a middle-aged Rasta shopkeeper from Riverton, for example, referred to the image of industrial smokestacks as a "progressive, money-making thing," and also thought it aesthetically pleasing. Wishi/Marchena residents, who inhaled the refinery's emissions day after day, also had relatively positive associations with the oil refinery, emphasizing its economic contributions, as I discuss in more detail later in the chapter. Across both islands, many people I spoke to referred to images of industrial air pollution as "pretty" or a "nice view." The interpretation of the visual aspects of atmospheric pollution—smoke, bellowing chimneys—in terms of progress and economic development is not specific to the Caribbean. Air pollution is suffused with cultural meaning, and environmental historians have showed that its construction as a social problem tends to be the result of sustained mobilization rather than a "natural" response to the physical presence of contamination. In Victorian Britain, for instance, smoke and smokestacks also symbolized economic productivity and the solution to poverty (DuPuis 2004; Thorsheim 2005). In the Caribbean, corporations, politicians, and international financial institutions have long supported hegemonic projects of development that associate industrialization with progress. In the light of such histories, it is perhaps not surprising that images of petrochemical plants and their emissions evoke positive responses.

This association of industrial development with progress and modernity perhaps also explains residents' widespread perceptions of wilderness—known as "bush" in Jamaica and *mondi* in Curaçao—as undeveloped, dangerous, or dirty. The appreciation and conservation of wild, untamed nature have been central features of North American and, to a lesser extent, European environmentalism. In contrast, wild nature often held negative associations for residents of the low-income Caribbean neighborhoods where I worked, with the exception of Seru Fortuna, where proximity to and levels of interaction with the *mondi* were greater. Reflecting on scenes of cacti or mangroves, Wishi/Marchena residents often associated the *mondi* with danger, whether in the form of prickly plants and wild animals, or lurking rapists and drug traffickers. In Riverton and Rae Town, many residents suggested that these landscapes were unclean, looked bad, and needed "cleaning up" and "development." This marking of development and wilderness as opposites is presumably what informed the racialized analysis of the Jamaican letter-writer mentioned in the previous chapter, who noted with regret that "we [Black Jamaicans] have bought into a notion of 'development' which cannot happen without a lot of concrete being poured, or re-arranging nature's design."[3] However, the repeated invocation of cleanliness and dirt in these discussions of wilderness also points to another distinct way that notions of pollution inform "Downtown environmentalism," in which a lack of human intervention means an absence of development and its sanitizing effects.

Environmental worldviews and subjectivities

The absence of a widespread appreciation of nature-as-wilderness need not indicate a wholesale lack of environmental consciousness. As discussed in the previous chapter, environmental professionals often expressed concern that low-income Jamaicans and Curaçaoans were alienated from nature, and emphasized that this could be understood as an underlying cause of environmental degradation. Geographer Elizabeth Thomas-Hope (1996, 10) demonstrates a similarly pessimistic perspective in her depiction of inner-city Kingston: "Children in Kingston's so-called 'garrison' communities, where green is the colour of a political party, not of vegetation, grow up in an environment devoid of nature. The power which they assert over their own environment reflects inner anger rather than positive interaction." This portrayal did not coincide with my findings. My research also included a survey intended to roughly measure environmental consciousness along a number of dimensions, including beliefs regarding limits to growth, anthropocentrism, and the balance of nature.[4] The discussions I had with residents in the four research neighborhoods in the context of this survey demonstrated that, to a significant extent, their environmental worldviews and beliefs were aligned with mainstream environmentalist thought. The survey results indicated that environmental consciousness—especially in terms of beliefs regarding the interconnectedness of humans and nature and the potentially disastrous impact of human activities on nature—was relatively widespread in low-income neighborhoods.

In contrast to professional environmentalists, whose analysis of environmental causation tended to be framed in scientific and technical terms, these residents' perspectives on human–nature relations were intimately connected to religious beliefs. The majority of residents expressed concern about the negative impact of human activities and lifestyles on nature, from the pollution of Kingston Harbor to the chopping down of trees and the indiscriminate construction of houses in Curaçao. On the whole, they rejected the idea of human exemptionalism: they felt that humans were not necessarily special or different from the rest of nature, as all were part of God's creation. I also found, across both islands, a very strong, almost apocalyptic expectation of environmental catastrophe. Residents explained their sense of imminent disaster by pointing to human interference with nature: drought follows deforestation, and frequent flooding follows land reclamation. However, they also understood natural disasters as indicators of divine wrath, and explained hurricanes and earthquakes as punishment for moral failures ranging from high murder rates to a more general lack of values. Residents did not necessarily embrace an ecocentric worldview—many felt that God had created humans to rule over the rest of nature, giving them dominion over all things. As Wayne, a young fisherman from Rae Town, explained to me, "as lion rule the jungle, so man rule the earth." Many people did emphasize that this God-given dominion entailed a responsibility to make use of natural resources wisely. Likewise, religious beliefs informed a widely shared optimism regarding the idea of limits to growth. The majority of residents felt strongly that there were no restrictions to the Earth's room or resources; as Omar, a middle-aged cook from Rae Town, maintained, "Father God no put no limits innit."

These perspectives on human–nature relations are suffused with Afro-Caribbean Christian religious beliefs. Catholicism in Curaçao, and various strands of Protestantism and Rastafari in Jamaica, formed the moral and philosophical underpinnings of residents' environmental worldviews and beliefs. While none of the professional environmentalists I interviewed made any reference to religion, low-income residents' reflections on human–nature relationships almost always included a mention of God (or, for Rastafari, Jah) or a reference to the Bible. Many people saw God as having laid the foundations for the relationship between humans and their natural environment but having left a measure of autonomy and responsibility to humankind. God had created a bounteous, limitless natural world specifically for the use of humans, but He also utilized natural forces such as earthquakes and hurricanes to express His displeasure at human wickedness.[5] In Jamaica, Rastafari is an important philosophical force in inner-city communities. Although the majority of Rae Town and Riverton residents identified as Christian, the influence of Rastafari was often apparent. The Rastafari concept of "ital livity" presents a specific, politicized version of the more general intertwining of the human, natural, and supernatural spheres. Ital livity, which is an important expression of Rastafari environmental ethics, refers to a lifestyle that eschews the artificiality and capitalist exploitation of "Babylon." It connects the exploitation of the natural world to racial and geopolitical inequity, and offers a philosophical alternative to both standard Christian environmental worldviews and mainstream secular environmentalism. The influence of this political philosophy was discernible in the discussions I had with residents about vegetarianism, organic agriculture, and the catastrophic overexploitation of natural resources in and beyond Jamaica.

The understandings that residents of low-income Caribbean neighborhoods have of environmental problems and human–nature relations are connected not only to religious beliefs, but also to how they imagine their own socio-ecological subject position. A focus on "environmental subjectivities" can shed light on the relation among environmental imaginaries, policies, and practices. In his work on the role of "environmentality" in conservation, Arun Agrawal (2005) points to the centrality of environmental subjectivities in understanding this relationship. Drawing on a longitudinal study of forestry management in the northern Indian region of Kumaon, he argues that achieving lasting changes in environmental practices and beliefs involves the making of new "environmental subjects." He defines these environmental subjects as "people who care about the environment. For these people, the environment is a conceptual category that organizes some of their thinking and a domain in conscious relation to which they perform some of their actions" (Agrawal 2005, 162).

As the previous discussions indicate, the people who live in ghettoized Caribbean neighborhoods such as Riverton and Seru Fortuna *do* care about the environment. They are environmental subjects to the extent that "the environment"—or *medio ambiente* in Curaçao—works as a significant conceptual category relevant to both their thinking and their action, although it is distinct from that of professional environmentalists: it is a broader category in which the natural, built, and social environments are entwined. In these low-income urban contexts, in which "the environment" as a domain is holistic rather than isolated, actions in relation to this domain are less likely to be in the realm of nature conservation than they are to involve micro-beautification efforts such as public clean-ups or the placing of potted plants in public space.

Agrawal describes the shifts in environmentalism that have occurred in India since British colonial rule, when Kumaon's villagers fought attempts to enclose and restrict access to their forests in the name of conservation. By the late twentieth century, as the mode of environmental regulation shifted to emphasize community forest management through village forest councils, increasing numbers of Kumaonis had come to embrace conservation in both their beliefs and their actions. Agrawal found that the extent to which villagers had become environmentally conscious depended on their practical involvement in forest conservation monitoring and enforcement. This connection, he suggests, shows that "environmental practice . . . is the key link between the regulatory rule that government is all about and imaginations that characterize particular subjects. In contrast, social identities such as gender and caste may play only a small role in shaping beliefs about what one considers to be appropriate environmental action" (Agrawal 2005, 163). He argues that involvement in different forms of social and environmental practice is key to understanding different forms of environmental self-formation or subjectivity.

While I agree with Agrawal that environmental anthropology has often privileged environmental imaginations and narratives over practices,[6] dismissing the importance of social identities in shaping environmental imaginations underestimates the entanglement of practice and social positioning. In Curaçao and Jamaica, identity categories such as race/color and class do not determine environmental beliefs and interests in any direct or essentialist way. However, in the highly segregated contexts of Willemstad and Kingston, these social identities are mapped closely onto place, with social and spatial positioning being closely related. Given the unequal distribution of environmental goods and hazards, such spatially differentiated identities do to a large extent limit socio-ecological practice.

Most of the residents with whom I worked did not encounter, or interact with, the same "nature" or "environment" that professional environmentalists were concerned with conserving. Even those Rae Town or Seru Fortuna residents who were involved in fishing or urban farming had a very different type of practical relationship to the "green" coastal or peri-urban environment than did NGO or government workers, who tended to emphasize the intrinsic or ecosystem value of these environments. Compared to these Uptown environmentalists, Downtown residents did, however, interact more frequently and intimately with the "brown" environment in the form of garbage, sewage, and air pollution. Dealing with waste products and toxic emissions is a form of everyday practice that should also be understood in relation to the formation of environmental subjects. Collecting recyclables from the dump, avoiding sewage that flowed freely down the street, or dusting off the fine layer of soot that floated down from the refinery's smokestacks—these mundane socio-ecological practices helped define subjects' interests in terms of brown rather than green agenda concerns. As outlined in the previous chapters, the segregation of urban mobilities and of residential and professional location along socio-economic and ethno-racial lines results in very different levels of exposure to pollution, to the materiality of dirt and dust. This connection between class–color identities and place-based social and environmental practice goes a long way toward explaining the socially and geographically uneven distribution of "green" and "brown" environmental subjectivities.

Socio-ecological marginality

Beyond its different orientation in environmental subjectivity, Downtown environmentalism is also distinct from Uptown environmentalism in its emergent framing of environmental problems in terms of marginality, neglect, and justice. This divergence came out clearly in Curaçao in relation to the Isla oil refinery, although I observed distinct differences between the ways that Wishi/Marchena and Seru Fortuna residents framed its air pollution. Despite widespread associations of industrial development with progress, not everyone was equally willing to view this type of activity as beneficial. Seru Fortuna residents recognized the economic benefits of the oil refinery but, compared to their counterparts in Wishi/Marchena, also emphasized the harmful effects of its emissions on human health. They were also much more cynical about where the money generated by the refinery's activities ended up. Employing environmental justice discourse, they noted that while the pollution affected Wishi/Marchena and adjacent downwind neighborhoods, the economic benefits accrued elsewhere. Maria, an elderly housewife from Seru Fortuna, told me: "The pollution is truly bad. It's supposed to be good for the economy, but it doesn't make the people rich, just the government." Ron, a youth worker from the same neighborhood, saw the profits as accumulating outside of Curaçao rather than to the government per se: "It does generate money, but I don't see the added value. It does bad things to Wishi/Marchena. Other people benefit from the refinery, but not this country." He continued: "They should fine Shell, but nobody has the nerve." Speaking from a greater physical and social distance from the refinery than their counterparts in Wishi/Marchena, Maria, Ron, and various other Seru Fortuna residents related environmental problems to local and global inequities. Their statements contributed to a local environmental justice discourse, in which *marginal* Curaçaoans suffer in the face of powerful corporate and government interests.

A nascent discourse of environmental justice was evident in a different way in Wishi/Marchena. While the refinery featured almost as a blind spot in their discourse, many residents framed the dilapidated state of their neighborhood, and specifically the presence of open dumpsites and litter, in terms of political neglect. Lettie, an elderly lady from Suriname who had been living in Curaçao since the 1940s, raged:

> They've been promising to clean up the mess here for a long time now. All kinds of garbage they dump here! It's people from other areas who

come here and do it. I can't even walk on the street for fear I'll break my leg. There's garbage everywhere and they don't do anything. Elections are coming but why should I vote? None of them do anything!

We were sitting by the window inside her house as she spoke, and she pointed at an empty lot with trees, bushes, weeds, and garbage nearby as she continued:

Look at that bush outside! [The solid waste management agency] Selikor won't come and clean it up; they come pick up our garbage every Wednesday but they won't clean that up. It's alright now because it's dry, but when it rains it just grows and grows! The people who own the lot have gone to Holland. You have iguanas and rats in there. People can hide in the *mondi*, people who do bad things. They dump dead dogs here, it's really a mess!

In such narratives, garbage symbolizes difference and danger—people from other areas, people who do bad things. But garbage was also visible, smell-able proof of the *marginal* position that the neighborhood and its residents occupied in the minds of the political elite. In fact, residents felt that their neighborhoods only received political attention around election time. Juni, an unemployed Seru Fortuna resident in his thirties, described his neighborhood as a political plaything: "This is a *bario* where politics are played out; all the political parties come here to make promises and get votes."

Similar accounts of environmental degradation as an indicator of political neglect were prevalent in Kingston. Miss Pauline, a middle-aged shopkeeper from Riverton, complained: "The place want some help from government, but it look like the politicians don't want to help the people." In addition to air pollution and garbage, urban flooding also produced environmental suffering that was interpreted as following from the political neglect of certain types of places and people. In a 2013 incident, heavy rains led to severe flooding on Sunlight Street, a street in the inner-city neighborhood of Trench Town. In a video clip that soon went viral within Jamaica,[7] an irate woman named Rosie described the situation to a cameraman from the local television channel CVM:

Everything in the house flood out. . . . From me live here at Sunlight Street, from me two months old, just born out of me mother . . . me never have seen my yard flood out yet. . . . So anybody see it them lie, cause

we never see it yet! And we want back everything! Laptop, phone . . .
name-brand furniture, name-brand bed, and name-brand car . . .

Standing in the middle of Sunlight Street, she leaned into the microphone,
gesturing animatedly at the camera. In the background, a street full of mud
and garbage, a gully with a broken cover, and ramshackle zinc fences marked
the scene as a "ghetto" space. Moving on from naming the goods that had
been damaged, Rosie began to list the health risks the flooding posed, in particular to young children:

> Baby can catch meningitis, shit-water and gully water. . . . My nephew's
> babies . . . she flood out too with her babies, nice pretty clean-skin baby
> them, flood out, not a pimples, mosquito bite—nothing! Right now,
> you know what happened to them? They need to go to hospital! And
> we need all type of something to clean out the germs! And the fly them
> starting in the house now and you no come look again, and it cannot
> go on like this!

The cameraman interrupted Rosie to ask what had caused the flooding. This
question caused her to become even more incensed, perhaps because wealthier Jamaicans often blame the poor for living in flood-prone areas such as
along gully banks. This flooding, in contrast, had been caused by improper
construction practices of workers rebuilding a nearby bridge.

> What cause it?? The workmen them cause everything, with how they
> cut the bridge, and none of them no come in the yard to come look
> what's going on! If they would just fix up right there so, the house would
> not flood out. It's the bridge cause everything! It's this big contract that's
> going on. . . . We need justice! Real justice we need! Justice we need!

As she called for justice, onlookers in the background laughed and nodded
in agreement. By shouting "We want justice," a phrase that is central to the
repertoire of protest of the Jamaican poor, Rosie situated the plight that she
and her neighbors were facing within a broader context of political neglect
and misrecognition of inner-city residents. As Hume N. Johnson argues,
the Jamaican street protests in which this call for justice is most commonly
voiced are expressions of "the need to be affirmed as a citizen who is important and who possesses rights deserving of recognition" (Johnson 2008, 174).

Emphasizing the lack of outside interest in the plight of inner-city residents affected by the flooding, Rosie went on to demand that the contractor in charge of the faulty bridgework be held responsible.

> Nobody no come to look, only the cameraman, it can't work so, we want justice! Justice! We need justice! . . . The germs and nasty . . . right now the flies start take over the place. Call the contractor, we need the contractor! . . . Jeyes! Dettol! Soap powder! All type of thing to clean out the house! The baby them what take meningitis, them a sick and dead. We want justice! We need justice!

What interests me most here are the connections Rosie made between dirt, wealth, health, and justice. In addition to emphasizing the material damages that accompanied the flooding, her account pointed to the risk of bacterial infections and skin conditions caused by the sewage and polluted gully water flowing into the houses on Sunlight Street, and ended with a demand for disinfectants such as Jeyes and Dettol to get rid of the germs and flies. Her emphasis on "name-brand" goods and "nice pretty clean-skin" children, together with her listing of the multiple cleaning supplies needed to disinfect the house, can be read as a contestation of the urban naturalism that conflates poor people and places with pollution and pathology. Her account is an assertion of the prosperous, healthy, and sanitary nature of her household, despite its location by a gully. It also forcefully proposes that urban pollution be read as environmental injustice, with inner-city residents suffering as they are ignored and neglected by Uptown politicians and wealthy contractors.

The television station's video was watched hundreds of thousands of times on YouTube. Its popularity is perhaps explained by the theatrical delivery of Rosie's tirade; many online commenters found her Jamaican Creole phrases and body language comical, while others called her crazy or suggested that she was high on cocaine. In addition, commenters contrasted her claim to a clean, affluent household environment with her "ghetto" appearance and residence. Many of them expressed disbelief that ghetto residents would possess the goods (laptop, phone, expensive furniture, flatscreen television) that she listed as having been "flooded out." These comments reflect a number of common prejudices toward inner-city residents, and in fact a number of more critical commenters pointed to a YouTube trend in which videos of low-income Black people were posted as entertainment. More specifically, certain comments evidenced the blame-the-victim explanations of environmental hazards discussed in detail in earlier chapters. One commenter declared that "those people build their houses next to gullies and river beds so as soon as a little rain falls the water takes its natural course and they expect the government to pay for it and it is not fair to the rest of the country." Rosie preempted this derogatory explanation by stating that her street "never flood out yet" and that anybody's claims to the contrary were lies. The many views and comments that this video received mark it as something of a public event in the digital transnational sphere of social media. Within this virtual public sphere, differently situated Jamaicans posited relations of environmental causality and allocated blame in different ways, both reaffirming and contesting the dominant poverty–pollution–pathology frame.

A similar perspective on brown environmental problems in terms of neglect and injustice is also articulated in the lyrics to Bounty Killer's dancehall song with which this chapter begins: "Poor people surround by danger / fly and the roach and giant mosquita / sewage water weh fill wid pure bacteria . . . long time the MP him nuh come near yah." The song connects disease-bearing pests and sewage water flowing across the roads to a lack of concern for the well-being of inner-city residents on the part of politicians. In addition, it makes direct connections between the different types of danger that citizens who live in inner-city neighborhoods face: violent crime and environmental hazards.

In their study of the poorest neighborhoods of Buenos Aires, Javier Auyero and Agustín Burbano de Lara (2012) also found that residents perceived clear interrelations among poverty, physical violence, and environmental hazards. Urban exclusion involves the exposure of poor people's bodies to multiple forms of harm, which are distributed unequally across the city's biophysical landscape. These researchers argue that understandings of the lived experience of urban marginality must take into account these various dimensions of harm: "Phenomenologically speaking, violence, infrastructural deprivation, and environmental hazards appear together in the lives of the marginalized" (Auyero and Burbano de Lara 2012, 533). In both Kingston and Willemstad, concentrations of environmental risk similarly coincide with concentrations of widespread material deprivation, inadequate infrastructure, and everyday physical violence. Perhaps even more so than in Buenos Aires, these Caribbean urban landscapes have historically been interwoven intimately with experiences of both raced and classed injustice. Spatially concentrated environmental risk is easily understood within these emotionally resonant frameworks.

Such understandings of environmental injustice both clash and co-exist with dominant urban naturalisms. Low-income Jamaicans and Curaçaoans

often perceived pollution as ethical and moral issues, but in multiple contradictory ways. Explanations that held so-called "nasty" people responsible
for the state of Kingston's gullies reproduced the urban naturalism of mutually reinforcing moral deficiencies and physically polluted environments. The
association of illegal dumpsites with Dominicans and prostitutes, or with
other "bad" neighborhoods such as Scharloo, similarly endorsed or redi-
rected such naturalisms, rather than contesting them. However, residents of
the different neighborhoods also articulated critiques of these conflations
when they pointed to the structural causes of neighborhood pollution: irregular garbage collection services, the lack of toilets, greedy corporations, and
lying politicians. These different framings of pollution—which form the
emergent, ambiguous contours of a Downtown environmentalism—suggest
that its mobilization as an effective social movement frame might not be a
straightforward endeavor.

Like David fighting Goliath

While many residents of low-income neighborhoods in Kingston and
Willemstad saw brown environmental issues as related to broader urban
inequalities and political neglect, and sometimes framed them explicitly as
forms of injustice, they were not involved in sustained mobilization against
these issues. With its focus on urban pollution but its lack of sustained
activism, the "Downtown environmentalism" I have sketched in this chapter diverges from much of the literature on environmental injustice. Those
anthropologists who have attended most directly to urban spaces and brown
environmental problems have tended to take a social movement studies
approach. Working mainly in U.S. cities, ethnographers have explored the
mobilization of low-income communities of color in opposition to environmental injustice (e.g., Bullard 2000; Checker 2001, 2005, 2011; Sze 2007).
In her study of African American community activism against environmental racism in Augusta, Georgia, Melissa Checker (2005) analyzes the various connections between race and the environment, from the racialization of
those places that are most vulnerable to polluting industries to racially differentiated environmental priorities. She explains how residents of the polluted
African American neighborhood of Hyde Park did not see "the environment"
as something that needed protection from human interference. Rather, it featured as a toxic threat to residents' health and well-being from which *they*
needed to be protected.

While emphasizing the structural inequalities that produce environmental racism, these accounts of the environmental justice movement highlight the agency of minoritized non-elites affected by urban pollution. Grassroots environmental justice activists may not always be successful in their struggles against polluting industries and negligent governments, but they play an active role in raising awareness and influencing NGO and state policy and legislation. This social movement focus in ethnographic studies of environmental injustice has meant, however, that less attention has been paid to urban communities without significant grassroots mobilization. How can we understand environmental knowledge and practice in polluted neighborhoods characterized more by passivity and resignation than by activism and indignation?

This question arises most pertinently in the case of Wishi/Marchena, a neighborhood that has been exposed to toxic emissions for many decades. The oil refinery is the neighborhood's defining characteristic, to the extent that the *bario* organization sold t-shirts decorated with the Isla's smokestacks during community events. Despite intermittent attempts to impose environmental regulations on the industry, the Isla has continued to flout this legislation with impunity. While I encountered general feelings of resentment about this situation during my stay in the neighborhood, many residents appeared to perceive it as something permanent and unalterable. The refinery had been around for so long, and protests and legal action and political promises did not seem to have resulted in any real changes. Kenneth Valpoort, a teacher and social worker who was also an active trade unionist, was one of the *bario*'s longtime leaders. Sitting in the yard of a school where he had been asked to act as a judge in a student competition, he explained the results of collective action in the past to me.

In 1988, we organized a demonstration against the pollution, Shell, the Isla. We did this together with [the environmental NGO] *Amigu di Tera* and another group. We got together more than 800 people—it was the largest demonstration ever organized in Curaçao after May 30 [in 1969][8]; it was a positive march. We did it three times, also in 1989 and 1990; after that it lost its effectiveness. But what happened? We didn't achieve anything. It was like David fighting Goliath. We wanted to take the Isla to court—it's still ongoing. But they [the government] were negotiating with the [Venezuelan oil company] PDVSA for the extension of their contract, and the lieutenant governor—at the time it was Mr. Elmer Wilsoe—told us we had to keep a low profile: he was afraid we would obstruct the contract negotiations. He told us to let the lawsuit and everything go. So that's what happened with the Isla.

Since these demonstrations, many people had become rather blasé about the problem. Despite the resentment expressed by many Wishi/Marchena residents, a considerable number of others admitted or insisted that they were not very concerned about the refinery and spoke of the serious air pollution as if it did not really affect them. When I first began working in the neighborhood, I introduced myself as researching environmental problems. This emphasis would prompt critical statements on the refinery and complaints about its smell and the soot that covered everything. However, some of these criticisms struck me as a bit rote, and I changed my introduction to stress my interest in the neighborhood more broadly and asked residents to tell me what they saw as its good points and its bad points. The majority did not prioritize the refinery as one of the *bario*'s main problems, mentioning unemployment, crime, or Dominican migrants as their chief concerns. Francis, a male nurse, explained that for many residents, health issues had ceased to be an urgent concern, and that the neighborhood's positive characteristics were more important:

> People have grown immune to the refinery, we've learned to live with the gas. I would be lying if I said it affected my health. It's become a part of our lives, it doesn't really bother us. A lot of people who work for Shell have always lived in this *bario*. What is more important to us is that this is a peaceful neighborhood in a central location. Besides, since they made the chimneys higher, there is less soot.

This relatively mild appraisal of the Isla can be understood when viewed through the historical entanglement of the refinery's development with that of the neighborhood and of Curaçao as a whole. While general opinion seemed to have turned against the refinery since the late 1980s, many older residents in particular found it difficult to speak negatively of it without also mentioning its contribution to the island's prosperity. Giovanni, a football coach in his mid-fifties, sighed as he spoke of the refinery: "The famous Shell . . . which has spoiled all of everything. But . . . without Shell it would have been a ghost town around here. He left it behind all spoiled and they don't want to clean it up." Despite the diminishing significance of the oil industry to the Curaçaoan economy, it was not hard to find residents who felt that the refinery's economic benefits still outweighed its purported disadvantages to community health and the environment. Historically, Wishi/Marchena had housed Curaçaoan manual laborers employed by Shell, and a number of residents were still employed at the PDVSA-run refinery. Tante, a housewife in her late sixties whose husband used to work for Shell, remarked without much bitterness that "the money is good, the smell is bad." Kitty, a seventy-nine-year-old lady from the island of Nevis who had moved to Curaçao in 1956 during the refinery's boom years, told me more sharply: "If they don't have Shell, Curaçao gone! Else we don't get pension. ... We have to live with it. Some people talk stupid and say it must go. But tourists come and go—this is your bread!"

The economic significance that many older residents in particular attributed to the Isla was intertwined with the emotional importance the refinery continued to have for them. For migrants such as Kitty, the refinery was what had enabled her to move from poverty elsewhere in the Caribbean to relative prosperity in Curaçao. Local and colonial governments encouraged the idea that the island's wealth, compared to the rest of the region, was attributable to Shell. This sentiment was also reproduced through the education system. Yvette, an NGO leader whose father had migrated to Curaçao from St. Lucia before she was born, told me that when she was growing up, the *fraters* (friars) who taught at many of the island's Catholic schools would tell their pupils: "If the lights of the refinery go out, Curaçao's light will dim as well." Half a century later, this equation of the island's well-being with that of the refinery made it hard for many older Curaçaoans to take an unequivocally critical stance toward the oil industry. As noted previously, however, residents from Seru Fortuna, an area whose history was much less entwined with the Isla, held pointedly different views regarding its role. In discussions of the refinery, they generally emphasized its polluting effects and the resulting harm to human health and the environment, associating it with social inequity.

Unlike in the biblical story, David has not won the battle with Goliath in Curaçao. Protest marches such as those held in 1989 and the two following years were discouraged by the government and seemed to many to have had little effect. In fact, they did have some results. The protests led to public disclosure of the fact that the refinery was exempt from having to apply for a nuisance permit (*hindervergunning*), the main instrument of environmental legislation. Following an updated nuisance law in 1994, the refinery received its first nuisance permit in 1997. While the restrictions set by this permit were so limited that they rendered it a largely toothless document, the fact that the refinery was subject to environmental regulation for the first time

in its history was an important symbolic shift. The environmental organizations that had marched with Wishi/Marchena residents filed a suit against
the permit's extremely lenient conditions, but as of 2015 the government had
still not revised these conditions. In the meantime, the refinery continued
to breach the conditions of the original permit, which were rarely enforced.

Kenneth Valpoort, the Wishi/Marchena *bario* leader introduced earlier,
saw the degradation of the neighborhood's physical environment as inseparable from residents' feelings of helplessness and lack of ownership for their
surroundings. He perceived the refinery's impunity as undermining a sense
of collective agency:

> We need a healthy infrastructure, a healthy environment, if it can
> be changed. Infrastructure, with good roads, asphalt, streetlights,
> sidewalks, cleanups. It's a mental change. So it's mental and physical
> infrastructure, one can't change without the other. To change the
> neighborhood you must change the people, is what I say. They have to
> say: "Hey, it's my community," and be proud. Say: "It's mine." It can be
> frustrating trying to keep your community's environment clean when
> you see the refinery, and it's the biggest polluter and no one is bother-
> ing them, and they don't give anything to the community. They don't
> get fines, they aren't punished in any way. And when we protest they
> [the Isla] say: "Don't forget, some people who live in your area work
> for us too."

Following past attempts in Wishi/Marchena to mobilize against the oil
refinery, the neighborhood's belief in collective action seemed to have waned
to the extent that most residents seemed to accept the everyday pollution as
a given. As noted previously, few ethnographies of urban pollution engage
with such instances of grassroots resignation in which there is widespread
skepticism regarding the possibility of substantial change. Javier Auyero and
Débora Alejandra Swistun's (2009) research on environmental suffering
in Flammable, a heavily contaminated neighborhood in Buenos Aires, is a
notable exception in this regard. Their ethnography seeks to relate "a story of
a people's confusion, mistakes, and/or blindness regarding the toxicity that
surrounds them ... a story of silent habituation to contamination and of
almost complete absence of mass protest against toxic onslaught" (2009, 4).

Studying the lived experience of toxic hazards in Flammable, where air,
soil, and water were all severely polluted by over seven decades of petrochemical industrial activity, Auyero and Swistun encountered widespread

misrecognition of the sources and effects of this contamination. They explain the absence of grassroots mobilization in Flammable through the concept of "toxic uncertainty," a mix of confusion and denial produced through inconsistent and contradictory governmental interventions and expert opinions. In addition, they locate impediments to collective action in the internal divisions among residents and in the somewhat hopeful but endless waiting for outside interventions of government officials, lawyers, doctors, journalists, and the polluting corporations. The socio-political production of toxic uncertainty and the related practice of perpetual waiting, they argue, work to paralyze marginalized urban residents and as such are central to those residents' submission to, and reproduction of, systems of socio-ecological domination.

This analysis of residents as inclined to collective inaction and inadvertently complicit in their own environmental suffering has many parallels with what I encountered in Wishi/Marchena. I understand the lack of grassroots environmental activism as stemming from an institutionally inculcated hesitancy to criticize the Isla, combined with residents' pessimistic perception of their ability to effect change in the face of vested political economic interests. I came across somewhat similar processes in Riverton, where residents also tended to downplay the health risks associated with living and working next to the garbage dump and would instead stress the economic advantages of their location. The misrecognition by people living in these areas of the structural conditions of their socio-ecological marginalization is an important part of systems of social domination. However, an overemphasis on habituation and powerlessness also risks depicting residents as passive victims who lack agency. As Anja Nygren (2012, 354) notes, "Even if they are relatively powerless, local inhabitants can hardly be passive playthings, condemned to live in a 'reality' totally dictated by other, more powerful actors."

Other authors also caution against narratives that neglect the agency of the urban poor, especially when such narratives tap into historical constructions of racialized apathy. Melissa Checker (2005) warns of the dangers of "culture of poverty" and "underclass" theories that represent African American urban communities as disorganized, passive, and incapable of sustained activism. As Deborah Thomas (2009) has shown in detail, culturalist research on the Afro-Caribbean poor has been complicit in reproducing similar stereotypes of urban disorder and deviance. Indeed, as I outlined in Chapter Four, residents of all four research neighborhoods in Curaçao and Jamaica valued their place-based networks of friends and family. The place attachment they expressed was not so much related to the physical characteristics of these polluted communities as it was to their social unity. For many of them, their neighborhood's social life and support networks were its main attraction. In Wishi/Marchena, both collectively organized events such as the *dia di bario* and individual efforts to beautify public spaces made it plain that residents were neither passive nor apathetic. Perhaps unlike residents of Flammable and similar polluted areas, moving away from the neighborhood was not impossible for Wishi/Marchena residents. Accessing affordable government-subsidized housing in other low-income *barios* or migrating to the Netherlands were viable options that some residents did in fact pursue. But in addition to a misrecognition of their structural environmental vulnerability, what kept many residents in the neighborhood in the face of toxic threat was a commitment to durable social networks of trust and support.

An absence of sustained environmental protest does not mean an absence of agency; it can also result from a measured assessment of social, economic, and ecological benefits and threats. In addition, the relative lack of organized grassroots environmental protests in the Caribbean—as compared to Latin America, for example[9]—might suggest a need to reimagine environmental activism beyond singular or unified movements. In Jamaica, and especially its low-income urban communities, the influence of less structured, plural movements such as Rastafari and its political philosophy suggest the relevance of attending to less explicitly organized grassroots influences on environmental ethics.

Conclusion

"Downtown environmentalism" is a loosely organized set of environmental imaginaries, narratives, and practices that I encountered in environmentally degraded and hazardous urban areas in Willemstad and Kingston. On the whole, residents were more concerned with the brown environmental problems that had a direct impact on their communities and their everyday practices than with relatively distant green issues related to biodiversity conservation or climate change. They tended to associate urban pollution with other social, cultural, and political concerns: urban environmental problems featured as the combined and interrelated effects of ecological and infrastructure degradation, poverty, violence and crime, and political neglect. This broader perspective contrasted with professional environmentalists' depiction of "environmental problems" as a distinct domain that was largely separate from social problems. Seeing "nature" or "the environment" as a separate domain of thought and action is by no means a universal tendency; in many cases, processes of learning and unlearning underlie the ease with which we make these distinctions.

The "Uptown environmentalism" of NGO and government professionals stressed the need for educational campaigns to achieve lasting change in environmental beliefs and behaviors. Implicitly or explicitly, such policies tend to culturalize environmental problems, drawing on explanatory frames rooted in culture rather than in political economy. In highly urbanized contexts, emphasizing the need for appreciation of endangered flora and fauna while largely ignoring the air pollution, flooding, and waste management issues that affect low-income neighborhoods amounts to a disregard for the realities and priorities of the urban poor. "Downtown environmentalism" presents an emergent alternative environmental imaginary that politicizes urban pollution and frames the unequal distribution of environmental goods and hazards in terms of poverty, race, and place. Yet, as is most clear in the case of Wishi/Marchena's position vis-à-vis Curaçao's Isla oil refinery, mobilizing against pollution and its unequal distribution has proven extremely difficult.

CODA

In February 2012, the Riverton dumpsite caught fire, and billowing clouds of smoke affected large sections of Kingston for over a week. While improper management of the dump usually only affected Riverton residents, the air pollution now became a major nuisance in wealthier neighborhoods. NEPA found that levels of particulate matter were "very high risk" in sites up to a kilometer away from the fire and "high risk" in sites within a two-kilometer radius.[1] In March 2015, an even worse fire, allegedly lit intentionally, raged for nearly two weeks. With over half of the dump area burning, the entire urban area was affected by the smoke, as was the neighboring city of Portmore. Air quality was classified as "very high risk" within a five-kilometer radius, with high concentrations of toxic emissions such as benzene and sulphur dioxide (NEPA 2015). Schools were closed, operations were suspended at Kingston's port, and hundreds of people sought medical help. If wealthier Jamaicans could usually write off the pollution associated with the dump as an unfortunate local issue, these fires made it a matter of national concern.

Riverton's mounds of garbage could even be read in terms of global environmental problems, as a 2012 cartoon in the *Jamaica Observer* demonstrated (see Figure 8.1). Drawn by the cartoonist Clovis, the image shows a towering heap of burning garbage, with plumes of dark smoke drifting off in the distance and a dead dog lying splayed in the foreground, next to a sign proclaiming the Riverton City Dump. A light-skinned "climate change minister" wearing a suit and dark glasses and protecting himself from the fumes with a gas mask and an umbrella gestures toward the fire. "This is bad, this is really bad!!" he exclaims in concern, apparently suddenly realizing that solid waste management might be part of his portfolio.[2] The minister's skin color, formal attire, and use of "proper" English

FIGURE 8.1 Cartoon by Clovis, *Jamaica Observer*, February 17, 2012

all serve to emphasize his distance from the life-world of Riverton, while his gas mask and umbrella highlight the extent to which Uptown environmental officials can shield themselves from exposure to the pollution that the urban poor cannot avoid.

A more politicized perspective on pollution also began to emerge among certain elite environmental professionals. In a *Jamaica Gleaner* column commenting on the 2015 fire, Peter Espeut, a Jamaican environmentalist who would generally be categorized as White or Brown, suggested that "maybe now that the wind has changed, and the smoke from the burning Riverton dump has gone uptown, we will see an improvement in how Jamaica handles solid waste. As long [as] it is only poor black people who are afflicted by deadly air pollution, nothing will change. Thank God for the winds of change that blew from the dump, uptown to Barbican, Norbrook, Cherry Gardens and Stony Hill."[3] Such an explicit and public reference to the classed and racialized geographies that shape environmental priorities, by an environmental professional who would generally be privileged by these same geographies, is relatively new and potentially transformative.

As I have argued throughout this book, Caribbean environmentalisms should be understood in relation to a historically developed politics of difference. All ecologies are political—but equally, all politics are embedded in the natural and built environments. A fuller understanding of the reproduction, contestation, and transformation of raced and classed inequalities requires attention not only to urban space, but also to the social production of "nature" and "the environment." Different environmental priorities, imaginaries, knowledges, and practices reflect and reinforce the spatialization of socio-economic and ethno-racial difference. Environments and environmental problems are constructed and explained through divergent and apparently conflicting frames, two of which I have glossed here as Uptown and Downtown environmentalism. Broadly speaking, these different forms of environmentalism offer, respectively, culturalist and politicized explanations of environmental degradation.

My focus on two forms of environmentalism may suggest an overly dualist reading of urban life. However, as my elaboration in the previous chapters demonstrated, Uptown and Downtown environmentalism share certain elements—in both Jamaica and Curaçao, low-income urban residents also draw on culturalist discourse that blames pollution on "nasty people," while some professional environmentalists have begun to move toward more politicized positions, and to emphasize the connection between green and brown agenda issues. Yet binary oppositions between "Uptown" and "Downtown," between *bario lujo* and *bario marginal*, do continue to structure socio-ecological relations, even in these relatively small island communities. While socio-spatial divisions in terms of class, skin color, and urban space are dynamic social constructions rather than essential or absolute categories of difference, such categories are central to the lived experience of residents of Kingston and Willemstad. Moreover, these socially constructed differences are made material through inequalities and disconnects in physical environmental infrastructure and services, such as the partial reach of a sewage system, uneven access to garbage disposal, or the location of an oil refinery—what Stephen Graham and Simon Marvin (2001) have termed "splintering urbanism." The material and emplaced dimension of urban environmental experiences means that, despite the small scale of the two cities discussed here, pollution often remains a problem that is primarily concentrated in low-income areas.

Studying the connections between environmentalism and urban inequalities involves a perspective that goes beyond explicit conflicts over environmental action and meaning. An environmental anthropology oriented toward social justice must also focus on the gaps in environmental attention, the issues that are ignored rather than addressed. Why are elites and the middle classes predisposed toward an interest in green environmental problems and not brown agenda issues? The focus of Uptown environmentalism, which tends to elide problems related to air pollution, sewage, and garbage, reflects the transnational, national, and local social and physical spaces within which environmental professionals move. Their activities are connected to global epistemic circuits that emphasize biodiversity and conservation. Nationally, their priorities are informed by the islands' economic reliance on nature-based tourism and by the increased importance of being green to processes of class distinction. More than just reflecting current national and transnational concerns, however, the lack of attention to urban pollution is connected to specific Caribbean urban geographies and histories. The segregated character of city life and urban mobilities means that environmental professionals are much less exposed to the everyday inner-city realities of urban pollution. In addition, historically developed associations that persistently connect the spaces in which the Afro-Caribbean lower classes live and work with moral and physical pollution serve to obscure the social and ecological urgency of addressing brown environmental problems.

A commitment to environmental justice and urban pollution need not preclude a commitment to conservation and other green issues. As the Clovis cartoon shows by linking local pollution to global climate change, brown and green issues are often connected, especially in small island environments. Combating ecological vulnerability does not require excluding or exacerbating social vulnerabilities. The environmental issues that preoccupy many low-income urban residents—sewage, garbage, air pollution, and floods—are connected to professionally prioritized issues such as biodiversity and the protection of coastal and marine ecosystems. Marine pollution, for instance, is intrinsically related to land-based, urban problems such as wastewater and solid waste management; much of the uncollected garbage and unrefined sewage polluting poor neighborhoods and clogging gullies ends up in the sea and washes up on beaches, degrading coastal ecosystems. The urban and industrial pollution that endangers human health, particularly in low-income areas, has similar harmful effects on nonhuman species and, as in the case of methane emissions from landfills, can contribute to climate change. Ecological vulnerability is aggravated when causes of social vulnerability, such as limited access to basic services and infrastructure, and insecure land tenure, are left unchecked. Conversely, including the socially vulnerable in environmental protection and conservation programs, both in and outside

urban areas, has the potential to provide a social and financial boost to dis-
enfranchised citizens.

A few recent instances suggest a gradual move among some environmental professionals toward making such connections between urban issues and
conservation. In Curaçao, a promising move by the ENGO Amigu di Tera
involved a lawsuit against the island government. The court case sought to halt
government plans to develop a major new housing development in Wèchi, an
area close to Seru Fortuna that had been designated as a conservation zone
within national planning legislation. The government and the public housing agency FKP argued that the development would provide urgently needed
low-income housing—although the real estate developer contracted to construct the new neighborhood clearly had the intention of building enough
middle-income houses to make a real profit. Hints were dropped that the
ENGO's commitment was to nature rather than to the more pressing problems that poor people faced, analogous to the framing of Jamaican environmentalists as "anti-development," described in Chapter Six. However, in this
case, Amigu di Tera made its case by stressing the government's responsibility
and its commitment (professed in urban policy documents) to combat urban
sprawl and improve the living conditions in *marginal barios* by renovating
existing housing and investing in dilapidated infrastructure. Constructing
new neighborhoods, the ENGO argued, not only contributed to urban
sprawl and the associated encroachment on the conservation areas of the
'mondi, but also served to distract citizens from the government's failure to
address housing and other infrastructural problems in existing low-income
neighborhoods.[4] Such new narratives are promising in their recognition of
first, the interconnectedness of various environmental problems, and second,
the relation between environmental and socio-political issues. They demonstrate the compatibility of green and brown issues, and of the concerns of
elites and those of the urban poor.

Over the past few decades, anthropologists have paid increasing attention to environmental degradation, calling for a consideration of the cultural dimensions of the global environmental crisis. While earlier versions
of ecological anthropology (or cultural ecology) sometimes presented apo-
litical analyses of human–environment relations, the emergence of political
ecology has resulted in increasingly politicized approaches. Critical environmental anthropologists have focused on the ways that conservation, often
in connection to development, becomes a site of governmentality (Agrawal
2005; Li 2007; West 2006). Other research has studied environmental epis-
temologies, relating culturally specific alternative paradigms of sustainability

and conservation to colonially constructed difference and the possibility of imagining and realizing radically different worlds (Escobar 2008). Much of this work has engaged critically with the conservation agendas propagated by environmentalist organizations in and beyond the global North. However, it is perhaps precisely this engagement with conservationist agendas that has inadvertently narrowed our understanding within environmental anthropology of what constitutes an environmental problem. Notwithstanding a strong interest in exploring the constructed character of "nature" and "the environment," the study of these constructs within the field has predominantly taken place outside of cities. This inattention to urban space works to reproduce a nature–culture distinction in which the city features implicitly or explicitly as anti-nature. This omission has also inhibited the anthropological analysis of garbage or industrial pollution as environmental problems. By locating environmental anthropology squarely in the city, I have sought to underline the need for a meta-deconstruction, that is, for attention to persistent city–nature dichotomies that inform the priorities and field sites of researchers.

Meanwhile, urban anthropology has displayed limited interest in the importance of the social production of nature and the environment to city life. This has often involved a misrecognition of the role of environmental issues in structuring urban inequalities. As Javier Auyero and Débora Alejandra Swistun emphasize, "that environmental factors are key determinants in the reproduction of destitution and inequity is a matter about which scholars (us included) have remained silent for too long" (2009, 18). Only recently have a number of urban anthropologists expressed a more explicit interest in the environmental injustice of unequal exposure to pollution (e.g., Checker 2005) or in the infrastructural violence that disconnects marginalized groups from the material networks that are necessary for sewage disposal or access to potable water (Rodgers and O'Neill 2012; Anand 2012). This engagement with the materiality of urban environmental inequities and its socio-political ramifications should be extended to incorporate cultural politics more explicitly. The discursive-material production of urban ecologies not only is a problem of unequal exposure or access for differently situated urban groups, but is also central to the construction and reproduction of categories of social difference.

By linking the cultural politics of the environment to the spatial politics of urban inequality, the concept of urban naturalism can bridge some of these divides between environmental anthropology and urban anthropology. It serves to elucidate the interconnections among the social, natural, and built environments by highlighting the material-ecological basis of the production of social difference. The conflation of urban places, people, and cultural traits is central to processes of environmental meaning-making: it guides what can be recognized as an environmental problem and where such problems can be found, and it shapes who we come to see as qualified to propose solutions to these problems and who we believe must be restricted or reeducated as part of these solutions.

A focus on these interconnections can also help us understand how urban environmental inequalities both persist and change over time. My interest in the historical chapters in this book has been to explore how colonial imaginaries and interventions may have prefigured more recent intersections of environmentalism and the politics of difference. Tracing such connections involves attending to the diverse elements of socio-ecological assemblages, which include specific tropes, narratives, sanitation infrastructure, flows of wastewater, airborne emissions, urban neighborhoods, and tropical landscapes. Studying how these various elements articulate, separate, and are rearticulated across different historical eras and episodes enables an analysis that recognizes the lasting effects of colonialism without eliding important changes that have occurred over time. This also allows a comparison between different cities and islands that highlights how certain articulations are specific to a singular place, with its own unique history, morphology, and demography, even as other articulations may have a broader applicability across the region.

In the Caribbean, the material and social production of urban pollution cannot be seen outside of histories of colonialism and institutionalized racism. Caribbean islands and cities are landscapes that contain traces of the region's long colonial era, from the protected areas established in Jamaica by the British colonial government to the lasting environmental impact of Shell's refinery, a Dutch corporate-governmental giant that has been able to pollute with impunity. Understanding how colonialism matters in contemporary environmentalism, urban pollution, and the production of difference involves recognizing the various reworkings of these traces. This involves less of an emphasis on "the artifacts of empire as dead matter or remnants of a defunct regime" and more of an increased attentiveness to "their reappropriations and strategic and active positioning within the politics of the present" (Stoler 2008, 196). In Jamaica and Curaçao, environmentalists who speak and act from classed and raced positions draw on historically resonant tropes of paradise and representations of the region as a space of nature, reworking these natural images in the context of tourism economies and global conservationist networks. Differently raced residents of ghettoized neighborhoods reproduce, deflect, and challenge the colonially rooted conviction that pollution is a natural attribute of certain types of people and places.

This ethnography has sought to trace the roots of such patterns of socio-ecological thought and practice in Caribbean island and urban landscapes. It has done so not only to show how the association of poverty, pollution, and pathology is a historical and social construction, but also to demonstrate that the project of "uprooting" these discursive entanglements involves under-standing how these associations are both reworked and undone through the materiality of rotting trash and foul-smelling smoke, perfumed bodies and derelict houses, sealed-off SUVs and pristine nature parks. By parsing the cultural politics of urban ecologies, we can de-naturalize those entrenched hierarchies that make the unequal distribution of physical environmental hazards appear "natural."

NOTES

CHAPTER 1

1. While the English terms "Uptown" and "Downtown" are used explicitly in the Jamaican context to denote distinct classed and racialized spaces, they parallel Papiamentu terms used in Curaçao, where *barios* (neighborhoods) that are *riku* (rich) or *lujo* (luxurious) are contrasted with those that are *marginal, popular,* or *di hende humilde* (of humble people). These different socio-spatial designations are discussed in more detail in Chapter 4.

2. The term "brown environmental problems" refers to the so-called "brown agenda," which prioritizes local, more immediate problems. Brown environmental problems affect mainly the poor, and their impact is primarily on human health. This is in contrast with the global environmental movement's green agenda, which generally prioritizes dispersed and delayed problems that will affect future generations. Problems ranking high on this green agenda tend to be those that mainly impact ecosystem health, and the scale at which they operate is global or regional (McGranahan and Satterthwaite 2002).

3. In fact, this ideal type of ethnographic subject did not originally dwell in the Caribbean either, given the region's problematic anthropological status as "in but not of the West" (see Trouillot 1992; Mintz 1996).

4. Anne Rademacher's (2011) anthropological work, which explores competing definitions of problems and solutions related to the decline of Kathmandu's riverscape, and the connections between urban ecologies and state making, is an important exception.

CHAPTER 2

1. Caribbean urbanism is discussed in the section that follows; for more on Caribbean ecocriticism, see DeLoughrey (2004); DeLoughrey et al. (2005); and Campbell and Somerville (2007).

2. Much of this section draws on the general histories of Kingston provided by Clarke (2006a, 2006b) and Howard (2005).

3. The survey found that the outer walls of 70 percent of the houses were made of boards, while 50 percent of all housing was classified as poor ("damages to the structure, cracked/missing window panes/blades/doors") and 10 percent as very poor ("not fit for human habitation"). In addition, for 64 percent of households, toilet facilities consisted of a pit latrine (SDC 1999a).

4. An SDC survey classified half of Rae Town's available housing stock as good or very good; the other half was characterized as very poor, or not fit for human habitation. Most households had piped water, electricity, and toilets connected to the sewage system, and the community's central location removed some of the obstacles to healthcare and education facilities (SDC 1999b).

5. There are hardly any fish left in the harbor itself, which has become heavily contaminated by a steady flow of untreated sewage and recurring industrial accidents, such as the leaking of 300 tons of sulphuric acid into the harbor in September 2009. Due to pollution of the harbor over an extended period, the harbor floor contained high levels of heavy metals and other toxic matter; government dredging of the harbor (to facilitate the passage of larger ships) resulted in the redistribution of polluted sediment in and around the harbor, significantly damaging the marine life, an effect immediately felt by the fishermen. See Petre Williams-Raynor, Sulphuric Acid Spill at Kingston Harbour, *Jamaica Observer*, September 13, 2009.

6. This section draws primarily on Gill (2008); Römer (1991); and Rupert (2012, 103–162).

7. A 1789 population breakdown of Willemstad lists 47 percent as enslaved Blacks, 22.7 percent as Free Blacks and "Coloreds," 8.9 percent as Sephardic Jews, 17.3 percent as White Protestants, and 4.2 percent as free White servants, out of a total of 11,543 inhabitants (Rupert 2012, 134).

8. In 2012, Curaçao's GDP per capita was US$18,360, compared to Jamaica's US$8,421.

9. See van der Torn (1999) and DCMR Milieudienst Rijnland (2004) for documentation of the refinery's health hazards for downwind communities.

10. See Habitantenan spantá ke pa trata ku bashamentu di shushi ilegal na Seru Fortuna, *RNW*, July 11, 2012, accessed December 31, 2012, at http://www.rnw.nl/papiaments/article/habitantenan-spant%C3%A1-ke-pa-trata-ku-bashamentu-di-shushi-ilegal-na-seru-fortuna.

CHAPTER 3

1. In contrast to the image of the Caribbean island as a tropical paradise, the portrayal of the mainland Guyanas as mystical, wild landscapes has often been filtered through the myth of Eldorado.

2. Though the concerns expressed by these proto-environmentalists were predominantly related to "green" problems of resource depletion, Sachs (2003) argues that colonial figures such as Alexander von Humboldt did link the exploitation of natural resources to the exploitation of specific social groups, a connection resembling those made by environmental justice movements centuries later.

3. For two prominent exceptions, see De Barros (2002) on the entanglement of moral and sanitary discourse in colonial Georgetown, Guyana; and Martinez-Vergne (1999) on the imposition of bourgeois social norms in and through urban space in nineteenth-century San Juan, Puerto Rico.

4. Letter from Milroy to Grey, March 31, 1851, quoted in Milroy (1854, 114).

5. "Extract from the Presentment of the Grand Jury of Kingston," December 21, 1850, quoted in Milroy (1854, 42).

6. This skew Milroy observed was corroborated by John Parkin (1852) in his *Statistical Report of the Epidemic Cholera of Jamaica*.

7. For more on the explanation for the disproportionate morbidity and mortality among the Black population, see Kiple (1985).

8. Letter from Macaulay to Peel, March 1, 1853, quoted in Milroy (1854, 136).

9. Letter from Ambassador Loudon in Washington to the Minister of Foreign Affairs De Marees Van Swinderen ("De Gezant te Washington Loudon aan de Minister van Buitenlandse Zaken De Marees Van Swinderen"), December 6, 1910. No. 1909/346. Received 17 December 1910 (B. Z., B 60, Exh. 26698). This and all other documents cited here in relation to the sanitary investigation are located in the National Archives Curaçao.

10. Letter from the Governor of Curaçao to the Minister of Colonies ("Van de Gouverneur van Curaçao aan de Minister van Koloniën"), July 25, 1912, No. 2464.

11. Letter from the Minister of the Navy to the Minister of Foreign Affairs ("Van de Minister van Marine aan de Minister van Buitenlandse Zaken"), May 3, 1911, Bureau B, No. 60.

12. Letter from the Governor of Curaçao to the Minister of Colonies ("Van de Gouverneur van Curaçao aan de Minister van Koloniën"), July 25, 1912, No. 2464. Decades later, the colonial government restricted prostitution in Curaçao to one state-regulated brothel that employed only migrants in order to "solve" the problem of streetwalkers, curb venereal disease, and safeguard the morality of local women (Kempadoo 2004). See Mayes (2009) for an excellent study of the regulation of prostitution in the Dominican town of San Pedro de Macoris, where spatial interventions made in the name of sanitation and morality were employed by both local elites and the U.S. occupying force to assert specific hierarchies along lines of race, gender, class, and nation.

13. Letter from the Attorney General to the Governor of Curaçao ("Van de Procureur-Generaal aan de Gouverneur van Curaçao"), December 18, 1914, No. 1226.

14. Letter from the Minister for War and Acting Minister of the Navy Colijn to the Minister of Colonies ("Van de Minister voor Oorlog en Ad Interim Minister van Marine Colijn aan de Minister van Koloniën"), March 20, 1913. Department van Marine, Bureau B, No. 40.

15. Letter from Dr. Lens to the Minister of Colonies ("Van Dr. Lens aan de Minister van Koloniën"), October 21, 1914.

16. Letter from the Governor of Curaçao to the Minister of Colonies ("Van de Gouverneur van Curaçao aan de Minister van Koloniën"), July 25, 1912, No. 2464. Nuyens went on to argue that it was too expensive to establish an urban sanitation department. Similarly, while he expressed the need to address the problem of sewage disposal, he emphasized the infrastructural difficulty and prohibitive costs of constructing an underground sewer system. He commended the suggestion that sewage be collected through a system of barrels but deemed this solution exceedingly costly as well.

CHAPTER 4

1. In researching how residents of these four neighborhoods perceived and constructed the urban environment and its various neighborhood components, I drew on two specific research methods. The first was repertory grid methodology, a quantifiable sorting method that I used to "identify the dimensions of appraisal that were employed in evaluating and comparing areas or environments" (Potter 2000, 104–105) and that used small cards with the names of neighborhoods to elicit concepts used to distinguish different urban areas. A second method involved sentence completion, a qualitative method also aimed at determining the manner in which different neighborhoods were perceived and constructed. On the whole, the way sentences were completed corresponded broadly with the categories found in the repertory grid method.

2. These experiences also reflect a broader Jamaican tendency to verbalize visual difference in public space. Others with a nonnormative appearance will go through public space accompanied by calls of "Tall Man," "Mawga Gyal" (if a woman is skinny), or "One-y" (if a person is missing an arm or a leg).

CHAPTER 5

1. For similar concepts of poor, ethnically "other" urban bodies, see Anderson (2006), writing on the colonial Philippines; and Guano (2004), writing on postcolonial Argentina. See Giroux (2007) on the "biopolitics of disposability" that target poor Black and Brown bodies in the United States.

2. Or the urban jungle; cf. Moore et al. (2003, 1).
3. EV, Nasty Habits, *Jamaica Observer*, June 19, 2006, accessed January 3, 2013, at http://www.jamaicaobserver.com/magazines/allwoman/107316_Nasty-habits. See Pelling (1999) for a similar blame-the-poor narrative in the context of urban flooding in Guyana.
4. While many Curaçaoans speak Dutch in addition to Papiamentu, Dutch-language media tend to be the domain of White expats and *koló kla* local elites.
5. Comments under Elisa Koek, Saliña Vervuilt door Trùks di Pan, *versegeperst.com*, July 13, 2007, accessed January 7, 2013, at http://www.versgeperst.com/nieuws/110567/salina-vervuilt-door-truk-di-pans.html. Translations are my own.
6. Comments under Elisa Koek, Tene Kòrsou Limpi!, *versegeperst.com*, August 30, 2011, accessed January 7, 2013, at http://www.versgeperst.com/column/117011/tene-korsou-limpi.html. Translations are my own.
7. See Thompson (2006, 135–155).
8. Dawn Ritch, A Search for Cultural Identity, *Jamaica Gleaner*, February 8, 2004.

CHAPTER 6

1. Dutch Caribbean Nature Alliance, About DCNA, accessed September 20, 2013, at http://www.dcnanature.org/about-dcna/.
2. Dutch Caribbean Nature Alliance, Trust Fund, accessed September 20, 2013, at http://www.dcnanature.org/about-dnca/trust-fund/.
3. Petre Williams, NEEC Gets New Boss, *Jamaica Observer*, March 9, 2008.
4. Petre Williams-Raynor, Storm over Blue Lagoon: Developers, Environmentalist Wage Bitter Battle over Blue Lagoon, *Jamaica Observer*, May 15, 2011, accessed August 20, 2013, at http://www.jamaicaobserver.com/news/Storm-over-Blue-Lagoon _8793030.
5. Tempest in a Teapot, *Jamaica Observer*, May 18, 2011.
6. David McFadden, Battle Brews in Jamaica Over Blue Lagoon's Fate: Commerce Might Trump Cove's Beauty, *Washington Post*, July 25, 2011, accessed August 20, 2013, at http://m.washingtontimes.com/news/2011/jul/25/battle-brews-in-jamaica-over-blue-lagoons-fate/.

CHAPTER 7

1. Like Riverton, Bactu, Seaview, Waterhouse, and Kintyre are names of Kingston "ghettos."
2. MP = Member of Parliament, representing one of sixty constituencies; councilors represent a total of 275 smaller electoral divisions within Jamaica.
3. Tempest in a Teapot, *Jamaica Observer*, May 18, 2011.

4. For an extensive analysis of the quantitative and qualitative results, and a more detailed discussion of the survey instrument, see Jaffe (2006, 2008).

5. See Chevannes (1994, 32–33) for a related interpretation of Jamaican views of the human, natural, and supernatural worlds. Similar versions of environmental thought can be found in the scarce ethno-ecological literature on the Caribbean (e.g., Ringel and Wylie 1979; Bonniol 1979).

6. In her research on the environment in Dominica, Thérèse Yarde (2012) also points out the extent to which environmental studies has concentrated on environmental thought over embodied experience.

7. http://www.youtube.com/watch?v=Mviu3RUtEnU. The clip originally aired on Jamaica's CVM television station. The original clip was spoofed multiple times, with men in wigs and miniskirts parodying Rosie's performance.

8. "May 30," or *trinta di mei*, refers to what is known as the "revolt" of 1969. Against a background of Curaçao's rigid socio-economic, racialized, and cultural gap between the privileged few and the masses, frustration with the status quo erupted when a labor protest developed into a full-scale revolt, and a large part of the old city center was looted, destroyed, or burnt down. Following the revolt, a process of "Antilleanization" helped break some colonial patterns, but in general the events did not lead to an overall political or social transformation. For more on the events and impact of *trinta di mei*, see Römer (1998, 54–57); and Oostindie (1999).

9. It is perhaps not coincidental in this regard that the most visible examples of environmental justice struggles in the region have been in the Spanish-speaking Caribbean, and particularly in Puerto Rico, where activists mobilized successfully against the U.S. Navy's use of the island of Vieques as a practice bombing range, which led to major soil and water contamination and negative impacts on human and ecological health (McCaffrey 2008; Baver 2012).

CHAPTER 8

1. High Risk Emissions from Riverton Fire—NEPA Air Quality Report, *Jamaican Observer*, April 4, 2012, accessed February 19, 2014, at http://www.jamaicaobserver.com/news/High-risk-emissions-from-Riverton-fire---NEPA-air-quality-report_11190402.

2. The Jamaican official's actual title is the "Minister of Water, Land, Environment and Climate Change." The National Solid Waste Management Authority is part of the portfolio of the minister of local government and community development.

3. Peter Espeut, The Winds of Change, *Jamaica Gleaner*, March 20, 2015, accessed at http://jamaica-gleaner.com/article/commentary/20150320/winds-change.

4. See, e.g., Elisa Koek, Amigu di Tera Wint, *versgeperst.com*, May 24, 2011, accessed March 4, 2014, at http://www.versgeperst.com/nieuws/104855/amigu-di-tera-wint.html.

REFERENCES

Adamson, Joni, Mei Mei Evans, and Rachel Stein, eds. 2002. *The Environmental Justice Reader: Politics, Poetics and Pedagogy*. Tucson: University of Arizona Press.

Agrawal, Arun. 2005. *Environmentality: Technologies of Government and the Making of Subjects*. Durham, NC: Duke University Press.

Allen, Rose Mary. 2003. Acceptatie of uitsluiting?: enkele belangrijke invalshoeken voor de discussie over beeldvorming over immigranten uit de regio en over de Curaçaoënaars. In *Emancipatie en acceptatie: Curaçao en Curaçaoenaars: Beeldvorming en identiteit onderveertig jaar na de slavernij*, ed. Rose Mary Allen, Coen Heijes, and Valdemar Marcha, pp. 72–90. Amsterdam: SWP.

———. 2010. The Complexity of National Identity Construction in Curaçao, Dutch Caribbean. *European Review of Latin American and Caribbean Studies* 89:117–125.

Alofs, Luc. 2011. *Onderhorigheid en separatisme: Koloniaal bestuur en lokale politiek op Aruba, 1816–1955*. Ph.D. thesis, Leiden University.

Anand, Nikhil. 2012. Municipal Disconnect: On Abject Water and Its Urban Infrastructures. *Ethnography* 13 (4): 487–509.

Anderson, Warwick. 2006. *Colonial Pathologies: American Tropical Medicine, Race, and Hygiene in the Philippines*. Durham, NC: Duke University Press.

Aoyagi, K., P. J. M. Nas, and J. W. Traphagan, eds. 1998. *Toward Sustainable Cities: Readings in the Anthropology of Urban Environments*. Leiden: Leiden Development Studies.

Appadurai, Arjun. 1988. Putting Hierarchy in Its Place. *Cultural Anthropology* 3 (1): 36–49.

Arabindoo, Pushpa. 2011. Mobilising for Water: Hydro-Politics of Rainwater Harvesting in Chennai. *International Journal of Urban Sustainable Development* 3 (1): 106–126.

Argyrou, Vassos. 2005. *The Logic of Environmentalism: Anthropology, Ecology and Postcoloniality*. New York and Oxford: Berghahn.

Arthur Andersen. 1996. *Programma "Sociaal vernieuwingsproces Wishi/Marchena en omgeving."* Curaçao: Arthur Andersen.

Austin-Broos, Diane. 1994. Race/Class: Jamaica's Discourse of Heritable Identity. *New West Indian Guide* 68 (3/4): 213–233.

Auyero, Javier. 2012. *Patients of the State: The Politics of Waiting in Argentina.* Durham, NC: Duke University Press.

Auyero, Javier, and Agustín Burbano de Lara. 2012. In Harm's Way at the Urban Margins. *Ethnography* 13 (4): 531–557.

Auyero, Javier, and Débora Alejandra Swistun. 2009. *Flammable: Environmental Suffering in an Argentine Shantytown.* Oxford: Oxford University Press.

Barrow, Christine. 1998. *Caribbean Portraits: Essays on Gender Ideologies and Identities.* Kingston, Jamaica: Ian Randle Publishers.

Barton, Gregory A. 2002. *Empire Forestry and the Origins of Environmentalism.* Cambridge: Cambridge University Press.

Baver, Sherrie. 2012. Environmental Struggles in Paradise: Puerto Rican Cases, Caribbean Lessons. *Caribbean Studies* 40 (1): 15–35.

Baviskar, Amita. 2003. Between Violence and Desire: Space, Power, and Identity in the Making of Metropolitan Delhi. *International Social Science Journal* 55 (175): 89–98.

Bewell, Alan. 1999. *Romanticism and Colonial Disease.* Baltimore: Johns Hopkins University Press.

Blokland, Talja. 2008. "You Got to Remember You Live in Public Housing": Place-Making in an American Housing Project. *Housing, Theory and Society* 25 (1): 31–46.

Bonniol, Jean-Luc. 1979. Perceptions of the Environment in a Small Island Community: Terre de Haut des Saintes. In *Perceptions of the Environment: A Selection of Interpretative Essays*, ed. Y. Renard, pp. 53–68. Barbados: Caribbean Conservation Association.

Bookchin, Murray. 1994. *Which Way for the Ecology Movement?* Edinburgh and San Francisco: AK Press.

Brown-Glaude, Winnifred R. 2011. *Higglers in Kingston: Women's Informal Work in Jamaica.* Nashville: Vanderbilt University Press.

Buell, Lawrence. 1995. *The Environmental Imagination: Thoreau, Nature Writing and the Formation of American Culture.* Cambridge, MA: Harvard University Press.

Bullard, Robert D. 1994. The Legacy of American Apartheid and Environmental Racism. *St. John's Journal of Legal Commentary* 9 (2): 445–474.

———. 2000. *Dumping in Dixie: Race, Class, and Environmental Quality.* Boulder, CO: Westview Press.

Burawoy, Michael, Joseph A. Blum, Sheba George, Zsuzsa Gille, and Millie Thayer. 2000. *Global Ethnography: Forces, Connections, and Imaginations in a Postmodern World.* Berkeley and Los Angeles: University of California Press.

Butler, Judith. 1990. *Gender Trouble: Feminism and the Subversion of Identity.* New York: Routledge.

———. 1993. *Bodies That Matter: On the Discursive Limits of "Sex."* New York: Routledge.

Caldeira, Teresa. 2000. *City of Walls: Crime, Segregation and Citizenship in São Paulo.* Berkeley: University of California Press.

Campbell, Chris, and Erin Somerville, eds. 2007. *"What Is the Earthly Paradise?" Ecocritical Responses to the Caribbean.* Cambridge: Cambridge Scholars Publishing.

Cañizares-Esguerra, Jorge, Matt D. Childs, and James Sidbury, eds. 2013. *The Black Urban Atlantic in the Age of the Slave Trade.* Philadelphia: University of Pennsylvania Press.

Carnegie, Charles V. 2014. The Loss of the Verandah: Kingston's Constricted Postcolonial Geographies. *Social and Economic Studies* 63 (2): 59–85.

Carrier, James G. 2003. Mind, Gaze and Engagement: Understanding the Environment. *Journal of Material Culture* 8 (1): 5–23.

Central Bureau of Statistics (CBS). 1993. *Third Population and Housing Census Netherlands Antilles 1992.* Willemstad: CBS.

———. 2002. *Fourth Population and Housing Census Netherlands Antilles 2001.* Volume 2, *Selected Tables.* Willemstad: CBS.

———. 2004. Census 2001, unpublished statistical data.

Centrale Gezondheidsraad. 1913. *Rapport omtrent de voorzieningen die op sanitair gebied te Willemstad waren te treffen ten einde deze haven te doen beantwoorden aan de hoogere eischen die het, met het oog op de opening van het Panamakanaal te verwachten grooter scheepvaartverkeer, zal stellen.* Willemstad: Centrale Gezondheidsraad.

Checker, Melissa. 2001. "Like Nixon Coming to China": Finding Common Ground in a Multi-Ethnic Coalition for Environmental Justice. *Anthropological Quarterly* 74 (3): 135–146.

———. 2005. *Polluted Promises: Environmental Racism and the Search for Justice in a Southern Town.* New York and London: New York University Press.

———. 2008. Eco-apartheid and Global Greenwaves: African Diasporic Environmental Justice Movements. *Souls* 10 (4): 390–408.

———. 2011. Wiped Out by the "Greenwave": Environmental Gentrification and the Paradoxical Politics of Urban Sustainability. *City & Society* 23 (2): 210–229.

Chevannes, Barry. 1994. *Rastafari: Roots and Ideology.* Syracuse, NY: Syracuse University Press.

———. 2001. Jamaican Diasporic Identity: The Metaphor of Yaad. In *Nation Dance: Religion, Identity and Cultural Difference in the Caribbean,* ed. P. Taylor, pp. 129–137. Bloomington and Indianapolis: Indiana University Press.

Chevannes, Barry and Herbert Gayle. 1998. *Solid Waste Management: Profiles of Inner City Communities in the Kingston Metropolitan Area.* Kingston: UWI Mona, Faculty of Social Sciences.

Clarke, Colin G. 2006a. *Decolonizing the Colonial City: Urbanization and Stratification in Kingston, Jamaica*. Oxford: Oxford University Press.

———. 2006b. *Kingston, Jamaica: Urban Development and Social Change, 1692–2002*. Kingston: Ian Randle Publishers.

Comaroff, J., and J. L. Comaroff. 2001. Naturing the Nation: Aliens, Apocalypse, and the Postcolonial State. *Social Identities* 7 (2): 233–265.

Commonwealth Secretariat. 2002. *Jamaica: Master Plan for Sustainable Tourism Development*. London: Commonwealth Secretariat.

Cronon, William, ed. 1996. *Uncommon Ground: Rethinking the Human Place in Nature*. New York: W. W. Norton.

Cresswell, Tim. 2006. *On the Move: Mobility in the Modern Western World*. New York and Oxford: Routledge.

Cross, Malcolm. 1979. *Urbanization and Urban Growth in the Caribbean: An Essay on Social Change in Dependent Societies*. Cambridge: Cambridge University Press.

Curaçao Tourism Board (CTB). 2005. *Update of Curaçao Tourism Development Plan (2005–2009)*. Willemstad: CTB.

Curtin, Philip D. 1989. *Death by Migration: Europe's Encounter with the Tropical World in the Nineteenth Century*. Cambridge: Cambridge University Press.

Dash, J. Michael. 1998. *The Other America: Caribbean Literature in a New World Context*. Charlottesville: University Press of Virginia.

Dutch Caribbean Nature Alliance (DCNA). 2013. *DCNA Annual Report 2012*. Kralendijk: DNCA.

DCMR Milieudienst Rijnmond and Stichting WTTZ. 2004. *Fact-Finding Missie Isla Raffinaderij Curaçao*. DCMR Milieudienst Rijnmond.

De Barros, Juanita. 2002. *Order and Place in a Colonial City: Patterns of Struggle and Resistance in Georgetown, British Guiana, 1889–1924*. Montreal: McGill-Queens University Press.

de Bruijn, Jeanne, and Maartje Groot. 2014. *Regionale Migratie en Integratie op Curaçao*. Willemstad: SOAW.

Dear, Michael. 2005. Comparative Urbanism. *Urban Geography* 26 (3): 247–251.

DeLoughrey, Elizabeth. 2004. Island Ecologies and Caribbean Literatures. *Tijdschrift voor Economische en Sociale Geografie* 95 (3): 298–310.

DeLoughrey, Elizabeth M., Renée K. Gosson, and George B. Handley, eds. 2005. *Caribbean Literature and the Environment: Between Nature and Culture*. Charlottesville: University of Virginia Press.

Dillman, Jefferson. 2015. *Colonizing Paradise: Landscape and Empire in the British West Indies*. Tuscaloosa: University of Alabama Press.

Dinzey-Flores, Zaire Zenit. 2013. *Locked In, Locked Out: Gated Communities in a Puerto Rican City*. Philadelphia: University of Pennsylvania Press.

Dixon, John, Mark Levine, and Rob McAuley. 2006. Locating Impropriety: Street Drinking, Moral Order, and the Ideological Dilemma of Public Space. *Political Psychology* 27 (2): 187–206.

Dodman, David R. 2004. Community Perspectives on Urban Environmental Problems in Kingston, Jamaica. *Social and Economic Studies* 53 (3): 31–59.

Douglas, M. T. 2002 [1966]. *Purity and Danger: An Analysis of Concepts of Pollution and Taboo.* London: Routledge.

Dove, Michael R., Percy E. Sajise, and Amity A. Doolittle, eds. 2011. *Beyond the Sacred Forest: Complicating Conservation in Southeast Asia.* Durham, NC: Duke University Press.

Drayton, Richard. 2000. *Nature's Government: Science, Imperial Britain, and the "Improvement" of the World.* New Haven, CT: Yale University Press.

Driver, Felix. 2004. Imagining the Tropics: Views and Visions of the Tropical World. *Progress in Human Geography* 25 (1): 1–17.

DuPuis, E. Melanie, ed. 2004. *Smoke and Mirrors: The Politics and Culture of Air Pollution.* New York: New York University Press.

Dwivedi, Ranjit. 2001. Environmental Movements in the Global South: Issues of Livelihood and Beyond. *International Sociology* 16 (1): 11–31.

Edmond, Rod. 2005. Returning Fears: Tropical Disease and the Metropolis. In *Tropical Visions in an Age of Empire*, ed. Felix Driver and Luciana Martins, pp. 175–194. Chicago: University of Chicago Press.

Environmental Foundation of Jamaica (EFJ). 2005. *Financial Statements, 31 July 2005.* Accessed at http://www.efj.org.jm/sites/default/files/efj_2005_audit_fin_stmt.pdf, November 20, 2015.

Ernstson, Henrik, Mary Lawhon, and James Duminy. 2014. Conceptual Vectors of African Urbanism: "Engaged Theory-Making" and "Platforms of Engagement." *Regional Studies* 48 (9): 1563–1577.

Escobar, Arturo. 2008. *Territories of Difference: Place, Movements, Life, Redes.* Durham: Duke University Press.

Eyre, L. A. 1997. Self-Help Housing in Jamaica. In: *Self-Help Housing, the Poor, and the State in the Caribbean*, ed. Robert B. Potter and Denis Conway, pp. 75–101. Knoxville: University of Tennessee Press.

Ferguson, Therese, and Elizabeth Thomas-Hope. 2006. Environmental Education and Constructions of Sustainable Development in Jamaica. In *Sustainable Development: National Aspirations, Local Implementation*, ed. Jennifer Hill, Alan Terry, and Wendy Woodland, pp. 91–113. Aldershot, UK: Ashgate.

Ford, J. C., and A. A. C. Finlay. 1903. *The Handbook of Jamaica for 1903, Comprising Historical, Statistical and General Information Concerning the Island, Compiled from Official and Other Reliable Sources.* Kingston, Jamaica: Government Printing Office.

Foucault, Michel. 1977. *Discipline and Punish: The Birth of the Prison*, trans. A. Sheridan. New York: Pantheon Books.

———. 1980. *Power/Knowledge: Selected Interviews and Other Writings, 1972–1977.* New York: Pantheon Books.

Gandy, Matthew. 2004. Rethinking Urban Metabolism: Water, Space and the Modern City. *City* 8 (3):363–379.

Garner, Andrew. 2009. Uncivil Society: Local Stakeholders and Environmental Protection in Jamaica. In *Virtualism, Governance and Practice: Vision and Execution in Environmental Conservation*, ed. James G. Carrier and Paige West, pp. 134–154. Oxford and New York: Berghahn Books.

Garrard, Greg. 2004. *Ecocriticism*. London: Routledge.

———. 2012. Worlds Without Us: Some Types of Disanthropy. *SubStance* 41 (1): 40–60.

Geoghegan, Tighe. 2009. Creolising Conservation: Caribbean Responses to Global Trends in Environmental Management. In *Virtualism, Governance and Practice: Vision and Execution in Environmental Conservation*, ed. James G. Carrier and Paige West, pp. 112–133. Oxford and New York: Berghahn Books.

George, H., W. Hoogbergen, S. Huybregts, D. Kruijt, W. de Luca, and R. Wijngaarde. 2003. *Atakando Probesa: Armoedebestrijding door Integrale Wijkaanpak*. Amsterdam: Rozenberg.

George, Kemi. 2009. Framing Vulnerability in Jamaica's Cockpit Country. In *Global Change and Caribbean Vulnerability: Environment, Economy and Society at Risk*, ed. Duncan McGregor, David Dodman, and David Barker, pp. 142–164. Kingston, Jamaica: University of the West Indies Press.

Gieryn, Thomas F. 2000. A Space for Place in Sociology. *Annual Review of Sociology* 26 (1): 463–496.

Gill, Ronald G. 2008. *Een eeuw architectuur op Curaçao: De architectuur en stedenbouw van de twintigste eeuw op Curaçao*. Willemstad: Stichting Het Curaçaosch Museum.

Giroux, Henry A. 2007. Violence, Katrina, and the Biopolitics of Disposability. *Theory, Culture and Society* 24 (7/8): 305–309.

Goldberg, Daniel Theo. 1993. "Polluting the Body Politic": Racist Discourse and Urban Location. In *Racism, the City and the State*, ed. M. Cross and Michael Keith, pp. 45–60. Oxford and New York: Routledge.

Goldman, Michael, and Rachel A. Schurman. 2000. Closing the "Great Divide": New Social Theory on Society and Nature. *Annual Review of Sociology* 26:563–584.

Goldstein, Daniel. 2004. *The Spectacular City: Violence and Performance in Urban Bolivia*. Durham, NC: Duke University Press.

Gotham, Kevin Fox, and Krista Brumley. 2002. Using Space: Agency and Identity in a Public-Housing Development. *City and Community* 13: 267–289.

Graham, Stephen, and Simon Marvin. 2001. *Splintering Urbanism: Networked Infrastructures, Technological Mobilities and the Urban Condition*. London and New York: Routledge.

Gregory, Derek. 1995. Imaginative Geographies. *Progress in Human Geography* 19 (4): 447–485.

Grove, Richard H. 1995. *Green Imperialism: Colonial Expansion, Tropical Island Edens and the Origins of Environmentalism, 1600–1860.* Cambridge: Cambridge University Press.

———. 1997. *Ecology, Climate and Empire: Colonialism and Global Environmental History, 1400–1940.* Cambridge: White Horse Press.

Guano, Emanuela. 2004. The Denial of Citizenship: "Barbaric" Buenos Aires and the Middle-Class Imaginary. *City & Society* 16 (1): 69–97.

Guha, Ramachandra, and José Martinez-Alier. 1998. *Varieties of Environmentalism: Essays North and South.* New Delhi: Oxford University Press.

Gupta, Akhil, and James Ferguson. 1992. Beyond "Culture": Space, Identity, and the Politics of Difference. *Cultural Anthropology* 7 (1): 6–23.

Haas, Peter M. 1992. Introduction: Epistemic Communities and International Policy Coordination. *International Organization* 46:1–35.

Hajer, Maarten A. 1995. *The Politics of Environmental Discourse: Ecological Modernization and the Policy Process.* Oxford: Oxford University Press.

Harper, Douglas. 2002. Talking About Pictures: A Case for Photo Elicitation. *Visual Studies* 17 (1): 13–26.

Hartert, Ernst. 1893. XXIX: On the Birds of the Islands of Aruba, Curaçao, and Bonaire. *Ibis* 35 (3): 289–338.

Harvey, David. 1996. *Justice, Nature and the Geography of Difference.* Oxford: Blackwell.

Head, L., and P. Muir. 2006. Suburban Life and the Boundaries of Nature: Resilience and Rupture in Australian Backyard Gardens. *Transactions of the Institute of British Geographers* 31 (4): 505–524.

Heynen, Nik. 2003. The Scalar Production of Injustice Within the Urban Forest. *Antipode* 35:980–998.

Higgins, Robert R. 1994. Race, Pollution, and the Mastery of Nature. *Environmental Ethics* 16 (3): 251–264.

Holmes, Douglas R., and George E. Marcus. 2005. Cultures of Expertise and the Management of Globalization: Toward the Re-Functioning of Ethnography. In *Global Assemblages: Technology, Politics, and Ethics as Anthropological Problems*, ed. Aihwa Ong and Stephen J. Collier, pp. 235–252. Malden, MA: Blackwell.

Hope Enterprises Ltd. 1999. *NEEC Campaign Pretest Report: A Qualitative Assessment.* Kingston, Jamaica: NEEC and CGR Communications Ltd.

Howard, David. 2005. *Kingston: A Cultural and Literary History.* Kingston, Jamaica: Ian Randle Publishers.

Ioris, Antonio Augusto Rossotto. 2012. Applying the Strategic-Relational Approach to Urban Political Ecology: The Water Management Problems of the Baixada Fluminense, Rio de Janeiro, Brazil. *Antipode* 44 (1): 122–150.

Jácome, Francine. 2006. Environmental Movements in the Caribbean. In *Beyond Sun and Sand: Caribbean Environmentalisms*, ed. L. Baver and B. D. Lynch, pp. 17–31. New Brunswick and London: Rutgers University Press.

Jaffe, Rivke. 2006. A View from the Concrete Jungle: Diverging Environmentalisms in the Urban Caribbean. *New West Indian Guide* 80 (3/4): 221–243.

———. 2008. As Lion Rule the Jungle, So Man Rule the Earth: Perceptions of Nature and the Environment in Two Caribbean Cities. *Wadabagei: A Journal of the Caribbean and Its Diaspora* 11 (3): 46–69.

———. 2009. Conflicting Environments: Negotiating Social and Ecological Vulnerabilities in Urban Jamaica and Curaçao. In *Global Change and Caribbean Vulnerability: Environment, Economy and Society at Risk*, ed. Duncan McGregor, David Dodman, and David Barker, pp. 317–335. Kingston, Jamaica: University of the West Indies Press.

———. 2010. Ital Chic: Rastafari, Resistance, and the Politics of Consumption in Jamaica. *Small Axe* 14 (1): 30–45.

Jaffe, Rivke, Ad de Bruijne, and Aart Schalkwijk. 2008. The Caribbean City: An Introduction. In *The Caribbean City*, ed. Rivke Jaffe, pp. 1–23. Kingston/ Leiden: Ian Randle Publishers/KITLV.

Jaffe, Rivke, and Anouk de Koning. 2016. *Introducing Urban Anthropology*. London and New York: Routledge.

Johnson, Hume Nicola. 2008. Performing Protest in Jamaica: The Mass Media as Stage. *International Journal of Media & Cultural Politics* 4 (2): 163–182.

Kaika, Maria. 2005. *City of Flows: Modernity, Nature and the City*. London and New York: Routledge.

Kempadoo, Kamala. 2004. *Sexing the Caribbean: Gender, Race and Sexual Labor*. New York and London: Routledge.

Khan, Shalini. 2010. *Infectious Entanglements: Literary and Medical Representations of Disease in the Post/Colonial Caribbean*. Ph.D. thesis, Queen's University.

King, Anthony D. 1990. *Urbanism, Colonialism, and the World-Economy: Cultural and Spatial Foundations of the World Urban System*. New York: Routledge.

Kiple, K. F. 1985. Cholera and Race in the Caribbean. *Journal of Latin American Studies* 17 (1): 157–177.

Kitchen, Lawrence. 2013. Are Trees Always "Good"? Urban Political Ecology and Environmental Justice in the Valleys of South Wales. *International Journal of Urban and Regional Research* 37 (6): 1968–1983.

Klaufus, Christien. 2012. The Symbolic Dimension of Mobility: Architecture and Social Status in Ecuadorian Informal Settlements. *International Journal of Urban and Regional Research* 36 (4): 689–705.

Knorr Cetina, Karin. 1999. *Epistemic Cultures: How the Sciences Make Knowledge*. Cambridge, MA: Harvard University Press.

Latour, Bruno. 1993. *We Have Never Been Modern*. Cambridge, MA: Harvard University Press.

Lawhon, Mary, Henrik Ernstson, and Jonathan Silver. 2014. Provincializing Urban Political Ecology: Towards a Situated UPE Through African Urbanism. *Antipode* 46 (2): 497–516.

Ledgister, F. S. J. 2012. Revolutionising Democracy in 1970s Jamaica: D. K. Duncan and the Quest for a Better World. Paper presented at the Caribbean Studies Association 37th Annual Conference, Le Gosier, Guadeloupe, May 28–June 1.

Lefebvre, Henri. 1991. *The Production of Space*. Oxford: Blackwell Publishing.

Levy, Catherine. 1996. The Environmental NGO Movement in Jamaica. *Jamaica Journal* 26: 22–25.

Li, Tania Murray. 2007. *The Will to Improve*. Durham, NC: Duke University Press.

Light, Andrew. 2001. The Urban Blind Spot in Environmental Ethics. *Environmental Politics* 10 (1): 7–35.

Livingstone, David N. 1999. Tropical Climate and Moral Hygiene: The Anatomy of a Victorian Debate. *British Journal for the History of Science* 32 (112): 93–110.

Lora-Wainwright, Anna, Yiyun Zhang, Yunmei Wu, and Benjamin Van Rooij. 2012. Learning to Live with Pollution: The Making of Environmental Subjects in a Chinese Industrialized Village. *China Journal* 68: 106–124.

Lundy, Patricia. 1999. Fragmented Community Action or New Social Movement? A Study of Environmentalism in Jamaica. *International Sociology* 14:83–102.

Malkki, Liisa. 1992. National Geographic: The Rooting of Peoples and the Territorialization of National Identity Among Scholars and Refugees. *Cultural Anthropology* 7 (1): 24–44.

Martinez-Vergne, Teresita. 1999. *Shaping the Discourse on Space: Charity and Its Wards in Nineteenth-Century San Juan, Puerto Rico*. Austin: University of Texas Press.

Mawdsley, Emma. 2004. India's Middle Classes and the Environment. *Development and Change* 35 (1): 79–103.

Mayes, April J. 2009. Tolerating Sex: Prostitution, Gender, and Governance in the Dominican Republic, 1880s–1924. In *Health and Medicine in the Circum-Caribbean, 1800–1968*, ed. J. De Barros, S. Palmer, and D. Wright, pp. 121–141. Oxford and New York: Routledge.

McCaffrey, Katherine T. 2008. The Struggle for Environmental Justice in Vieques, Puerto Rico. In *Environmental Justice in Latin America: Problems, Promise and Practice*, ed. David V. Carruthers, pp. 263–285. Cambridge, MA: MIT Press.

McDonogh, Gary Wray. 2003. Myth, Space and Virtue: Bars, Gender and Change in Barcelona's *Barrio Chino*. In *The Anthropology of Space and Place: Locating Culture*, ed. Setha Low and Denise Lawrence-Zúñiga, pp. 264–283. Malden, MA: Blackwell.

McFarlane, Colin. 2010. The Comparative City: Knowledge, Learning, Urbanism. *International Journal of Urban and Regional Research* 34 (4): 725–742.

McGranahan, Gordon, and David Satterthwaite. 2002. Environmental Health or Ecological Sustainability? Reconciling the Brown and Green Agendas in Urban Development. In *Planning in Cities: Sustainability and Growth in the Developing World*, ed. R. Zetter and R. White, pp. 43–57. London: ITDG Publishing.

Mills, Charles W. 2001. Black Trash. In *Faces of Environmental Racism: Confronting Issues of Global Justice*, ed. L. Westra and B. E. Lawson, pp. 73–94. Lanham, MD: Rowman and Littlefield.

Milroy, Gavin. 1854 [1852]. *The Report on the Cholera in Jamaica and on the General Sanitary Condition and Wants of the Island*. London: George Edward Eyre and William Spottiswoode.

Ministry of Social Development, Labor and Welfare (SOAW). 2012a. *Buurtprofiel Wishi: Een beeld van de zone Wishi te Curaçao*. Willemstad: SOAW.

———. 2012b. *Buurtprofiel Fortuna: Een beeld van de zone Fortuna te Curaçao*. Willemstad: SOAW.

———. 2014. *Building a Life, Building a Nation: Facts and Faces of Regional Migration and Integration in Curaçao*. Willemstad: SOAW.

Mintz, Sidney W. 1996. Enduring Substances, Trying Theories: The Caribbean Region as "Oikoumenê." *Journal of the Royal Anthropological Institute* 2 (2): 289–311.

Mitchell, W. J. T. 2002. Imperial Landscape. In *Landscape and Power*, 2nd ed., ed. W. J. T. Mitchell, pp. 5–34. Chicago: University of Chicago Press.

Mohammed, Asad. 2008. Colonial Influences on Urban Form in the Caribbean: Illustrated by Port of Spain, Trinidad and Tobago. In *The Caribbean City*, ed. R. Jaffe. Kingston/Leiden: Ian Randle Publishers/KITLV.

Mohammed, Patricia, ed. 2002. *Gendered Realities: Essays in Caribbean Feminist Thought*. Kingston, Jamaica: University of West Indies Press.

Moore, Donald S., Anand Pandian, and Jake Kosek. 2003. Introduction: The Cultural Politics of Race and Nature: Terrains of Power and Practice. In *Race, Nature, and the Politics of Difference*, ed. D. S. Moore, J. Kosek, and A. Pandian, pp. 1–70. Durham and London: Duke University Press.

Nader, Louise. 1980. The Vertical Slice: Hierarchies and Children. In *Hierarchy and Society: Anthropological Perspectives on Bureaucracy*, ed. G. Britain and R. Cohen, pp. 31–43. Philadelphia: Institute for the Study of Human Issues.

National Resource Conservation Agency (NRCA). 1997. *Jamaica State of the Environment Report*. Kingston, Jamaica: NRCA.

National Environment and Planning Agency (NEPA). 1999. *JANEAP (Jamaica National Environmental Action Plan) 1999–2002*. Kingston, Jamaica: NEPA.

———. 2002. *JANEAP (Jamaica National Environmental Action Plan): 2002 Status Report*. Kingston, Jamaica: NEPA.

———. 2006. *JANEAP (Jamaica National Environmental Action Plan) 2006–2009*. Kingston, Jamaica: NEPA.

———. 2011. *State of the Environment Report 2010*. Kingston, Jamaica: NEPA.

———. 2015. *Report on Ambient Air Quality Monitoring Conducted in the Kingston Metropolitan Area (KMA) in Response to the Fire at the Riverton City Solid Waste Disposal Facility (11–30 March 2015)*. Kingston, Jamaica: NEPA.

Nelson, Velvet. 2007. Traces of the Past: The Cycle of Expectation in Caribbean Tourism Representations. *Journal of Tourism and Cultural Change* 5 (1): 1–16.

Nettleford, Rex. 1978. *Caribbean Cultural Identity: The Case of Jamaica*. Los Angeles: CAAS.

Nijman, Jan. 2007a. Introduction: Comparative Urbanism. *Urban Geography* 28 (1): 1–6.

———. 2007b. Place-Particularity and "Deep Analogies": A Comparative Essay on Miami's Rise as a World City. *Urban Geography* 28 (1): 92–107.

Noble, Greg. 2005. The Discomfort of Strangers: Racism, Incivility and Ontological Security in a Relaxed and Comfortable Nation. *Journal of Intercultural Studies* 26 (1–2): 107–120.

Nygren, Anja. 2012. Review of Javier Auyero and Débora Alejandra Swistun, *Flammable: Environmental Suffering in an Argentine Shantytown*. *Critique of Anthropology* 32: 353–355.

Olsen, J. 1999. *Nature and Nationalism: Right-Wing Ecology and the Politics of Identity in Contemporary Germany*. New York: St. Martin's Press.

Oostindie, Gert, ed. 1999. *Curaçao, 30 Mei 1969: Verhalen over de Revolte*. Amsterdam: Amsterdam University Press.

Osborne, T., and N. Rose. 1999. Governing Cities: Notes on the Spatialisation of Virtue. *Environment and Planning D: Society and Space* 17 (6): 743.

Otuokon, Susan, and Shauna-Lee Chai. 2009. Building Capacity and Resilience to Adapt to Change: The Case of the Blue and John Crow Mountains National Park. In *Global Change and Caribbean Vulnerability: Environment, Economy and Society at Risk*, ed. Duncan McGregor, David Dodman, and David Barker, pp. 165–193. Kingston, Jamaica: University of the West Indies Press.

Parkin, John 1852. *Statistical Report of the Epidemic Cholera of Jamaica*. London: William H. Allen; Highley & Son.

Paton, Diana. 2004. *No Bond but the Law: Punishment, Race, and Gender in Jamaican State Formation, 1780–1870*. Durham, NC: Duke University Press.

Pelling, Mark. 1999. The Political Ecology of Flood Hazard in Urban Guyana. *Geoforum* 30 (3): 249–261.

Pellow, David Naguib. 2005. Environmental Racism: Inequality in a Toxic World. In *The Blackwell Companion to Social Inequalities*, ed. Mary Romero and Eric Margolis, pp. 147–164. Malden, MA, and Oxford: Blackwell.

Potter, Robert B. 1989. Urbanization, Planning and Development in the Caribbean: An Introduction. In *Urbanization, Planning and Development in the Caribbean*, ed. R. B. Potter, pp. 1–20. London: Mansell.

———. 2000. *The Urban Caribbean in an Era of Global Change*. Aldershot, UK: Ashgate.

Prashad, Vijay. 1994. Native Dirt/Imperial Ordure: The Cholera of 1832 and the Morbid Resolutions of Modernity. *Journal of Historical Sociology* 7 (3): 243–260.

Pulido, Laura. 1996. A Critical Review of the Methodology of Environmental Racism Research. *Antipode* 28 (2): 142–159.

———. 2000. Rethinking Environmental Racism: White Privilege and Urban Development in Southern California. *Annals of the Association of American Geographers* 90 (1): 12–40.

Rademacher, Anne. 2011. *Reigning the River: Urban Ecologies and Political Transformation in Kathmandu*. Durham, NC: Duke University Press.

Ramphall, Davin. 1997. Postmodernism and the Rewriting of Caribbean Radical Development Thinking. *Social and Economic Studies* 46:1–30.

Raymond, Mark. 2013. Locating Caribbean Architecture: Narratives and Strategies. *Small Axe* 17 (2): 186–202.

Ren, Julie, and Jason Luger. 2015. Comparative Urbanism and the "Asian City": Implications for Research and Theory. *International Journal of Urban and Regional Research* 39 (1): 145–156.

Ringel, Gail, and Jonathan Wylie. 1979. God's Work: Perceptions of the Environment in Dominica. In *Perceptions of the Environment: A Selection of Interpretative Essays*, ed. Yves Renard, pp. 39–50. Barbados: Caribbean Conservation Association.

Robbins, Paul. 2004. *Political Ecology: A Critical Introduction*. Oxford: Blackwell.

Robbins, Paul, and Julie Sharp. 2003. The Lawn-Chemical Economy and Its Discontents. *Antipode* 35 (5): 955–979.

Robinson, Jennifer. 2004. In the Tracks of Comparative Urbanism: Difference, Urban Modernity and the Primitive. *Urban Geography* 25 (8): 709–723.

———. 2011. Cities in a World of Cities: The Comparative Gesture. *International Journal of Urban and Regional Research* 35 (1): 1–23.

Robinson, Wirt. 1895. *A Flying Trip to the Tropics: A Record of an Ornithological Visit to the United States of Colombia, South America and to the Island of Curaçao, West Indies, in the Year 1892*. Cambridge: Riverside Press.

Robotham, Don. 2000. Blackening the Jamaican Nation: The Travails of a Black Bourgeoisie in a Globalized World. *Identities: Global Studies in Culture and Power* 7 (1): 1–37.

Rodgers, Dennis. 2004. "Disembedding" the City: Crime, Insecurity and Spatial Organization in Managua, Nicaragua. *Environment and Urbanization* 16 (2): 113–124.

Rodgers, Dennis, and Bruce O'Neill. 2012. Infrastructural Violence: Introduction to the Special Issue. *Ethnography* 13 (4): 401–412.

Römer, René A. 1991. *De sociale geschiedenis van Willemstad: Haar wijken en hun bewoners*. UNA-Cahier 35. Willemstad: Universiteit van de Nederlandse Antillen.

———. 1993. Flexibiliteit en spontaniteit: De samenhang tussen samenleving, cultuur en architectuur van Curaçao. *Bulletin KNOB* 92 (1/2): 4–6.

———. 1998. *De Curaçaose Samenleving*. Curaçao: Amigoe N.V.

Rotenburg, Robert. 2014. Nature. In *The Blackwell Companion to Urban Anthropology*, ed. Donald Nonini, pp. 381–393. Oxford: Wiley-Blackwell.

Roy, Ananya. 2009. The 21st-Century Metropolis: New Geographies of Theory. *Regional Studies* 43 (6): 819–830.

Rupert, Linda M. 2012. *Creolization and Contraband: Curaçao in the Early Modern Atlantic World*. Athens: University of Georgia Press.

Sachs, Aaron. 2003. The Ultimate "Other": Post-Colonialism and Alexander von Humboldt's Ecological Relationship with Nature. *History and Theory* 42 (4): 111–135.

Said, Edward. 1978. *Orientalism*. New York: Pantheon.

Sandler, Ronald D., and Phaedra C. Pezzullo, eds. 2007. *Environmental Justice and Environmentalism: The Social Justice Challenge to the Environmental Movement*. Cambridge, MA: MIT Press.

Satterthwaite, David. 2003. The Links Between Poverty and the Environment in Urban Areas of Africa, Asia and Latin America. *Annals of the AAPSS* 590:73–92.

Scanlan, John. 2005. *On Garbage*. London: Reaktion Books.

Secor, Anna J. 2002. The Veil and Urban Space in Istanbul: Women's Dress, Mobility and Islamic Knowledge. *Gender, Place and Culture* 9 (1): 5–22.

Sheller, Mimi. 2003. *Consuming the Caribbean: From Arawaks to Zombies*. London: Routledge.

———. 2004. Natural Hedonism: The Invention of Caribbean Islands as Tropical Playgrounds. In *Tourism in the Caribbean: Trends, Development, Prospects*, ed. David Timothy Duval, pp. 23–38. London and New York: Routledge.

———. 2012. *Citizenship from Below: Erotic Agency and Caribbean Freedom*. Durham and London: Duke University Press.

Sheller, Mimi, and John Urry, eds. 2006. *Mobile Technologies of the City*. London and New York: Routledge.

Singh, Neera M. 2013. The Affective Labor of Growing Forests and the Becoming of Environmental Subjects: Rethinking Environmentality in Odisha, India. *Geoforum* 47: 189–198.

Sletto, Bjørn Ingmunn. 2005. A Swamp and Its Subjects: Conservation Politics, Surveillance and Resistance in Trinidad, the West Indies. *Geoforum* 36 (1): 77–93.

Slocum, Karla, and Deborah A. Thomas. 2003. Rethinking Global and Area Studies: Insights from Caribbeanist Anthropology. *American Anthropologist* 105 (3): 553–565.

Small, Mario Luis. 2004. *Villa Victoria: The Transformation of Social Capital in a Boston Barrio*. Chicago: University of Chicago Press.

Smith, Neil. 1990 [1984]. *Uneven Development: Nature, Capitalism and the Production of Space*, 2nd ed. Oxford: Blackwell.

Social Development Commission (SDC). 1999a. *Riverton Meadows Community Profile*. Kingston, Jamaica: SDC.

———. 1999b. *Rae Town Community Profile*. Kingston, Jamaica: SDC.

Statistical Institute of Jamaica (STATIN). 2003. *Population Census 2001*. Vol. 1, *Country Report*. Kingston, Jamaica: STATIN.

Stepan, Nancy Leyes. 2001. *Picturing Tropical Nature*. Ithaca, NY: Cornell University Press.

Strachan, Ian Gregory. 2002. *Paradise and Plantation: Tourism and Culture in the Anglophone Caribbean*. Charlottesville: University of Virginia Press.

Stoler, Ann Laura. 2008. Imperial Debris: Reflections on Ruins and Ruination. *Cultural Anthropology* 23 (2): 191–219.

———. 2013. Introduction: "The Rot Remains": From Ruins to Ruination. In *Imperial Debris: On Ruins and Ruination*, ed. Ann Laura Stoler, pp. 1–35. Durham, NC: Duke University Press.

Swyngedouw, Erik. 1997. Power, Nature, and the City: The Conquest of Water and the Political Ecology of Urbanization in Guayaquil, Ecuador: 1880–1990. *Environment and Planning A* 29 (2): 311–332.

———. 2004. *Social Power and the Urbanization of Water: Flows of Power*. Oxford: Oxford University Press.

Sze, Julie. 2007. *Noxious New York: The Racial Politics of Urban Health and Environmental Justice*. Cambridge, MA: MIT Press.

Taylor, Dorceta E. 2000. The Rise of the Environmental Justice Paradigm: Injustice Framing and the Social Construction of Environmental Discourses. *American Behavioral Scientist* 43 (4): 508–580.

Taylor, Frank Fonda. 1993. *To Hell with Paradise: A History of the Jamaican Tourist Industry*. Pittsburgh: University of Pittsburgh Press.

Thomas, Deborah A. 2004. *Modern Blackness: Nationalism, Globalization and the Politics of Culture in Jamaica*. Durham, NC: Duke University Press.

———. 2009. The Violence of Diaspora: Governmentality, Class Cultures, and Circulations. *Radical History Review* 103:83–104.

———. 2011. *Exceptional Violence: Embodied Citizenship in Transnational Jamaica*. Durham, NC: Duke University Press.

Thomas, Deborah A., and Karla Slocum. 2008. Caribbean Studies, Anthropology, and US Academic Realignments. *Souls* 10 (2): 123–137.

Thomas, Herbert T. 1890. *Untrodden Jamaica*. Kingston, Jamaica: Aston W. Gardner & Co.

Thomas-Hope, Elizabeth. 1996. *The Environmental Dilemma in Caribbean Context*. Grace, Kennedy Foundation Lecture. Kingston, Jamaica: Grace, Kennedy Foundation.

Thompson, Krista. 2006. *An Eye for the Tropics: Tourism, Photography and Framing the Caribbean Picturesque*. Durham, NC: Duke University Press.

Thompson, Michael. 1979. *Rubbish Theory: The Creation and Destruction of Value*. Oxford: Oxford University Press.

Thorsheim, Peter. 2005. *Inventing Pollution: Coal, Smoke and Culture in Britain Since 1800*. Athens: Ohio University Press.

Tobin, Beth Fowkes. 2005. *Colonizing Nature: The Tropics in British Arts and Letters, 1760–1820*. Philadelphia: University of Pennsylvania Press.

Tomalin, E. 2004. Bio-divinity and Biodiversity: Perspectives on Religion and Environmental Conservation in India. *Numen: International Review for the History of Religions* 51:265–295.

Trouillot, Michel-Rolph. 1992. The Caribbean Region: An Open Frontier in Anthropological Theory. *Annual Review of Anthropology* 21:19–42.

Tsing, Anna Lowenhaupt. 2005. *Friction: An Ethnography of Global Connection.* Durham, NC: Duke University Press.

Uitvoeringsorganisatie Stichting Ontwikkeling Nederlandse Antillen (USONA). 2008. *Nature and Environment as Assets: Evaluation of the NEPP 2004–2007.* Willemstad: USONA.

Ulysse, Gina. 2007. *Downtown Ladies: Informal Commercial Importers, a Haitian Anthropologist, and Self-Making in Jamaica.* Chicago: University of Chicago Press.

van der Torn, P. 1999. *Health Complaints and Air Pollution from the Isla Refinery in Curaçao: With Special Emphasis to the Response to Irregular Situations.* Rotterdam: Public Health Service of Rotterdam and Surroundings.

van der Woud, Auke. 2010. *Koninkrijk vol sloppen: Achterbuurten en vuil in de negentiende eeuw.* Amsterdam: Prometheus.

van Paddenburg, Gerrit Gijsbert. 1819. *Beschrijving van het eiland Curaçao en onderhoorige eilanden.* Haarlem: Françaois Bohn.

Verrest, Hebe, and Rivke Jaffe. 2012. Bipolar Antagonism and Multi-Polar Coexistence: Conceptualizing Difference and Shaping Fear in Two Caribbean Cities. *Social and Cultural Geography* 13 (7): 625–644.

Vomil/Mina. 1998. *Nota Duurzaam Toerisme voor de Nederlandse Antillen.* Curaçao: Vomil/Mina.

———. 1999. *Voortgangsrapportage van de Contourennota van het Natuur- en Milieubeleid van de Nederlandse Antillen 1996–2000.* Willemstad: Vomil/Mina.

———. 2000. *Natuurbeleid van de Nederlandse Antillen: Aan de Dageraad van een Nieuw Millennium 2000–2005.* Willemstad: Vomil/Mina.

———. 2001. *Meerjarenplan Milieu- en Natuurbeleid Nederlandse Antillen 2001–2005.* Curaçao: Vomil/Mina.

———. 2004. *Nature and Environment Policy Plan Netherlands Antilles, 2004–2007.* Willemstad: Vomil/Mina.

Wacquant, Loïc. 1993. Urban Outcasts: Stigma and Division in the Black American Ghetto and the French Urban Periphery. *International Journal of Urban and Regional Research* 17 (3): 366–383.

———. 2007. *Urban Outcasts: A Comparative Sociology of Advanced Marginality.* London: Polity.

Waley, Paul. 2012. Japanese Cities in Chinese Perspective: Towards a Contextual, Regional Approach to Comparative Urbanism. *Urban Geography* 33 (6): 816–828.

Watts, David. 1987. *The West Indies: Patterns of Development, Culture, and Environmental Change Since 1492.* Cambridge: Cambridge University Press.

Weeber, Leon. 2004. *Leefsituatie in enkele achterstandsbuurten van Curaçao: Historische achtergronden en statistische feiten.* Willemstad: CBS.

West, Paige. 2006. *Conservation Is Our Government Now: The Politics of Ecology in Papua New Guinea.* Durham, NC: Duke University Press.

Wheeler, Elizabeth A. 1996. *Unthinkable Cities: Kingston and Los Angeles*. Ph.D. diss., University of California, Berkeley.

Withers, Charles W. J. 1999. Geography, Enlightenment and the Paradise Question. In *Geography and Enlightenment*, ed. David N. Livingstone and Charles W. J. Withers, pp. 67–92. Chicago: University of Chicago Press.

Yarde, Thérèse. 2012. *Perceptions of Nature in the Caribbean Island of Dominica*. Ph.D. diss., University of Edinburgh.

INDEX

aesthetics, 26–27, 52, 127

affect, 121

African Americans, 94, 98, 127, 146, 151

agriculture
limited importance of, 36, 52
organic, 138
plantation, 5, 26, 28, 55, 67, 113

air-conditioning, 87–89, 121

anthropology, 4
Caribbeanist, 25–26
early, 9
environmental, 8–9, 140, 156–159
historical, 46
and space, 13–14, 75
urban, 9, 24, 159

architecture, 76, 83
and colonialism, 22, 26–27
See also built environment

area stigmatization, 77–79, 83, 91, 101

area studies, 23–25

assemblages, 46–47, 160

beautification, 34, 80, 83, 139, 152

biodiversity, 9, 16, 19, 110–113, 115, 118, 152, 157
hotspots, 6, 112

biopolitics, 56, 62, 64

bodies

and natural landscapes, 7, 51
as pollutants, 15, 67, 97–100, 104–105
and urban space, 14–15, 63, 66, 70–71, 85–90, 98

bodily adornment and modification, 70–71, 87

bodily regime, 71, 87–90

built environment, 5, 12, 17, 47, 83–84, 93, 156
and colonialism, 6, 8, 26–27, 44
See also architecture; urban planning

cacti, 1, 42, 133, 136

capitalism, 12, 25, 138
mercantile, 25, 27, 29

Caribbean studies, 24–27

cars, 38, 40, 41, 42, 87–91, 121

cholera, 29, 56–61, 73, 101

Christianity, 137–138

civilization
and cities, 7, 9, 48, 51, 97
and European colonialism 6–8, 13, 27, 49–51, 54, 56
and sanitary reform, 57
in Curaçao, 62–66
in Jamaica 58, 60–61
as opposed to nature, 10, 49–51, 109

class distinction. See social distinction